More Battlefields
of Canada

More Battlefields of Canada

Mary Beacock Fryer

Dundurn Press
Toronto and Oxford

Editor: Carol Anderson
Designer: Shawn Syms
Printed and bound in Canada by Best Gagne Printing Ltd., Louiseville, Quebec.

The publisher wishes to acknowledge the generous assistance and ongoing support of **The Canada Council, The Book Publishing Industry Development Program** of **The Department of Communications, The Ontario Arts Council, The Ontario Publishing Centre** of **The Ministry of Culture, Tourism and Recreation,** and **The Ontario Heritage Foundation.**
    Care has been taken to trace the ownership of copyright material used in the text (including the illustrations). The author and publisher welcome any information enabling them to rectify any reference or credit in subsequent editions.

J. Kirk Howard, Publisher

Canadian Cataloguing in Publication Data

Fryer, Mary Beacock, 1929–
    More Battlefields of Canada

Includes bibliographical references and index.
ISBN 1-55002-189-3

1. Battles – Canada. 2. Battlefields – Canada.
3. Canada – History, Military. I. Title.

FC226.F79   1993   971   C93-094432-1
F1028.F79   1993

Dundurn Press Limited	Dundurn Distribution	Dundurn Press Limited
2181 Queen Street East	73 Lime Walk	1823 Maryland Avenue
Suite 301	Headington, Oxford	P.O. Box 1000
Toronto, Canada	England	Niagara Falls, N.Y.
M4E 1E5	OX3 7AD	U.S.A. 14302-1000

Table of Contents

Acknowledgments

The author and publisher wish to thank the following for their informed comments on various chapters: Dr. Robert S. Allen, historian; Dr. Carl Benn, Curator, Military and Marine History, Toronto Historical Board; Mr. Henry Bosveld, Superintendent, Fort Malden National Historic Park, Amherstburg, Ontario; Dr. Ben Greenhous, Directorate of History, National Defence Headquarters, Ottawa; Mr. Stephen Mecredy, Fort Henry, Kingston, Ontario; Dr. Peter MacLeod, historian, Ottawa; Dr. Carman Miller, History Department, McGill University, Montreal; John R. Stroud, Hong Kong Veterans' Association; General J.L. Summers, Saskatoon; Associate Professor Wesley B. Turner, Department of History, Brock University, St. Catharines, Ontario.

Introduction

In 1986, Kirk Howard of Dundurn Press and I published *Battlefields of Canada*. Because we did not contemplate writing about every battlefield, we selected sixteen sites. We wanted to publish a small volume, a book that would be a lightweight, handy guide for anyone wanting to refer to it while walking around a site. We chose sites for various reasons – importance, special features and aspects, epoch, or regional distribution.

Before I began work on *Battlefields of Canada,* the editor of one of my earlier books, *King's Men,* told me I should not confine myself entirely to sites within Canada's present boundaries. Several sites, particularly in the United States, are legitimate Canadian battlefields. On the strength of this recommendation, we chose Fort Ticonderoga (Carillon), 1758, so important in the conflict between Britain and France, and a selection that brought an angry response from one American reviewer. For this second volume we chose Fort Astoria, 1812, a site of little historical importance but one that satisfied the desire to include a selection from the West Coast (across the Columbia River from Columbia, land that Britain might have claimed except for American agitation, fifty-four forty or fight!) to annex territory that would render Alaska contiguous with the United States. Britain compromised, sacrificing what became the State of Washington in order to retain the northern portion; hence, the name – British Columbia.

We resolved to go further afield this time. After selecting the Red River Expedition, 1870, and an episode from the 1885 Rebellion, we chose Paardeberg, South Africa. I visited the republic in 1991 and toured several sites there. The temptation to describe kopje and veld was overwhelming especially since so many characters prominent in Canadian events in 1870 and 1885 fought there.

Again, some battlefields chosen are historic sites and so are easy to visit, to see the reconstruction of events; others have vanished. The Battle of York, 1813, was on surroundings vastly different from the present-day reconstruction, but today Fort York commemorates the event. Paardeberg is virtually unaltered. Lundy's Lane is in a built-up area; a restored Fort Erie beckons. Hardly a trace remains of Fort La Tour, in downtown Saint John, New Brunswick, but Annapolis Royal, Nova Scotia, is beautifully restored. We made do with a non-battlefield in Alberta because of its bizarre nature. There is a Cree versus Blackfoot site at Lethbridge, but an internecine war there paled beside the performance of native warriors at Cut Knife Hill and Creek.

Rather than neglect Prince Edward Island, we recalled its importance as a source of food to Louisbourg. Red River is hardly a battlefield; the true drama lies in the struggle to reach the two Forts Garry, a route that can still be traversed. And we felt, in view of present interest in the future of Hong Kong and the numbers who visit there, that we should remember the events of 1941 and their sombre aftermath.

We decided to repeat the chronology from *Battlefields of Canada*, which ends in 1885, in order to fill in gaps between sites we chose from later times, and we again included a list of books for readers who wish to discover more about the sites.

Mary Beacock Fryer
Toronto, 1993

I

Acadian Civil War:
Saint-Étienne de La Tour
versus Menou d'Aulnay

The historic rivalry between England and France in North America is well-known to students of Canadian history. Less well-known are the hostilities that occurred between factions within the French colonial administration. The Acadian civil war was the result of bloody competition between Charles de Saint-Étienne de La Tour (1593–1666) and Charles de Menou d'Aulnay (1604–1650). Because of mismanagement in France, each man governed a portion of Acadia, with mutual hatred. The quarrel between La Tour and d'Aulnay helped to prevent the evolution of a strong French presence in Acadia. The people who were truly in control, of course, were the Micmacs.

Two sites figure prominently in the La Tour–d'Aulnay battles. Some of the action took place at Port Royal (now Annapolis Royal) in Nova Scotia, now a popular, restored historic site. The other site, Fort La Tour, is obscure. A marker at Portland Point, in Saint John, New Brunswick, helps identify the spot, which was also the setting of earlier native activity and, later, European settlement. Archaeological diggings were carried out in the 1950s, after which the site was covered. Today, it is little more than a grassy mound among the many port facilities. A toll bridge runs from Portland Point across the harbour, linking the main core of Saint John with West Saint John. For the natives, the French, and the later English settlers, Portland Point commanded a fine overview of the harbour and made a strong defensive position.

Both England and France envisioned that their colonies would become great sources of wealth. The French government wanted to collect taxes on this wealth, but could not afford to finance the establishment of colonies. Instead, merchants and traders established posts at their own expense, and in return they received monopolies over certain areas. In their own ships they brought from France goods to trade with the native people, in exchange, primarily, for furs, but also for salt, fish, and timber. To operate this trade the French created a number of early commercial companies before settling on the Compagnie de la Nouvelle France, with branches in both Canada and Acadia. This company operated until 1627, when Louis XIII and Cardinal Richelieu, Louis XIII's chief minister, authorized the Companie des Cent Associés to operate in Canada.

Charles de La Tour represented certain mercantile interests. When he was fourteen, in 1606, Charles and his father Claude sailed with a party from Dieppe to Port Royal, Acadia, to settle in the colony founded by Pierre du Gua de Monts and his assistant Samuel de Champlain. They soon returned to France, however, because de Monts's trading monopoly was cancelled and he was ordered to evacuate the settlement. In 1610 they sailed with a party to reoccupy Port Royal. After that settlement was destroyed by a force from Virginia in 1613, the La Tours lived with the natives and later rebuilt part of Port Royal. Charles remained in the neighbourhood, but Claude again returned to France. Charles married a native woman and fathered three daughters. By 1623, he was the leader of Acadia, and had shifted his headquarters from Port Royal to the neighbourhood of Cape Sable, an island on the southeast coast of Nova Scotia, and built a post, which he named Fort Lomeron in honour of David Lomeron, an agent in La Rochelle. This post was also known as Fort St. Louis.

In the meantime, England asserted its claim. In 1621, James I (and James VI of Scotland) awarded Acadia to the Scottish poet and courtier Sir William Alexander, and renamed it Nova Scotia. By 1627, after much wavering, Charles de La Tour's post was the only one in Acadia still in French hands. The following year, Claude de La Tour set out for the colony on a French ship. It was captured, along with three other vessels, by David and Lewis Kirke, brothers who commanded three English warships. Claude was taken to England, where he quickly switched loyalties and was awarded a baronetcy in Nova Scotia. He also accepted a second baronetcy for his son Charles, who did not desire the honour. Charles remained loyal to France, a situation his father failed to understand. In 1630, Claude arrived off Fort Lomeron aboard an English ship and came ashore to insist that Charles change his allegiance, because Acadia was now officially an English (Scottish) colony. His son refused. Claude returned to the ship and began firing on the post. But Charles defended the fort, and Claude was forced to abandon the battle. When Louis XIII heard the news, he rewarded Charles by making him governor of Acadia. Later Claude and Charles reconciled, and Claude made his home in Acadia near Cape Sable.

Of the two French combatants in Acadia, d'Aulnay was the better-connected. He was a nobleman and King's councillor, and keen to make a fortune through trade. As well, he was a relative of Cardinal Richelieu, the man who controlled France.

In 1632, Acadia was returned to France by the Treaty of Saint-Germain-en-Laye. D'Aulnay arrived as an assistant to Isaac de Razilly, newly appointed governor of Port Royal. Accompanied by 3,200 men, they evicted some Scottish settlers and began another rebuilding of Port Royal. Three years later, in 1635, Charles de La Tour received a grant of land at the mouth of the Saint

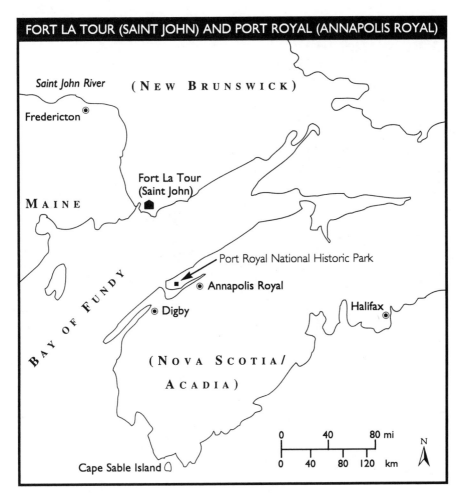

FORT LA TOUR (SAINT JOHN) AND PORT ROYAL (ANNAPOLIS ROYAL)

Saint John River

(N E W   B R U N S W I C K)

Fredericton

Fort La Tour
(Saint John)

M A I N E

Port Royal National Historic Park

Annapolis Royal

Digby

Halifax

B A Y   o f   F U N D Y

(N O V A   S C O T I A /
A C A D I A)

Cape Sable Island

0   40   80 mi
0   40   80   120   km

N

John River, and began to build a new trading post on Portland Point. He called it Fort Sainte Marie, but it was better known as Fort La Tour. At about the same time, Governor Razilly died at Port Royal and his brother, Claude, succeeded him. Claude de Razilly did not come out to Acadia; instead, he delegated d'Aulnay as governor in his absence. Relations between Governor Razilly and Charles de La Tour had always been harmonious, but the appointment of d'Aulnay initiated a decade of violence. By 1638, the French government tried to solve the problem of two governors sharing the same territory, and had partitioned Acadia. The situation worsened, however, because the French, with their vague notion of the geography of Acadia, had not drawn a clear line of demarcation between the territories of La Tour and d'Aulnay.

The king gave La Tour peninsular Nova Scotia but not Port Royal, the focus of the settlement in that peninsula. He gave d'Aulnay land north of the Bay of Fundy but not Fort La Tour, which stood on that very shore. The

Metro Toronto Reference Library, John Ross Robertson Collection

Annapolis Royal, Nova Scotia. Originally founded by the French as Port Royal, this harbour and settlement changed hands many times.

governors thus faced each other from fortified positions across the Bay of Fundy, each surrounded by the other's territory. To complicate matters, the two rivals were expected to cooperate by sharing expenses. In 1640, however, when La Tour sailed across to Port Royal, entered the Annapolis Basin, and landed, d'Aulnay refused to let him enter his habitation. Immediately the two came to blows.

That same year saw a change in La Tour's domestic arrangements. He married the heroic Françoise-Marie Jacquelin. Women of the right class were scarce in Acadia; La Tour had had to seek his wife in France. He was unable to go himself because he was fully occupied rendering his fortress impregnable against an attack by d'Aulnay. He sent a colleague in his place to find a suitable bride and arrange to bring her to Acadia. The colleague selected Mademoiselle Jacquelin, and the marriage took place when Françoise-Marie arrived.

Fort La Tour, as it was now generally known, had become the centre of a formidable habitation. Its yellow roof was a notable landmark; the main buildings were surrounded by a palisade. A native village lay to the northwest, an area still called Indiantown, and in between were outbuildings. Three cannon faced the harbour, ready to defend the fort from a sea attack. A deep ditch circled the landward side. There must have been gun platforms, but archaeologists have not found any such remains. The principal bastion was of masonry, the walls two feet thick. It stood at the northwest corner of the gate-house compound, facing the harbour. The single gun had an 8.5-centimetre (3 1/2-inch) bore and could fire four- to six-pound balls. The other emplacements were redans of wood and stone. In this heavily fortified home, Françoise-Marie gave birth to just one child, a son. Life might have been serene if not for d'Aulnay's schemes.

D'Aulnay went to France, where he arranged to have all shipments of trade goods to La Tour stopped. La Tour then went to Boston to recruit mercenaries to help him defend his habitation. In 1642, d'Aulnay sailed again for France, in order to find a wife, Jeanne Motin, and to complain about La Tour, who was ordered to come home to answer d'Aulnay's charges. To ensure that her husband could not be imprisoned, Madame La Tour went in his stead. After filing counter-complaints, she received authorization from the Compagnie de la Nouvelle France to send her husband the ship *Saint-Clément,* which carried soldiers and supplies to Fort La Tour.

When d'Aulnay's sources reported on the coming ship, he sent three of his own ships to blockade Fort La Tour. Charles de La Tour slipped away, probably in a small boat, reached the *Saint Clément,* and persuaded the captain to sail to Boston. There he met with the vice-admiral of France, who gave him permission to seek out assistance from firms belonging to the local Puritans. La Tour mortgaged some property, hired four ships, about seventy men, soldiers, and English volunteers, and sailed for his habitation.

When La Tour's rented fleet hove into view, d'Aulnay hastened to Port Royal, with La Tour's ships in hot pursuit. La Tour demanded compensation. When d'Aulnay declined to negotiate, La Tour landed with a few of his soldiers and thirty English volunteers and burned the mill in the settlement. D'Aulnay, of course, complained bitterly, and the French government fingered La Tour as the aggressor. Madame La Tour again went to France, no small task at that time, when an Atlantic crossing sometimes took more than two months. She tried to arrange for supplies to be sent to Fort La Tour, but the government rejected the request and denied her permission to leave the country. She resorted to a disguise, escaped to England, and returned home, probably through Boston.

Unfortunately for the La Tours, d'Aulnay had the ear of the King. He hired soldiers in France, bought a warship and reached Port Royal in September 1644. He also signed a peace treaty with the New Englanders at Boston. Both d'Aulnay and La Tour were conducting business with the English in Massachusetts, although the Compagnie de la Nouvelle France supposedly held a monopoly. Boston merchants favoured La Tour – they thought d'Aulnay to be much the more dangerous of the two.

In February 1645, La Tour was in Boston, in search of supplies of food and trade goods. By that time, d'Aulnay had acquired a new sixteen-gun flagship, named, of course, the *Grand Cardinal.* He attacked Fort La Tour but was held off. By April, he had learned from deserters that La Tour was again in

Boston, and so on the 13th he arrived at the fort with his ships and 200 men. This time he sent a party of men ashore with two cannon and orders to set up a battery close to the palisade. When the guns were in place, d'Aulnay sailed the *Grand Cardinal* in close to the fort and called to the garrison to surrender. The garrison of only forty-seven men, a few of them professional soldiers, responded with cannon shot and jeers. On the principal bastion someone ran up a red flag, the symbol of defiance. Fort La Tour's garrison was severely outgunned as well as outnumbered. D'Aulnay had smaller guns on his other ships, in addition to the battery that the men had built ashore. The same disparity in the numbers of men applied to the stocks of ammunition – supplies inside the fort were limited, but d'Aulnay had more than enough.

Madame La Tour took command of the defence. Throughout the siege, two surgeons and the apothecary brought the wounded into shelter and tended them. On the afternoon of 16 April, Easter Day, d'Aulnay withdrew, and Madame La Tour allowed the garrison to rest in the now badly damaged fort. An acrid smell, of burnt powder mingled with blood and charred timber, permeated the air. D'Aulnay prepared for a final assault on the weakened position. The advance began an hour before sundown. D'Aulnay's men were thirsting for a fight and crazed by his promise of pillage. The landing force joined the men at d'Aulnay's gun battery near the palisade, and soon penetrated the fort through a gaping hole in a parapet.

Madame La Tour and the survivors were not beaten yet. They rushed at the intruders with musket-butt, pike, halberd, and sword. Madame implored them not to give in unless d'Aulnay promised quarter to everyone. The dissembling d'Aulnay gave his word, but reneged as soon as he entered the fort, claiming that he would not have made such a promise had he known how few defenders had held him at bay. What followed was a grisly nightmare for Madame and her brave defenders.

Madame La Tour's garrison had to be punished for the heavy losses inflicted on d'Aulnay's men. He exacted a frightful price – eight had been killed and several were wounded. Madame La Tour was bound, a heavy rope was wound round her neck, and she was forced to watch while all but two of her surviving men were murdered by slow strangulation – "hanged and strangled," rather than a quick, neck-breaking drop. Of the two who were spared, one was reported to be the executioner, and the other may have been a Swiss mercenary. Among the executed were seven or eight men from Boston who had joined La Tour's service. D'Aulnay had shown exactly what a dangerous man he could be.

D'Aulnay allowed Madame some freedom, until he caught her trying to arrange for a native to carry a message to Boston. He confined her and threatened to send her to France to stand trial for treason. Thoroughly intimidated, haunted by fears of long imprisonment and likely execution as a traitor that would certainly be preceded by torture, this brave woman could stand her cap-

New Brunswick Museum

Mme. Françoise-Marie de La Tour. In the absence of her husband, the brave woman commanded the garrison of Fort La Tour, and died only days later.

tor's cruelty no longer. Three weeks after the fall of the fort, the broken Madame La Tour died. D'Aulnay ordered her burial behind the fort among the dead soldiers, and he allowed her honours for the courage she had shown. He then placed her son in the care of a female servant, and sent him to France.

D'Aulnay rebuilt Fort La Tour, strengthened it by adding a second fort, and turned it into a profitable trading post again. Once they heard of his success, the King and Queen sent him congratulations for dealing with what they had been persuaded to believe was a traitor. Meanwhile, La Tour remained in Boston, trying to raise a relief expedition. Word of the destruction of his habitation and the death of his beloved wife reached him before he was ready. In his desperation to raise money, he mortgaged everything he possessed. The indenture was signed on 13 May (old calendar; by the new calendar the date was 23 May 1645. The English retained the old calendar until 1747, but the French had already adopted the new calendar. Thus, in French records, Fort La Tour fell on 16 April, but in English sources the date was 6 April).

The next year, La Tour moved to Quebec, where Governor Huault de Montmagny welcomed him. He spent the following four years trading, and on one occasion he fought with the Huron nation against the Iroquois.

D'Aulnay, meanwhile, attacked forts belonging to the Compagnie de la Nouvelle France on behalf of a private breakaway company, the Compagnie de Razilly-Condonnier. The many cries of protest to France made no difference – d'Aulnay's position seemed unassailable – until a May day in 1650.

A canoe bearing d'Aulnay and a servant overturned as it was coming into Port Royal. Both d'Aulnay and the servant drowned. He left his wife, Jeanne Motin, with eight young children, four boys and four girls. When La Tour learned of d'Aulnay's fate, he decided it was safe to go to France to present his side of the story. He was soon restored to royal favour, along with his property and a commission as governor of all Acadia. He recruited colonists and reached Port Royal in the summer of 1653. He showed Madame d'Aulnay the royal order returning Fort La Tour to him, and they quickly came to an amicable arrangement. Madame was a more agreeable person than her late husband, and evidence suggests that her grief was short-lived.

La Tour was deeply in debt, after mortgaging all his property except that returned to him by the king. Madame d'Aulnay was also saddled with debts because so much of her husband's resources had gone into defeating and restoring Fort La Tour. Both faced the fact that the rivalry had almost ruined them, and became determined to end the quarrelling. Madame d'Aulnay accepted Charles de La Tour's offer of marriage, and they had five children together. What happened to the son d'Aulnay sent to France is not known.

La Tour's troubles with a fellow Frenchman were over, but he still could not sit back and relax. An expedition sent by the Protector, Oliver Cromwell, in 1654, captured Fort La Tour, and Charles was sent to England as a prisoner. In 1656, he saw Cromwell, who refused to return his property and would only allow him the baronetcy in Nova Scotia that his father had obtained for him, a title that La Tour had never acknowledged. Cromwell imposed other conditions: La Tour was to give his allegiance to England, pay what he owed the Boston merchants, and provide for the cost of an English garrison then being maintained at Fort La Tour. La Tour accepted all three conditions; he had no choice.

To pay his debts, La Tour formed a partnership with two English traders, but was always uncomfortable over the allegiance he now owed England. He soon sold out to his partners, and moved with his wife and family to Cape Sable, his earlier habitation at the southeastern tip of Nova Scotia. He died there in 1666, bringing to a final end one of the more fascinating eras in the history of Acadia.

II

The First Capture
of Quebec, 1629

Quebec has been captured four times. The best-known instance is the summer-long siege that ended with the battle between Wolfe and Montcalm on the Plains of Abraham. Today, approximately half of this field is preserved as a park, where visitors may stroll and envisage what happened there in 1759. The other sites are obscured by development, but the Kirke expedition and the rest are worth recalling along with the famous Plains.

When King Charles I of England declared war on France in March 1627, he was motivated, at least in part, by his desire to demonstrate solidarity with the persecuted French Huguenots. To English merchants, the war provided the opportunity to wrest a colony from France. They formed the Company of Merchant Adventurers in Canada. The King granted the company a monopoly for the St. Lawrence trade in furs that carried with it an obligation to establish colonies. In the spring of 1628, the Adventurers financed an expedition against Quebec, where Samuel de Champlain, founder of the stronghold in 1608, was in command.

A prime mover behind the establishment of the Adventurers was Gervase Kirke, a merchant of London and Dieppe. Kirke had five sons, David (c. 1597–1654), Lewis (Louis), Thomas, John, and James. All were born to a Huguenot mother in Dieppe, and all were considered French citizens by France. The expedition would be led by Gervase's eldest son, David, with Lewis as his second-in-command. (This was the expedition referred to in Chapter I, when Claude de La Tour was captured.)

Another member of the Company of Merchant Adventurers was William Alexander Jr., whose father, Sir William, had held the fief to Nova Scotia since 1621. It comprised Sable Island, Cape Breton, the Acadian peninsula, and present-day New Brunswick; Nova Scotia was, of course, France's Acadia. The younger William hoped to secure the removal of all French, to complete his father's dream of Nova Scotia becoming a distinctly Scottish colony. (England and Scotland were still separate countries in 1627, sharing a Stuart monarch

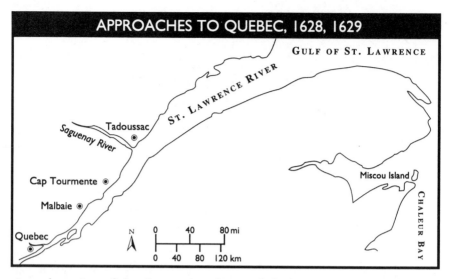

APPROACHES TO QUEBEC, 1628, 1629

GULF OF ST. LAWRENCE

ST. LAWRENCE RIVER

Tadoussac

Saguenay River

Cap Tourmente

Miscou Island

Malbaie

CHALEUR BAY

Quebec

N

0   40   80 mi

0   40   80   120 km

since the union of the Crowns in 1603; each had its own government.) Sir William himself did not join the Company of Adventurers because of a disagreement with the Kirkes over a claim he held to a large seigneury along the St. Lawrence. For political considerations, Sir William had placed his interests in his son's hands.

Champlain's Quebec, the most important French settlement in Canada, amounted to hardly more than seventy people, and a mere twenty were considered permanent residents. On low ground facing the St. Lawrence lay Champlain's original habitation, begun in 1608 and rebuilt in stone in 1624, a storehouse and the Recollect house. A wooden Fort St. Louis was under construction on Cape Diamond, and close by on the heights lay Louis Hébert's "enclosure," land considered a royal fief. Hébert (c. 1575–1627) was the man French Canadians claim as their common ancestor. Down in the valley of the St. Charles River were buildings of the Recollects and Jesuits – Recollects on the right bank, Jesuits on the left. Some eighteen to twenty acres (eight hectares) of land had been cleared, not enough to grow crops for the entire settlement. The population of New France amounted to 127 souls – 107 in Canada, scarcely twenty in Acadia – compared to 2,400 in the English colonies to the south. Champlain held the trade monopoly in 1627. He had lost it in 1621 to the Sieurs de Caën but had managed to regain it; nevertheless, the de Caëns had remained active in the Canadian trade.

Champlain had been absent in France from 1624 to 1626, as he tended to colony business and marital problems. His wife, Hélène Bouillé, did not like Canada. They had been married in 1610 when she was twelve and he forty-three. She had accompanied her husband to Canada in 1620, but had refused to return with him. Now she was planning to become a nun, and he sought to remove her from his will.

The French had outposts at Miscou island, Tadoussac, and Cape Tourmente. Miscou Island lay in the mouth of Chaleur Bay, on the south side; Tadoussac, at the opening of the Saguenay River, had been a trading station for many years; Cape Tourmente lay forty-eight kilometres (thirty miles) downstream from Quebec itself. All were inhabited intermittently.

Rivalling the Company of Merchant Adventurers to Canada was the French Company of the Hundred Associates, a revamped Compagnie de la Nouvelle France, that had received a trade monopoly for all of New France. Like the Adventurers, the Hundred was expected to strengthen Quebec. Clearly the Adventurers and the Hundred were on a collision course. The latter planned a French supply expedition for Quebec, but some members hesitated to send it during wartime, for fear of the powerful English navy.

Meanwhile, the Kirkes, acting on a letter of marque from England, fitted out three ships and set forth in March. Soon afterwards the French decided to send the relief supply fleet to Quebec, because the colony was so desperately short of food. By the time the fleet, commanded by Claude Rougement de Brison, left France, the Kirkes were far ahead.

David Kirke's force seized the habitation at Miscou, which had few or no residents at the time. Sailing round the Gaspé Peninsula, bound for the Gulf of St. Lawrence, Kirke captured first a Basque ship, and then an advance French supply ship. He occupied Tadoussac, and dispatched a party of fifteen to raze the settlement at Cape Tourmente. The party returned with a few prisoners, whom David Kirke freed before re-embarking. The prisoners hurried to Quebec to alert Champlain. Kirke sent some Basques with a letter demanding that Champlain surrender, but he bluffed them with a brazenness that succeeded. Quebec was facing starvation, nearly out of food and ammunition, but the Kirkes had no idea how bad the situation was, and instead withdrew. Quebec was safe for the moment, and all would be well if the supply fleet did not encounter the English. An open, oared shallop sailed in, carrying one of Champlain's agents, who reported that the fleet had reached Gaspé Bay. Champlain took heart, but before long he could hear distant guns.

The Kirkes did find the supply fleet. Rougemont tried to steal past the three English ships under cover of fog but, on 17 July, David Kirke sighted the ships below Tadoussac. After each side fired off some 1,200 shots, Rougemont asked for terms. Champlain recorded later that Rougemont had been "more brave than wise." He ought to have stayed at Gaspé Bay until informers had assured him the Kirkes were well out in the Gulf. The Hundred Associates had lost a staggering 164,760 livres in goods; a livre was approximately the same as an English pound at that time. The Kirkes captured a fortune, but missed an opportunity to take Quebec, not to mention Charles de La Tour's barely defended fort on Cape Sable Island. Where they could easily have taken both habitations, their triumph instead was booty.

Father Louis Hennepin, *A New Discovery of a Vast Country in America,* 1698, vol. II

Champlain's Habitation, or *The Taking of Quebec by the English.*

Second Expedition against Quebec, 1629

Before making a second attempt to remove the French, the Kirkes and William Alexander Jr. formed the Anglo-Scotch Company. Their intent was to take over Canada, and to plant two Scottish colonies in Nova Scotia/Acadia, one on Cape Breton Island, the other at Port Royal (Annapolis Royal) in peninsular Nova Scotia. William Jr. left with two shiploads of colonists and soldiers and landed at Port Royal, close to the site of the then-deserted French settlement of 1605–1613. The workers first built Fort Charles to protect themselves. At about the same time, sixty more Scottish settlers left home for Cape Breton, led by James Stewart Lord Ochiltree. They built Fort Rosmar on the site of what would become Louisbourg fortress.

At Quebec, the situation was now desperate. Out of food, Champlain had sent his people to see whether any of the natives could spare something, and scouts had headed east, hoping that fishermen could help out. Others had been scouring the forest for acorns and roots. Fish were plentiful around Quebec, but, except for eels, people could not catch many because of the lack of nets, lines, and hooks. Champlain received word that a ship was close, the vanguard of a larger fleet, and he sent a messenger to Gaspé Bay with instructions to hurry back as soon as he had news.

When the English ships reached Tadoussac, David Kirke sent his brothers, Lewis and Thomas, ahead with three ships to demand that Champlain surrender. Not long after they departed, Emery de Caën reached Gaspé from France with the single ship. Happy that Quebec would soon be relieved, and

Cape (Cap) Tourmente. The cape was the setting for one of the outposts to Quebec. The monochrome grey wash and gouache over pencil was done by Lucius O'Brien in the 1880s.

satisfied that the fleet could not be far behind, the messenger left to bring the good news to Champlain. Unfortunately, he was taken prisoner and held at Tadoussac. De Caën continued on his way, unaware that most of David Kirke's strength was at Tadoussac. His ship ran aground nearby, but as Kirke attempted to close in, it refloated and De Caën escaped. His luck did not last, for when he was off Malbaie he encountered Thomas Kirke and his ship. The two vessels exchanged shots, but Thomas's crew succeeded in boarding the French ship. From De Caën, Thomas learned for the first time that their countries were at peace – France and England had signed the Treaty of Susa on 24 April 1629. Unsure of whether Thomas had been told the truth, the Kirkes pursued their plan to take Quebec.

On 19 July, Lewis and Thomas captured a party that Champlain had sent out to meet De Caën's relief ship. The two Kirkes sailed on, took shelter behind Pointe Lévis, and sent a small boat with a messenger and a white flag to Champlain. Aware that his relief ship had been taken and he could hold out no longer, Champlain agreed to surrender. The only foodstuffs left were small quantities of peas and Indian corn, a few acorns, and 1,200 eels. Lewis and Thomas went ashore on 20 July, backed by 150 men.

The rest of the French relief fleet learned that the English were in Quebec when they were near Cape Breton. Before turning back, the French attacked the Scots at Fort Rosmar and forced them to evacuate their fledgling settlement. The French built a new fort close by, left forty men as a garrison, and returned home to France.

At Quebec, Lewis and Thomas Kirke arranged to leave a strong garrison and plenty of supplies before they packed up their prisoners for the journey to England and repatriation. Champlain and the first load of prisoners reached Tadoussac on 1 August. When Champlain first came to stay in Canada, he brought out some promising young men to live among the natives, where they could learn aboriginal languages and customs. He was outraged to recognize two of them, Étienne Brûlé and Nicolas Marsolet, among the English, and furious to learn that both had defected to the enemy Iroquois and had served as guides for the Kirkes.

With the French who had sailed for England went Emery de Caën and the Jesuit Father Jean de Brébeuf. The French left Quebec on 9 September, but two families, the widow of Louis Hébert and her children, and the Couillarts, elected to remain. Champlain reached Dover on 29 October, loudly protesting the seizure of Quebec in peacetime and demanding that it be returned immediately. He was further outraged at the Kirkes, French citizens, and traitors who were beneath contempt.

For three years the English retained Quebec, improving the settlement and deriving some wealth from the fur trade. All the French possessions that had been captured were then returned, after some tricky negotiations between

Charles I and Louis XIII. Queen Henrietta Marie of England was Louis's sister, and only a small portion of her dowry had yet been paid. Short of funds, Charles agreed that he would part with the properties taken in New France if Louis would part with more of the dowry money. In 1632, the monarchs signed the Treaty of Saint Germain-en-Laye, and Port Royal and Quebec again became French. The Kirkes and their trading partners lost 6,000 pounds in investments they had made in Canada, a damaging sum, yet a pittance compared with the booty of the summer of 1628.

Champlain returned in 1633, by which time Étienne Brûlé had left the Iroquois and was again living among the Hurons. When these native allies learned that the French were back, they turned on Brûlé and murdered him. Father Jean de Brébeuf returned to work among the Hurons, and was cruelly murdered when the Iroquois destroyed their Huron rivals in the 1640s. Sir William Alexander was created Earl of Stirling, while David Kirke, knighted in 1633, later became a governor of Newfoundland. Champlain died of a stroke in Quebec on Christmas Day, 1635. His successor was Charles Huault de Montmagny.

III

Le Moyne d'Iberville's Battlegrounds: Hudson Bay and Newfoundland

A truly heroic, and utterly ruthless, crusader for France in its struggles with England for supremacy in North America was Canadian-born Pierre Le Moyne d'Iberville et d'Ardillières (1661–1706). Iberville was one of twelve sons of Charles Le Moyne de Longueuil et de Châteauguay. Near the close of the seventeenth century, Iberville attacked Hudson's Bay Company forts, on James and Hudson Bays, on five different occasions. Between the fourth and fifth attacks, he ravaged most of the English settlements in Newfoundland. Visitors who take the Polar Bear Express to Moosonee, Ontario, usually cross the Moose River to Moose Factory on Hayes Island, the original site for the Hudson's Bay Company trading post. Moose Factory, or Moose Fort, as it was known in the 1680s, is the most accessible of the historic fur forts.

In 1668, two disgruntled French traders, Pierre-Esprit Radisson and Médard Chouart des Groseilliers, went to England. They were angry over the exorbitant tax on furs that the government of New France demanded. They proposed trading through Hudson Bay to circumvent the colonial administration. Some merchants chartered the little *Nonsuch*, which, with Groseilliers aboard, sailed for the Bay that same year, returning with a fine load of pelts. A second ship, the *Eaglet*, carrying Radisson, had set out with the *Nonsuch*, but had turned back after a bad storm.

In 1670, King Charles II granted a charter to the "Governor and Company of Adventurers of England trading into Hudson's Bay." The Company was a great success. By 1686, the Adventurers' good fortune was too much for the French to tolerate, as they saw their source of furs undercut mainly because of colonial corruption. Governor Brisay de Denonville agreed to an expedition led by Pierre Chevalier de Troyes, to capture all the fur posts on James Bay – Moose Fort on the island, Charles Fort on the Rupert River, and Albany Fort at the mouth of the Albany River, and to turn them into French posts of the rival Compagnie du Nord (established by French mer-

Pierre Le Moyne d'Iberville

chants in 1682). Two of the Le Moyne brothers, Pierre d'Iberville and Jacques de Sainte-Hélène, commanded seventy voyageurs. Denonville added thirty French regulars, as a show of government support, but the expertise of the voyageurs promised positive results.

Four Encounters on the Bay

De Troyes's men left Montreal in mid-April 1686, in thirty-five canoes, up the Ottawa River to Lake Temiskaming, down the Abitibi and Moose Rivers, dragging canoes over ice, portaging, and paddling, for more than 1,300 kilometres (800 miles). By late June, after more than eighty days, they were on shore opposite Moose Fort, enclosed by a rectangular stockade and with bastions at the corners. The guns faced the bay; the fort was vulnerable to attack from the land, but the inhabitants did not expect invaders from either direction until the ice was out of Hudson Strait. Inside were seventeen men, none of them leaders. John Bridgar, the governor of Moose Fort, and his officers had left for Charles Fort on the Rupert River (later called Rupert House). As soon as they had paddled across the Moose River the French stormed the fort. Iberville, ahead of the others, gained entry only to have the gate swing shut, isolating him from his followers. He fought off all seventeen Bay men, thereby establishing a reputation as larger than life, until the French broke down the gate and he had some support. Outnumbered, the Company employees surrendered.

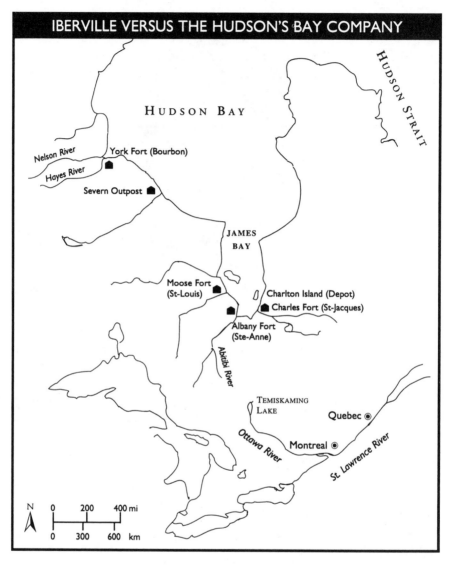

IBERVILLE VERSUS THE HUDSON'S BAY COMPANY

HUDSON STRAIT

HUDSON BAY

Nelson River

York Fort (Bourbon)

Hayes River

Severn Outpost

JAMES BAY

Moose Fort (St-Louis)

Charlton Island (Depot)

Charles Fort (St-Jacques)

Albany Fort (Ste-Anne)

Abitibi River

TEMISKAMING LAKE

Quebec

Ottawa River

Montreal

St. Lawrence River

N

| 0 | 200 | 400 mi |
| 0 | 300 | 600 km |

De Troyes then ordered the other posts taken. Charles Fort lay 170 kilometres (105 miles) to the east by land; Albany Fort was 160 kilometres (100 miles) to the northwest. They took Charles Fort on 3 July while Iberville and thirteen men captured the Company ship *Craven* that had brought Bridgar from Moose Fort. Jacques Le Moyne (Sainte-Hélène) attacked and destroyed a supply depot on Charlton Island, out in the bay. That left Albany Fort, with a garrison of thirty and the strongest defences. The French loaded siege guns from Charles Fort aboard the stolen *Craven*.

On 25 July, after they had fired some 140 shots into the fort, the chaplain came out waving a white cloth. De Troyes parlayed with the governor, Henry

Sergeant, in the middle of the Albany River. Each negotiator rode in a small boat. The French were so fatigued after taking two forts and the depot that De Troyes did not want Sergeant to see the condition they were in lest he have second thoughts. De Troyes allowed the English to keep their personal effects and sent them to Charlton Island to await the arrival of the next Company ships due from England. In August, De Troyes left for Quebec, and Iberville remained in command of forty men, to secure the French hold on James Bay.

To confuse matters, the French renamed the forts. They became Saint-Louis (Moose), Saint-Jacques (Charles/Rupert) and Saint-Anne (Albany). The French controlled James Bay, but the English were not excluded from the fur trade because they still had posts on Hudson Bay. They retained York Fort (York Factory) at the mouth of the Hayes River, and Port Nelson, on the opposite shore of the Hayes River near the mouth of the Nelson River. Iberville wintered in Moose/Saint-Louis Fort, while his supplies dwindled. When no ship arrived to relieve him in 1687, he returned to Quebec and then sailed for France to look for assistance so that he could remove the English entirely from the lucrative fur route.

He found the backers he needed, and in the spring of 1688 he sailed, first for Quebec where he had to arrange for a stock of furs there to be sent to France, and then for Hudson Bay. He had a fine new flagship, the armed escort frigate *Soleil d'Afrique,* a smaller vessel loaded with trade goods, and a commission, at age twenty-six, as commander-in-chief on Hudson Bay. By September he had anchored his flagship near Charlton Island and had sailed to Sainte-Anne/Albany with a crew of sixteen men in the smaller ship to pick up a load of furs.

When he attempted to sail out of the mouth of the Albany River, he found his way blockaded by two English ships. The eighteen-gun *Churchill* and the frigate *Yonge,* with eighty-five Company employees, had come to retake the fort. In command was Capt. John Marsh, assisted by William Bond, who gloried in the title of Company Admiral. Iberville sent men in canoes to cut the anchor lines on the markers indicating the channel, and the two English ships ran aground. Very soon all three vessels were icebound, stuck with one another's company for the winter.

Iberville now showed the vicious side of his nature. From the fort he was in a position to prevent the English from leaving an encampment they had made on shore, to hunt for fresh game. This he did, and caused an epidemic of scurvy. Captain Marsh died; Admiral Bond, who tried to hunt, was captured. Iberville invited the English surgeon to come and hunt, but when he did the French took him prisoner. Then Iberville mounted two cannon on a bluff above the English camp; the English surrendered. They lost three men in the fighting, but twenty-five died of scurvy or the cold. Iberville captured another English ship that arrived in July before he sailed for home. He landed in Quebec with all his prisoners and furs on 28 October.

Before his third encounter on the two bays, Iberville joined an expedition against the English colony of New York. England and France were officially again at war. Persuaded in part by John Churchill Duke of Marlborough, the governor of the Hudson's Bay Company, King William III (of Orange) declared war on France on 17 May 1689. The governor of New France, now Louis de Buade, comte de Palluau et de Frontenac, sent raiding parties of French and natives to the country around Schenectady. With Iberville were two of his brothers, Saint-Hélène (Jacques) and François Le Moyne de Bienville.

In July 1690, Iberville again sailed for Hudson Bay, this time intending to deal with York Fort. His expedition was not strong – three small ships, thirty guns, and eighty men. Arriving off York Fort in August, he found the inmates alerted and the site too well protected. When a much larger English ship of thirty-six guns approached, he tacked away and escaped. More in keeping with Iberville's capacities was New Severn, a recently built outpost of York Fort, at the mouth of the Severn River, 416 kilometres (250 miles) to the southeast. On his approach, the commander at Severn, Thomas Walsh, blew up one of the wooden buildings and disappeared. Iberville collected a stock of furs from an intact building and wintered on the east side of James Bay. He returned to Quebec in October 1691 and sailed from there for France.

Bureaucratic delays prevented Iberville from returning to Hudson Bay for three years. In 1692 he arrived at Quebec from France late in the season, and Governor Frontenac sent him instead to harass settlers on the coast of New England. Again, in 1693, because of contrary winds after he left France, the season grew too advanced. In New France, Iberville married Marie Thérèse Pollet, who spent most of her later life in France where their five children were born. In the autumn of 1692, when Iberville was absent, an English force of three frigates, one fire ship, 213 marines, eighty-two guns, and two years' supply of food reached James Bay. After wintering on the east side, the fleet sailed for Albany/Sainte-Anne Fort. They found it empty, except for an emaciated, half-crazed French blacksmith chained in the central blockhouse. They assumed that any other survivors must have set out in canoes hoping to reach Quebec. The Hudson's Bay Company was back in control of the Albany River.

By 1694, Iberville was able to return to his self-imposed task of eliminating the English. His target on this fourth encounter was York Fort, and he had two armed ships. He commanded the *Poli;* his brother Joseph Le Moyne de Serigny was in command of the *Salamandre.* They left Quebec early in August, and reached the entrance to the Hayes River by 24 September. Thomas Walsh, who had fled from New Severn in 1690, was now governor of York Fort. On his staff was Henry Kelsey, the future explorer. The only "troops" were an independent company of employees and fur traders, under the command of the deputy governor, Philip Parsons. These men had had little training. Armaments at the fort included thirty-two cannon and fourteen

National Archives of Canada, C-7963

York Factory

swivel guns, but all faced the sea. As at Moose Fort, Iberville found the side facing the forest unprotected.

He landed two guns, mounted them within range on the landward side, and fired a few warning shots. On the evening of 13 October (3 October old calendar, still in use by the English) he sent a delegate with a flag of truce to demand surrender. Henry Kelsey emerged to negotiate. If Iberville would wait until morning to allow the staff to sleep free of the noise of bombardment, Kelsey told Iberville that the fort would capitulate. The fifty-seven defenders surrendered as promised, to the horror of Company officers who later accused Walsh of cowardice. They knew that York Fort was well-supplied with food, guns and trade goods, but they were not aware that Walsh did not have enough firewood inside to withstand a long siege.

The French and their prisoners wintered at York Fort, which Iberville renamed Fort Bourbon. Scurvy took a severe toll on captors and captives alike. Among those who perished was Iberville's brother, Louis Le Moyne de Châteauguay. Iberville lingered through the summer, hoping to capture English supply ships expected any time. When they had not arrived by September, he left seventy men as a garrison at York/Fort Bourbon and sailed for France.

Newfoundland Interlude

Iberville reached La Rochelle in October with a load of furs. When he returned to Quebec, he received orders to attack English posts along the Atlantic coast, and to drive them from their settlements in Newfoundland. In his absence the English had a free hand on Hudson Bay. With five vessels and 400 men they retook York/Fort Bourbon and furs valued at 136,000 livres

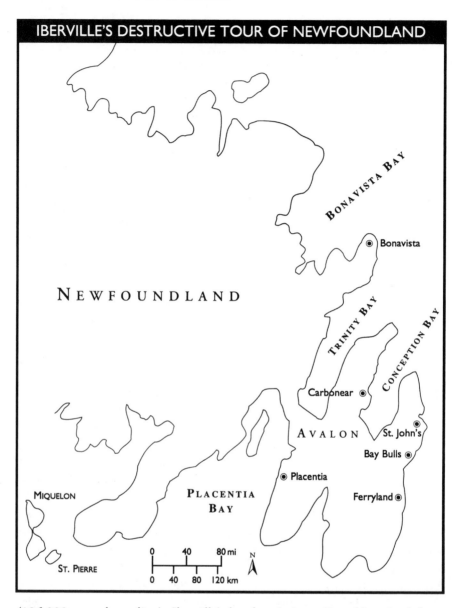

IBERVILLE'S DESTRUCTIVE TOUR OF NEWFOUNDLAND

NEWFOUNDLAND

BONAVISTA BAY

Bonavista

TRINITY BAY

CONCEPTION BAY

Carbonear

AVALON   St. John's

Bay Bulls

Placentia

MIQUELON

PLACENTIA
BAY

Ferryland

ST. PIERRE

0   40   80 mi   N

0   40   80   120 km

(136,000 pounds sterling). Iberville's brother Serigny (Joseph) arrived from France with supplies only hours later, and promptly turned back towards Hudson Strait.

Iberville left France for Quebec in the spring of 1696 with three ships stopping long enough to ask another of his brothers, Paul Le Moyne de Maricourt, to look for recruits to use against Newfoundland. With two frigates he sailed for the mouth of the Saint John River, where three English ships were blockading old Fort La Tour. He captured one English frigate; the other two ships escaped. In August, Iberville sailed on with some regulars from the Acadian garrison and natives to Fort William Henry, at the mouth of the Pemaquid River, 330 kilometres (200 miles) west along the coast from the Saint John River. Following a practice that had served him well, he unloaded some guns and set up a battery. The English surrendered, and Iberville sent the prisoners to Boston, destroyed the fort, and returned to Quebec in preparation for a winter campaign in Newfoundland.

In the three ships he had brought from France, Iberville sailed for Placentia – *Plaisance* – the French capital of Newfoundland. The French had founded the settlement in 1692, four years before Iberville arrived. They had built defences in what is now Castle Hill National Historic Park. (Some of the ruins on the site are English, built during a later period of English occupation.)

In 1696 the English and French shared – uneasily – the island. The French fishing villages were around Placentia Bay, the English ones along the east side of the Avalon peninsula from Ferryland to St. John's, the English capital, and along the Bonavista peninsula. Iberville had every intention of removing the English from the island permanently, and he intended to claim most of the enormous profits to be gained from the fishery as his booty. As was so often the case, just who was to be leader of this journey of pillage and looting was not agreed upon. The governor at Placentia, Jacques-François de Mombeton de Brouillan, assumed that he would command the garrison troops. Iberville could lead only the recruits he had brought from Quebec. Of the two, Brouillan was the more greedy, even more anxious to make his fortune than Iberville. After much wrangling, Captain Nicolas Daneau de Muy managed to bring about peace so that the expedition could commence.

Brouillan left by sea with his force on 29 October. Iberville set out by land on 1 November, to rendezvous with Brouillan at Ferryland, eighty kilometres (fifty miles) south of St. John's. After putting the settlement to the torch and commandeering all the stock of dried fish, they continued on to the capital, burning all settlements as they went. After a short siege, St. John's surrendered and was duly torched. Captain Jacques Testard de Montigny, of Iberville's force, almost obliterated the English fisheries along the eastern shores.

By the end of March 1696, only the settlements on Bonavista, and Carbonear, on the Avalon peninsula, were intact. Bonavista was saved by remoteness, Carbonear by a forceful merchant, William Pynne, who commanded the defenders of his community. Iberville and Brouillan had destroyed thirty-six settlements, taken 700 prisoners, and killed another 200 people. Iberville collected an enormous weight of dried cod – 200,000 quintals, 200,000 hundredweight (nine million kilograms). Such destruction was possible because the tiny fishing settlements were isolated and clung to the coast. Communication by land was slow, and during the winter boats often could not put out to carry warnings.

Before he could complete the eviction of the English, a squadron from France, under the command of Iberville's brother Serigny (Joseph), sailed into Placentia Bay. Serigny brought orders for Iberville to drop everything and sail for Hudson Bay. But his efforts in Newfoundland were in vain. Soon after he departed, an English squadron carrying 2,000 soldiers, under Sir John Gibson and Sir John Norris, reached St. John's. They convinced the displaced fishermen to return to their burnt-out villages and rebuild the fishery. On 5 September 1697, England and France signed the Treaty of Ryswick. All conquered territory was to be returned. England received Newfoundland; Acadia remained French. The treaty was overturned, however, when the French again established their capital at Placentia. In 1705, the governor, Daniel d'Auger de Subercase, led an expedition of 450 men against the English settlements. He captured Bay Bulls and Petty Harbour and sent a party to burn out the settlements along Conception and Trinity Bays. Again Carbonear survived, and Subercase did not attempt to take St. John's. Three years later, for greater strength, the militia at St. John's became the Royal Newfoundland Regiment. That change did not prevent another French conquest, however. In January 1709 they again captured St. John's, but, lacking the manpower to retain it, abandoned the English capital in April.

Iberville's Fifth, and Last, Battle on Hudson Bay

The fleet that Iberville led to Hudson Bay in the summer of 1697 was the largest the French had ever sent against the Company's posts. His flagship was the 44-gun *Pélican* . Three other ships followed, including the supply vessel *Profond.* After finding themselves stranded by ice for three weeks, the squadron was on the move by mid-August. Fog proved to be the next obstacle; the Pélican became separated from the rest of the fleet and arrived alone off York/Fort Bourbon on 4 September. Iberville had sent a party in a shallop to scout out the fort when he noticed three sails on the horizon, which he assumed to be the rest of his fleet. But he was wrong – the approaching sails belonged to three armed English ships. The *Hampshire*, with fifty-six guns, was a Royal Navy frigate, Captain John Fletcher commanding. The other two ships belonged to the Company: the *Dering* sported thirty-six guns, and the *Royal Hudson's Bay*, thirty-two. The enemy could thus mount 124 guns against the lone *Pélican's* forty-four. To make matter worse, some of the men in the *Pélican's* crew were still ashore, and forty were down with scurvy.

If there ever was a "mother" of all French sea battles in Canadian waters, this was the one. The *Pélican* was outgunned almost three to one, but Iberville was a master tactician. Finding himself positioned between the fort and the rapidly approaching enemy ships, he had the crew stretch rope at intervals along the deck, to be used as handholds should the surface become slippery with blood. He sent his gunners below to the gun deck to remove the covers and make ready to fight. He attempted to sail past the *Hampshire*, which swung broadside and fired into the *Pélican's* rigging, almost disabling the spars. From astern, the two Company ships were raining grape and canister shot.

For four hours the unequal duel kept on, as the unwieldy vessels tacked and hove to. The standing rigging of the *Pélican* was in shambles and the *Dering* had shot a huge hole in her bow. The *Hampshire* came close enough for Captain Fletcher to demand surrender, which Iberville fiercely rejected. He moved to windward of Fletcher and fired his own broadside. The *Hampshire* hit a shoal and quickly sank, drowning all hands. Iberville had already swung about to deal with the *Royal Hudson's Bay*. After firing once the Company ship surrendered.

When a sharp squall struck, the *Dering* ran for shelter in the Nelson River. Along the shore, Iberville's men were boarding the *Royal Hudson's Bay* when the storm reached them. The ship sank, and the survivors of both sides waded to the beach. On the *Pélican*, Iberville tried to anchor, but the ship grounded on a sand bar. They were much too far out to wade, so the crew had to swim in the icy waters, and eighteen drowned. The survivors could find little to eat, and they huddled around a fire for warmth.

At last, on 13 September, the other three French vessels appeared, but they tacked back and forth out of range of the fort's guns. The situation called for action from Iberville's few, who acted as many. Their firing from the trees beyond the stockade so distracted the English that the French ships were able to approach and land guns and soldiers farther along the shore. Once he saw the guns, Henry Baley, the governor of York/Fort Bourbon, surrendered and vanished into the forest.

All that remained in English hands was Albany Fort. Iberville was tempted, but with the season so far advanced he sailed for Quebec instead. Under the Treaty of Ryswick that returned Newfoundland to England, the forts at the bottom of James Bay were to be French, and York/Fort Bourbon would be returned to England. This did not happen, however – York/Bourbon remained French, while the English retained Albany Fort on James Bay. The matter was, at length, settled by the Treaty of Utrecht in 1713, when the Hudson's Bay Company was awarded all the posts. Thus, while some of the fortifications on Castle Hill at Placentia are of French origin, others were built later by the English.

After he reached Quebec in the late autumn of 1696, Iberville was transferred to a land that could not have been in starker contrast to the rugged land he had called home. The French required his unique talents to found the colony of Louisiana. As usual, he had a brother with him, now Jean-Baptiste Le Moyne de Bienville. Tour guides in New Orleans still remember the brothers as Frenchmen, not Canadians. In a city that treasures its French past, Pierre's title is pronounced with a long "i" rather than an "ee," and Jean-Baptiste's as "Beanville."

National Archives of Canada

Moose Factory

By the time the Treaty of Utrecht brought yet another temporary halt to the French-English conflict, Iberville was dead. After Louisiana, he marauded among England's West-Indian possessions, while engaging in trade between France and several other Caribbean islands. In 1706, he contracted malaria in Havana, Cuba, and died. He lies buried in the Church of San Cristobal, an unlikely resting place for a Canadian hero. France later awarded him the Cross of St. Louis, the first person of Canadian birth so honoured.

IV

Louisbourg, May–July 1758

Louisbourg, on Cape Breton Island, is among Canada's best-known battle sites. The restoration of part of the thirty-hectare (seventy-acre) national park is the most ambitious project of this type undertaken in the country. Each summer, thousands of visitors flock to the park, and see Louisbourg at the best time of the year. Construction of the original fortress on the cold, foggy, not-very-livable east coast of Cape Breton began as a result of the Treaty of Utrecht of 1713. France lost Acadia, as well as the claim to Newfoundland and the Hudson Bay Lowland. She retained Île Royale (Cape Breton) and Île Saint-Jean (Prince Edward Island). To control the Gulf of St. Lawrence and protect access to Quebec, the French began to build the fortress of Louisbourg in 1719.

In time, a complex community evolved on the site – soldiers, fishermen lured by the proximity of the Grand Banks, merchants, and civilian labourers all lived and worked here. Some of the fishermen also dwelt outside the walls along the shore. While cold, damp winters were a drawback, the excellent harbour was an asset. The fortress encircled a point jutting out into the Atlantic that formed the southern side of the harbour. The landward defences looked formidable – a row of walls and bastions enclosed the town, citadel, garrison barracks, and other government buildings. Near the centre of the narrow entrance to the harbour was an island, where a gun battery dictated that no enemy fleet should enter without a fight. Across the harbour was the Royal Battery , ready to fire on any ship that might pass the Island Battery at the harbour mouth. No one worried about the landward side – it faced an impenetrable swamp.

The land around the fortress was not especially fertile, and because of the almost continual cold the growing season was very brief. Île Saint-Jean, with its excellent soil and milder climate, served as a source of food for the fortress, and so was administered from there.

Louisbourg fell twice, in 1745 and 1758. If Maj.-Gen. Jeffery Amherst and his army of 27,000 soldiers and sailors had failed in 1758, he would have been a national disgrace. That it fell in 1745 was, human suffering aside, a comic opera.

The War of the Austrian Succession (King George's War) broke out in 1744. Angered over attacks on their merchant vessels by the French from

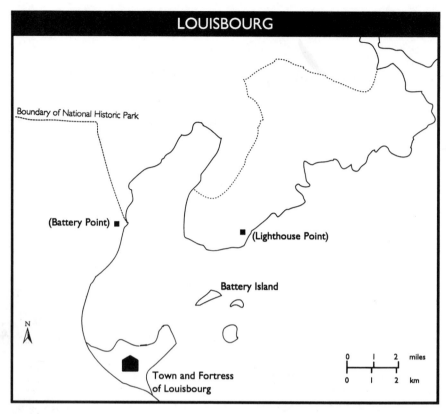

LOUISBOURG

Boundary of National Historic Park

(Battery Point) ■

■ (Lighthouse Point)

Battery Island

N

Town and Fortress
of Louisbourg

0   1   2   miles

0   1   2   km

Louisbourg, New Englanders formed an expedition, led by the businessman and militia officer William Pepperrell. The New Englanders landed on the shore of Gabarus Bay, to the south and west. Pepperrell and his rank amateurs marched, dragging heavy guns, into and across the impenetrable swamp. Here was a demonstration of "it could not be done but they did not know and went ahead and did it anyway." They captured the Royal Battery, turned its guns against the town, and proceeded to batter Louisbourg from there and from all the landward sides until the garrison surrendered. The New Englanders were furious when, at the signing of the Treaty of Aix-La-Chapelle in 1748, Britain agreed to return Louisbourg to France.

When the two countries were again at war in 1756, Louisbourg was an obvious target. The French had improved the shattered defences somewhat, but the fortress was far from invulnerable. In 1758, shortly before the attack, the troops had demolished the Royal Battery across the harbour to ensure that it could not be turned against them again. No longer so trustful of their swamp, they had ringed the eastern portion of Gabarus Bay with defensive lines of guns and trenches along the rise above the curving beach, and fronted them with felled trees and abatis. Amherst faced a more formidable obstacle than Pepperrell, but with a much stronger army.

Britain planned two powerful strikes against France's North American possessions for the summer of 1758. One, led by the commander-in-chief, Gen. James Abercrombie, would be against Fort Ticonderoga, on Lake Champlain. The other, an attack on Louisbourg, was commanded by the comparatively young and newly promoted Major-General Amherst (1717–1797). If both expeditions were successful and the season not too far advanced, Abercrombie and Amherst would move on towards Quebec. In the spring, Amherst's expedition began to assemble at Halifax.

The commander of Louisbourg was Augustine de Boschenry de Drucour (1702–1762), a seasoned naval captain and a knight of the order of Saint-Louis. The commander of the ten warships in the harbour was Jean-Antoine Charry Desgouttes. Drucour had 3,500 soldiers in his garrison – four regiments of regulars and twenty-four companies of *troupes de la marine* – and 4,000 sailors and militia. About 4,000 other residents were civilians.

The British expedition actually had two leaders. Amherst directed the ground force, and Adm. Edward Boscawen (1711–1761) the fleet. Boscawen was a grandson of Arabella Churchill, a sister of the 1st Duke of Marlborough. Amherst's three brigade commanders were Brig.-Gen. Edward Whitmore (1694–1761), the colonel of the 22nd Foot and a veteran of Hovenden Walker's disastrous failure against Quebec in 1711; Nova Scotia Gov. Charles Lawrence (1709–1761), who had years of experience in the Maritimes; and the most junior commander, but one who showed great promise, Brig.-Gen. James Wolfe (1727–1759). Boscawen's subordinate, Adm. Sir Charles Hardy, arrived in Halifax on 19 March to set up a blockade of the shipping routes towards Louisbourg, in order to prevent supplies and reinforcements from reaching the fortress. Britain put an embargo on all her ports from Nova Scotia to South Carolina, to conceal the extensive preparations required for the enterprise.

Regular troops came from Boston, New York City, and Philadelphia, as well as from the British Isles. The latter arrived in a convoy on 12 May with Admiral Boscawen. Amherst was still en route in the frigate HMS *Dublin*. The land force, 13,000 strong, included fourteen regiments of infantry, four companies of American rangers, a detachment of artillery, and some civilian workmen. Wolfe's was an élite division, composed of grenadiers from several regiments and a special light infantry battalion, the ranger companies and the 78th Fraser Highlanders. Boscawen's naval force comprised 157 vessels – 23 ships-of-the-line, 16 smaller warships, transports, and auxiliaries, 14,000 sailors and marines, and 1,842 guns. The French would be outnumbered by roughly four to one.

Boscawen made good use of his time while he waited for Amherst. While the soldiers drilled to make those from Britain fit after the long, cramped voyage, the sailors and marines practised moving troops ashore from small boats that the fleet had brought to serve as landing craft. By 29 May, although Amherst still had not arrived, Boscawen put to sea. He was worried that if the expedition required many weeks to subdue Louisbourg, he might risk being at sea during the September hurricane season. The fleet had barely cleared the harbour when the *Dublin* hove into view. Amherst boarded Boscawen's flagship for a conference on strategy.

The fleet bringing Lawrence's and Wolfe's divisions reached Gabarus Bay on 2 June and dropped anchors. Immediately, Amherst set out with Lawrence and Wolfe in a ship's boat to reconnoitre the shore, being careful not to draw too close. Before Amherst reached the fleet, the brigadiers had made a tentative plan to stage the landings to the east of Louisbourg, rather than to the west as Pepperrell had done. Now, Amherst decided he would also prefer to gain a beachhead to the west, from Gabarus Bay. Wolfe was dubious about the site, but did not strongly oppose it. Bad weather set in at once, causing concern about the fate of the ships bringing Whitmore's division. Soon the first ships appeared, however, and the last stragglers fought their way into the bay on the 6th and anchored with the others.

By 7 June the wind had dropped and the swells had subsided somewhat. Under cover of the firing of his ship's guns, Amherst landed one regiment and sent it east around Black Point to set up a small base at Lorembec. At night, he loaded the advance troops of his three brigades on the small boats, ready to confront, at first light, the 2,000 French regulars manning the lines above the beach. Wolfe's brigade faced L'Anse à la Cormorandière (Kennington Cove), the west end of Amherst's intended line, where the French entrenchments were the most heavily fortified. Lawrence was in the centre and Whitmore in the most exposed place on the east, nearest the walls.

The guns of the frigate *Kennington* and the snow *Halifax* would keep up a steady fire as each division moved, to ensure that the French gunners could not concentrate their firepower on any one spot on their lines. The assault began at 2:00 a.m. on 8 June, when a signal light appeared on Boscawen's masthead. Wolfe's division moved first, towards L'Anse à la Cormorandière. Lawrence and Whitmore slid west , following Wolfe. Smoke from the *Kennington* and *Halifax* helped obscure the movement of the divisions. At first, the firing from the French guns drove Wolfe's boats back, but then three of them slipped behind some rocky headland that blocked the view from the enemy line. The men waded ashore and climbed onto the dry rocks, followed by the rest of the division. Lawrence's division helped distract the French by making a feint farther east, at Simon's Point, while Whitmore made his pretended approach even closer to the town. Wolfe's division was already marching around the French left flank, when Lawrence and Whitmore moved to land at L'Anse à la Cormorandière in Wolfe's tracks. Wolfe's boldness – and luck – combined to gain Amherst a beachhead.

Demoralized by the threat to their left flank, the French abandoned their position and retreated inside the walls of Louisbourg. The three divisions went in hot pursuit, until guns on the fort's bastions brought them to a halt. In the mêlée the British took seventy prisoners. They then began to consolidate their position barely three kilometres (two miles) from the walls. Amherst hurried ashore, eager to build on this initial success, but Louisbourg's fabled bad weather intervened.

By the 11th, Amherst was able to land his light artillery, mainly 6-pounders, at the Lorembec outpost, but the sea was too rough for his 24- and 32-pounders, the guns he needed most. Island Battery, at the entrance to the harbour, was a priority. While Boscawen blockaded it, Amherst took Wolfe, 1,200 of his light troops, and some of the 6-pounders on a long march around the perimeter of the harbour, past the now-defunct Royal Battery and on to Lighthouse Point at the other end of the harbour, where they mounted a battery and set up another outpost. The rest of his army concentrated on laying out their own siege lines, digging trenches and setting up redoubts along the west side of the fortress. Whitmore commanded troops who were building the gun batteries. The men worked at night, to avoid drawing French fire. Good weather returned on the 16th, and Amherst began landing his heaviest guns and moving them to the siege lines.

Inside the fortress, Drucour admitted that his situation was hopeless, but would not give in. He had ample stocks of food and ammunition, and the longer he held out the more brightly shone his hope that the British could not reach Quebec that season.

Patriotic duty came first, but neither side neglected the chivalrous courtesies of the day. Amherst sent two pineapples as a gift for Madame Drucour.

National Archives of Canada, C-5907

View of Louisbourg. The artist was Captain Ince. Many British officers made sketches and later engraved them.

The burning of the French ships *Prudent* and *Bienfaisant* at the taking of Louisbourg in 1758.

The French commander retaliated by sending a bottle of champagne to Amherst and a box of sweetmeats to James Wolfe, now in command of the battery on Lighthouse Point. While that polite exchange took place, Amherst was coping with an outbreak of smallpox among carpenters from New England who had come with the expedition.

Drucour had more serious internal problems. Morale was so low that many troops deserted. He ordered sixteen who were apprehended hanged. The civilians suffered cruelly from the bombardment – their homes were in ruins. Drucour managed to persuade a reluctant Desgouttes to scuttle four of his precious ships, hoping to block the channel. This left only five French ships-of-the-line and one frigate to hold off the British fleet.

Throughout July the British extended their trenches, moving them ever closer to Louisbourg's walls. One night, 725 Frenchmen raided the British position near Black Point, captured an outpost, and broke through Amherst's lines before his men drove them back. In the sortie the French killed one infantry officer and captured four of his men, then took two officers and twenty-eight men of the grenadiers. Partisans and native allies of the French roamed outside the wall, but did little damage. Periods of bad weather continued to alternate with good.

At noon on the 21st, a ball from one of Amherst's siege guns hit Desgoutte's 74-gun *Entreprenant,* lighting her supply of powder. In the explosion the ship *Capricious,* anchored close to the *Entreprenant,* caught fire. Flames leapt from the *Capricious* to the *Célèbre.* By 4:00 p.m., while the

French boats scrambled to rescue sailors and extinguish the flames, the British had a field day, firing grapeshot at the doomed men.

Louisbourg was now a disaster area. It had been struck by some twenty mortars and many more cannon. The barracks and the inner citadel had burnt, and the Island Battery was almost useless. The only effective ships were the 74-gun *Prudent* and the 64-gun *Bienfaisant*. Most of the sailors were ashore, assisting the other defenders. During the night of the 25th, Amherst and Boscawen resolved to dispose of the two remaining French warships. They sent fifty small boats loaded with troops into the harbour. Some occupied the Island Battery, while the rest approached the *Prudent*. They found her aground and promptly set her ablaze. Then they towed the *Bienfaisant* beyond the range of the French guns and captured 152 of her crew. During the operation seven men lost their lives and nine were wounded.

In the morning, now that Boscawen was poised to enter the harbour (the four sunken warships apparently were no obstacle), Drucour sent a flag to Amherst and asked for terms. The surrender ceremony took place on 27 July. Amherst's losses had been light, but the French had lost the entire Louisbourg garrison and 2,400 sailors. Amherst soon learned that Abercrombie had failed to take Fort Ticonderoga, although he had an army of nearly 8,000 men and far outnumbered Montcalm, the French commander. While Boscawen took the French prisoners and part of his fleet back to England, Amherst remained with a large garrison to make repairs to the fortress. Abercrombie soon received a notice of his recall. Amherst replaced him as commander-in-chief and he sailed for the main headquarters in New York City. Wolfe, promoted to major-general, would lead the attack on Quebec in 1759. He lost his life during this successful capture of the rock. Whitmore remained at Louisbourg as governor of Cape Breton and the Island of St. John.

The French had another opportunity to be chivalrous during Amherst's expedition down the St. Lawrence to capture Montreal in 1760. As at Louisbourg, the French were determined to delay him as long as possible. Some 400 soldiers, sailors and militia, stationed at Fort Lévis, an island at the head of the most westerly rapids, stood in his way. As Amherst was drawing close in a whaleboat, soaked by spouting geysers from the hail of shots, the French commander, Captain Pierre Pouchot, saluted him. He returned it as best he could while attempting to wring out his dripping coattails. Pouchot held up Amherst's 10,000-man army for more than a week before giving in, and his resistance delayed the British a further week to repair Lévis and leave a garrison there.

While going home for leave of absence because of ill health, Edward Whitmore drowned at sea. Lawrence succumbed at New York City. When Amherst retired, he built a house at Riverhead, near Sevenoaks, England, his birthplace, and named his home "Montreal."

V

John Bradstreet's Attack on Fort Frontenac, August 1758

Asmall but significant battle took place at Kingston during the Seven Years' (French and Indian) War. The battle was important because, in capturing Fort Frontenac at a time when the French were deeply committed farther east, John Bradstreet cut them off from their inland possessions – Niagara, Detroit, Michilimackinac, Duquesne (Pittsburgh), and the colony of Louisiana, at the mouth of the Mississippi River. Two years before, soon after war had been declared in 1756, the commander-in-chief in New France, the Marquis de Montcalm, had captured the British forts at Oswego, destroyed them, and stolen eight British ships. Afterwards, the forts stood empty, and the French controlled the Great Lakes. During the summer of 1758, the British had begun building whaleboats at Oswego, to use in transporting troops when the right time came.

With the Royal Navy blockading the Gulf of St. Lawrence, the French used their fleet on Lake Ontario to send luxury goods to Fort Niagara, to be forwarded by bateau and canoe to Louisiana. Bradstreet's opponents at Fort Frontenac were Pierre-Jacques Payen de Noyan et de Chavoy, the governor, and Commodore René Hypolite Pépin *dit* La Force, who commanded nine ships.

Fort Frontenac stood on the site of the Tête de Pont Barracks (today, on Highway 2, at the west end of the LaSalle Causeway), on low ground inside the entrance to the Cataraqui River. A plaque stands near the entrance gate to the barracks. The fort was well placed to guard the waterway, but on both sides lay high ground. To the west, the streets of Kingston slope uphill; to the east, beyond Royal Military College, is Fort Henry, completed in the 1840s on the best defensive site in the vicinity. Some 100 kilometres (60 miles) downstream on the south side of the St. Lawrence stood another French fort, La Présentation (at Ogdensburg, New York); it also stood on low ground on a poor defensive site. La Présentation was half-mission, half-fort. In command was the belligerent Abbé François Piquet, who sent his Mohawk converts on raids against the British supply routes to Lake Ontario.

John Bradstreet (1714–1774) was born at Annapolis Royal, Nova Scotia, a son of Lieut. Edward Bradstreet of the British army, and Agathe de Saint-

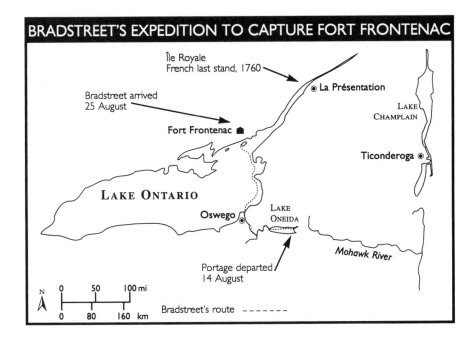

BRADSTREET'S EXPEDITION TO CAPTURE FORT FRONTENAC

Île Royale
French last stand, 1760

La Présentation

Bradstreet arrived
25 August

LAKE
CHAMPLAIN

Fort Frontenac

Ticonderoga

LAKE ONTARIO

Oswego

LAKE
ONEIDA

Mohawk River

Portage departed
14 August

N

0   50   100 mi

0   80   160   km

Bradstreet's route - - - - - - -

Étienne de La Tour (c. 1690–1739). Agathe's father was Jacques, a son of Charles de Saint-Étienne de La Tour, the victor in the Acadian civil war. Bradstreet was ambitious, both in commerce and as a soldier, although he felt he did not gain promotions in the British service as rapidly as he deserved because of his Acadian background.

He was a seasoned career officer, and had been at the capture of Louisbourg in 1745. By 1758, he was a lieutenant-colonel in the British army and a deputy quartermaster-general in America, responsible for organizing the movement of supplies and troops from Albany to Lake Champlain and to Lake Ontario. His duties included overseeing the construction of the required bateaux and whaleboats. He served under General James Abercrombie in the general's disastrous and ill-conceived attempt to capture Fort Ticonderoga, on Lake Champlain, from Montcalm on 8 July 1758. When Bradstreet suggested taking the French fort at Cataraqui, Abercrombie gave him permission and allowed him about 3,000 men. In the words of the well-known author on the war, Charles H. J. Snider, the smartest thing Abercrombie did was to send Bradstreet to Fort Frontenac.

So confident were the French that they controlled the upper St. Lawrence and Lake Ontario, the garrison was a mere 100 men, and only fifty of them were soldiers. Governor de Noyan was sixty-eight and rather infirm. René La Force (1728–1802) was in the prime of life, a swashbuckler suited to shifting luxury goods. Anchored in the harbour were his flagship *La Marquise de Vaudreuil*, the snow *Montcalm*, and the brigantine *Georges*. The latter two had been the *Halifax* and the *London* before the French captured them at Oswego and renamed them. Six smaller ships, most of them rowing schooners taken at Oswego, were tied to docks, loaded with trade goods, and nearly ready to sail for Fort Niagara.

Bradstreet's expedition set out in bateaux from Fort Stanwix, at the portage between the Mohawk River and Lake Oneida on 14 August, bound for Oswego. Most of his troops were colonial militiamen, but 150 were regulars from the 60th Regiment (in which Bradstreet had once held a captaincy). To man the boats came 200 whalers from New England and, to serve as scouts, a party of Oneida native allies. By the 21st they had reached Oswego, where a few whaleboats had been completed. Some of the troops went aboard, while others continued in the bateaux. Bradstreet had landed his men and some field guns to the west of Fort Frontenac by the afternoon of the 25th.

That night, La Force informed De Noyan that he had noticed Oneidas, certainly friends of the British, in the woods, and that there were British soldiers on the beach in a nearby bay. The commodore then went off to look after his fleet, and to load goods still in warehouses aboard his ships, in order to save them from capture so that he could resume his trading when the emergency was over.

On the 26th, Bradstreet's colonial artillerymen built a gun battery overlooking the fort from the west, and at dusk they began firing. The 27th was a Sunday, and during the saying of Mass, Bradstreet's gunners started firing again. Commodore La Force decided that the time had come to leave. The wind was light and from the northeast, not the best of conditions for sailing out of the harbour at Cataraqui, and worse for going downstream through the Thousand Islands towards La Présentation. La Force had no time to waste, nor could he take his entire fleet. He set sail with *La Marquise de Vaudreuil*, the *Montcalm*, and the *Georges*. The six smaller ships at the docks would have to be sacrificed, left at the mercy of the attacking force.

The three ships proved unmanageable in the light breeze, and they began sailing backwards "in irons," unable to tack into the wind. Soon, all three ran aground, and the situation grew desperate. La Force hurriedly transferred his crews to one of the rowing schooners and his men pulled out of the harbour and made for La Présentation. The commodore had no intention of letting his skilled sailors fall into enemy hands when he planned to fight another day. Behind him, De Noyan surrendered Fort Frontenac. Because of the governor's advanced age, Bradstreet allowed him to go to Montreal with the women and children. The rest of the captured garrison were sent to Albany, where they became prisoners of war.

Now that the British seemed about to return to Lake Ontario in force, the French needed a better fortification than low-lying La Présentation. They began building a stronghold on Île Royale (Chimney Island, New York), just

Mary Beacock Fryer

Fort Stanwix stood at the carrying place between the Mohawk River and Lake Oneida (now Rome, New York), a place well-known to Bradstreet. It is now a rebuilt historic site.

above the first set of rapids in the St. Lawrence. The fort was only partly finished in 1760 when Gen. Jeffery Amherst took his army of 10,000 men in whaleboats from Oswego to Montreal. The French made a gallant, last stand at Île Royale that held up Amherst for ten days, but they could not help Montreal – the city surrendered soon after Amherst arrived. Among the defenders on Île Royale were Commodore René La Force and his sailors.

La Force was destined to sail under two flags. He returned as commodore on Lake Ontario during the American Revolution, this time flying not the lilies of France, but the Red Jack of Great Britain.

John Bradstreet was promoted to full colonel, retroactive to 20 August 1758. In 1764, the war over, he led a small force to Sandusky, hoping to deal with the Ottawa war chief Pontiac, who was then menacing Detroit. He received an order to attack Pontiac's Shawnee and Delaware allies, but felt he lacked the strength to succeed and so remained where he was. Bradstreet was later accused of mismanagement. He continued as an acting deputy quartermaster-general, but it was merely a sinecure, for he was given little to do for the rest of his life. He died in New York City in 1774, and was buried at Trinity Church.

VI

Counterattack: Sainte-Foy, April–May 1760

E very year, thousands of visitors who come to Quebec City walk on the
Plains of Abraham, and remember Wolfe and Montcalm and September 1759. Quebec has been attacked more than once, however. On
some of these occasions, expeditions that set out to conquer the fortress on the
rock have failed. The very first attempt, that of the swashbuckling Kirke
brothers in 1628, did not succeed, but the brothers followed it with a temporary occupation the following year.

Tension between France and England (Great Britain after 1707, with the
union of the Parliaments), never really abated. Soon after a peace treaty came
into effect, provocation on both sides resumed, and a new war was declared.
Following the Kirkes', the next attempt came in 1690, a year after hostilities
had begun in King William's War, which was a conflict between New France
and her native allies on one side, and New England and the Iroquois nations
on the other. 90 ?

In May 1630, William Phips (1651–1695), the Provost Marshall of New
England, began his campaign against the French by attacking Port Royal. The
French surrendered there on 21 May. Phips was soon off on a second expedi-
tion, with 32 ships and 2,200 men, to subdue Quebec. They arrived on 16
October, late in the year to begin a campaign, and just two days after Louis de
Buade de Frontenac arrived from France for his second term as governor. With
Frontenac came 3,000 fresh troops, a disconcerting situation for Phips. For
three days his men sparred with the French militia until, disheartened by the
cold and fearful of being trapped by ice, Phips decided to withdraw. King
William's War ended in 1697 with the Treaty of Ryswick.

Hostilities began again in 1702, this time with the start of Queen Anne's
War, the War of the Spanish Succession. In September 1710, a force from
Boston captured Port Royal, the last occasion that it changed hands. The set-
tlement and the fort the French had started in 1608 have been known as
Annapolis Royal and Fort Anne ever since. The next year, 1711, a disastrous
expedition intended against Quebec was dubbed "the magnificent fiasco."
From Britain a substantial fleet set sail for Boston. From there, it joined with

New Englanders to prosecute the attack. The leader was Rear-Adm. Hovenden Walker (c. 1656–1725). By the time he left Boston, in July, he had nine warships, two bomb ketches, sixty troop transports, a miscellany of smaller boats, and 12,000 soldiers, sailors, and natives. A land force of 2,300 men, led by Colonel Francis Nicholson, a former governor of Virginia, set out in small boats from Albany, intending to rendezvous with the fleet outside Quebec. Walker's fleet came to grief on shoals along the north shore just at the mouth of the St. Lawrence River. After losing eight ships and 900 men, Walker abandoned the expedition and recalled Nicholson. The war ended in 1713 with the signing of the Treaty of Utrecht.

King George's War, the War of the Austrian Succession, began in 1744 and ended four years later with the Treaty of Aix-la-Chapelle. In this conflict, attention focused on Louisbourg; Quebec was not threatened.

The next outbreak of hostilities would be the last for France in North America. The Seven Years' War, the French and Indian War, began officially in 1756 and ended in 1763. Quebec was captured once, and then defended successfully. In September 1759, at the famous short, sharp battle on the Plains of Abraham, the British commander, Gen. James Wolfe, was killed in action, and his French opponent, the Marquis de Montcalm, was mortally wounded. The French regulars and the more numerous militia who escaped from the battlefield fell back on Montreal, to fight another day. Military leadership devolved on François de Lévis, Duc de Lévis, who had command of about 10,000 men, six small frigates, and good sources of supply.

Metro Toronto Reference Library, John Ross Robertson Collection

This work shows the ruins of Notre-Dame-des-Victoires church and other buildings in the Lower Town after the bombardment of Quebec in 1759.

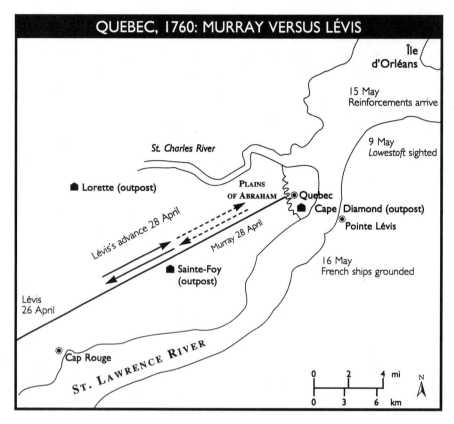

QUEBEC, 1760: MURRAY VERSUS LÉVIS

Île d'Orléans

15 May
Reinforcements arrive

9 May
Lowestoft sighted

St. Charles River

Lorette (outpost)

PLAINS OF ABRAHAM

Quebec

Cape Diamond (outpost)

Pointe Lévis

Lévis's advance 28 April

Murray 28 April

Sainte-Foy (outpost)

16 May
French ships grounded

Lévis
26 April

Cap Rouge

ST. LAWRENCE RIVER

0   2   4 mi

0   3   6 km

N

Wolfe's successor at Quebec was Brig.-Gen. James Murray (1721/22–1794), whose garrison amounted to scarcely 4,000 troops in the city. For naval defence he had five armed ships – two sloops and three smaller vessels. Adm. Charles Saunders, who had been responsible in large measure for Wolfe's victory, had taken the rest of his enormous fleet out of the St. Lawrence before freeze-up.

Murray faced a serious dilemma over how to ensure the survival of his garrison and the civilians in the neighbourhood through the coming winter. The walls of Quebec, inadequate before Wolfe's bombardment, were in deplorable condition. Fully a third of the dwellings were in ruins, as were most other buildings and fortifications. Murray put his able-bodied troops and many civilians to work repairing the damage. The country around the city was open, and Murray dispatched work parties considerable distances away, to forested land where they could cut enough firewood. He established posts at Lorette and Sainte-Foy, and sent guards with all his outside workers to combat any threat from French raiding parties.

Food was even scarcer than firewood. During the winter, in part owing to short rations, sickness and disease killed some 1,000 men, nearly five times the number who had died in battle on the Plains of Abraham. In February, a small

French force attempted to capture Pointe Lévis, but Murray's troops marched across the frozen St. Lawrence and drove them off. As spring approached, Murray's situation was a sorry one. Daily, he watched anxiously for the ice to go out, for the time when he could hope to see a relief ship coming. He sent a party of light infantrymen to take post at Cape Diamond, ready to warn him of the arrival of a French force from Montreal. On 23 April, the ice began to float away, a mixed blessing, since it was as great an advantage for Lévis as for the Royal Navy.

Lévis, who had had the winter to prepare, was ready. He set out with his six frigates and some 7,000 troops, sailing and marching, to Saint Augustin, twenty-five kilometres (fifteen miles) upriver from Quebec. All the French troops were ashore by 26 April. Forewarned by scouts, Murray ordered his outposts at Cape Diamond, Lorette, and Sainte-Foy evacuated. The road from the west now lay open to the French army. Early in the morning of the 28th, Murray decided to erect more defences. Accompanied by twenty field guns and artillerymen to operate them, Murray led 2,500 men out onto the Plains of Abraham and set them to digging a trench at right angles to the road. Before it was finished, French troops appeared on the road from Sainte-Foy. Murray resolved to attack at once, before Lévis could deploy his men. That first head-long rush took the French by surprise. They fell back, but soon regrouped and attacked. When Murray saw that the French had reached his flanks and were threatening to surround him, he ordered a withdrawal into the city. In their haste the men abandoned the twenty field guns, leaving a prize for Lévis. The French, now in command of the Plains of Abraham, set up camp as a preliminary to beginning a bombardment.

Metro Toronto Reference Library, John Ross Robertson Collection

Cape (Cap) Rouge. Here Lévis assembled the French troops for the counter-attack against Murray and the British troops at Quebec in 1760.

Inside the city, Murray had all the remotely able-bodied men and walking wounded working on preparations to withstand a siege. He sent a messenger in a small boat to find a way to warn General Jeffery Amherst of Quebec's impending plight. Amherst, the commander-in-chief, was then in New York City. A message reached him two weeks later, but responding to Murray's situation would take time. Suddenly, on 9 May, watchers in Quebec spotted a sail – either a cause for alarm, or for rejoicing. For some time the garrison waited tensely, fearful that the ship might fly the lilies of France. Observers burst into cheers when they were able to make out the Red Jack of the frigate *Lowestoft*. Help was at hand, although Lévis's bombardment did not abate.

Six days later, the first huge ship-of-the-line bringing two fresh regiments from Louisbourg (captured in 1758 by Amherst) appeared below the Île d'Orléans, followed by a second frigate. On 16 May, two more frigates arrived, sailed upstream and drove Lévis's six smaller ones aground. His naval support out of action, Lévis decamped and began marching his army back to Montreal. Like Murray before, he abandoned considerable artillery, as well as supplies. He had no way of knowing that a French relief fleet had reached the mouth of the St. Lawrence on 14 May, scarcely a week behind the British ships. On learning that the British had already reinforced Quebec, the French fleet retired to Chaleur Bay.

As 1760 began, Prime Minister Pitt had decided that this year he would put an end to French resistance in Canada. To achieve his goal he agreed to a massive input of troops and equipment. Three British armies would converge on Montreal. Amherst and 10,000 men, the largest force, would go by the Hudson-Mohawk and Oswego route, Lake Ontario and the St. Lawrence, to strike from the west. Lieut.-Col. William Haviland and 4,000 troops would leave Crown Point, on Lake Champlain, on 16 August, and would continue north along the Richelieu River. Murray received the order to take a fleet of small ships and open boats from Quebec. He left on 14 July with 2,500 soldiers, to seal off any escape route to the east. His would be the slowest passage, against the prevailing wind and current of the St. Lawrence.

Passing Trois-Rivières on 7 August, Murray kept his boats close to the south shore, out of range of a French gun battery on the opposite side. By the 27th, his ships were close to the east end of the Island of Montreal. He camped at Varennes as he waited for news of Haviland's and Amherst's progress. Most of his troops stayed on the ships. Some French regulars, who had married and had families in the colony, and many militia, surrendered to Murray while he was waiting at Varennes. He allowed the militiamen to go to their homes on parole. Because so many men had left, Lévis's army at Montreal was now reduced to 2,500 effectives. From Fort Chambly, on the Richelieu, Haviland's army cut overland and reached the south shore of the St. Lawrence opposite Montreal on 5 September. Amherst, who had left Oswego on 10 August, had finished shooting the rapids by the 6th and was fifteen kilometres (nine miles) from the city.

With all three armies now so close to Montreal, Lévis surrendered without a fight on 8 September. The North American phase of the Seven Years' War was finished, although peace between Britain and France would not come until 1763, when the war ended in Europe. By the Treaty of Paris, France ceded all her North American territory to Britain, except for the islands of Saint Pierre and Miquelon, and fishing rights off Newfoundland.

VII

Quebec:
Last Siege, 1775–1776

T he last attack on Quebec came from the south. It was part of an unfriendly rebel attempt to force Canada to join the American Revolution as the fourteenth colony. Wolfe's victory of 1759 was won on the Plains of Abraham; Murray's defence was on the same spot. The defence of 1775 was a street fight in the Lower Town, a battle that was re-enacted in October 1975. Staging the battle through the streets was impractical, however, and so the commemoration took place on the Plains of Abraham.

Although poorly fortified Montreal was captured, the key to the defence of Canada was the fortress atop the rock of Quebec. The rebellion in the Thirteen Colonies turned bloody in April 1775 when provoked British troops in Concord and Lexington, Massachusetts, fired on rebels. (Americans would call them "patriots," but from the Canadian viewpoint they were rebels and traitors.)

On 10 May, Benedict Arnold, an infamous turncoat, joined the leaders of the Green Mountain Boys, Ethan Allen and Seth Warner, and seized decaying Fort Ticonderoga, on Lake Champlain. Warner took Crown Point two days later. The invasion route to Canada lay open. The strongest post north of the boundary was Fort Saint Jean, on the Richelieu River. To make matters worse, the governor of Canada, Gen. Guy Carleton (1724–1808), had sent two regiments to besieged Boston, at the request of the commander-in-chief, Gen. Thomas Gage. That left only two below-strength regiments in Canada: the 7th Royal Fusiliers and the 26th Cameronians, comprising altogether 800 men.

The rebel invasion would be in two divisions, one to Montreal by the Richelieu route, and the other over the harsh, wilderness path up the Kennebec River, across a steep divide, and down the Chaudière River to the south shore of the St. Lawrence opposite Quebec. A rebel force of 1,500 under Gen. Richard Montgomery (1736–1775) left Crown Point on 30 August. Montgomery was a former British officer who had married into the rebel Livingston family. Some 1,200 men under Montgomery's second-in-command, Col. Benedict Arnold (1741–1801), left Cambridge, Massachusetts, on 18 September. After a journey likened to Hannibal crossing the Alps, Arnold arrived at Pointe Lévis, opposite Quebec, on 9 November, at the head of 600 starving scarecrows. Half of his men had turned back, fallen ill, or died.

Benson Lossing's Field Book of the American Revolution

Col. Benedict Arnold's men polled and portaged their boats up the Kennebec and down the Chaudière Rivers to reach Quebec.

In the meantime, Montgomery had been stalled at Fort Saint Jean since 5 September, because the defenders had kept up a sustained, stubborn resistance. Governor Carleton was in Montreal, making abortive plans to relieve Saint Jean. When he learned that the fort had capitulated on 2 November, he evacuated all troops in the Montreal area on ships, an operation completed by the 11th. Montgomery's rebels occupied the city on the 12th. Off Sorel, where a rebel advance party had built a gun battery, Carleton received a flag of truce and a demand that he surrender his fleet and troops. Carleton stalled for a time and discussed the situation with his deputy, Col. Robert Prescott. Both agreed that with Montreal subdued, it was imperative that the governor reach Quebec. If he could hold that fortress until reinforcements arrived from Britain, he would be in a position to retake Montreal. Joseph Bouchette, a captain of one of the ships, had him rowed, oars muffled, away from the fleet in a small boat. Carleton hoped that Colonel Prescott might yet escape. Most of the regulars were with him, or prisoners taken at Saint Jean, and Carleton would need every available soldier to hold Quebec.

At Trois-Rivières, Carleton learned that Benedict Arnold was at Pointe-aux-Trembles, another stumbling block. The *Fell,* a snow (a square-rigger with trysail aft of main), was there, en route to Quebec with some 7th Royal Fusiliers. Carleton joined them, and the *Fell* passed Arnold's position safely and reached the harbour of Quebec without incident.

In command during Carleton's absence was Lieut.-Col. Allan Maclean (1725–1798), a Gaelic-speaking Scots Highlander and ardent Jacobite who had been "out with the Prince" at Culloden. Maclean was a veteran of many campaigns. After an exile in the Scots Brigade in the Netherlands, he went home and joined the British army. He had been wounded at Ticonderoga in

1758, and had served with Murray's garrison in Quebec in 1761. In 1775 he had sailed to Boston with a King's commission to raise a provincial regiment, the Royal Highland Emigrants, from among Highlanders settled in all the colonies. The uniform for the new corps would be the red coat and the kilt worn by His Majesty's other Highland regiments.

When Maclean arrived in Montreal in August, looking for recruits, Carleton appointed him his second-in-command and posted him to Quebec. Maclean had left Quebec with reinforcements for Saint Jean in September, under orders to rendezvous with troops that Carleton was leading from Montreal. Maclean was south of Sorel when Carleton ordered him back to Quebec. The boats carrying the force Carleton raised in Montreal had been fired upon near St. Helen's Island, and he had lost his nerve. Maclean arrived in Quebec on 12 November to find a timorous Lieut.-Gov. Hector Cramahé talking of striking the flag. Ever since he had seen Benedict Arnold's raga-muffins across the St. Lawrence, Cramahé felt trapped. Brusquely, Maclean ordered all defeatist talk to cease; everyone must concentrate on defence.

The next day, Arnold appeared with his men on the Plains of Abraham, and sent a flag of truce demanding surrender. An infuriated Maclean refused to allow any gate to be opened to admit the flag. Since Arnold had no artillery he could do little, but he stayed encamped until the 18th. He moved west to Pointe-aux-Trembles when he learned that Montgomery was sailing from Montreal with reinforcements. On the 19th, the *Fell* brought Carleton, but the fleet he had left behind, Colonel Prescott, and all the soldiers had been captured. Valuable troops he badly needed were prisoners-of-war.

"A Return of Men for the Defence of the town of Quebec this 16th November 1775" had been compiled by order of Maclean:

	Officers	Privates
Royal Artillery	1	5
Recruits belonging to Royal Highland Emigrant Regiment	14	186
Lizard Frigate Marines	2	35
Seamen effective	19	114
Hunter Sloop	8	60
Magdaline arm'd Schooner	4	16
Charlotte arm'd Ship	4	46
Masters, Mates, Carpenters & Seamen belonging to the Transports & Merchant Ships that have not been impressed	0	74
Artificers & Carpenters	0	80

	Officers	Privates
British Militia, including officers		200
Canadian Militia, including officers		300
Royal Fusiliers on board the Fell & Providence arm'd vessels expected to arrive soon	3	60
Seamen belonging to said Vessels	18	72
	63	1,248

By British Militia, Maclean meant English-speaking troops under Col. William Caldwell, whose home was near Sainte-Foy. The Canadian militia were French-speaking men from the vicinity. Inside the city were about 500 civilians. The day after Carleton's return, on 20 November, he ordered compiled a "Return of Provisions in the Garrison":

Flour	1,950 barrels
Wheat, 7,840 Bushells will make	1,500 " " in flour
Rice in Tierces about 450 lb each	146
Bisket	1,100 Quintals
Butter	406 Firkins
Pease	800 Bushells

On 3 December, Gen. Montgomery reached Pointe-aux-Trembles with 600 reinforcements and the artillery Arnold had eagerly awaited. Ironically, the reinforcements had travelled aboard the ships captured off Sorel a fortnight before. The siege seemed about to commence. Maclean and Carleton slept in the Recollect Convent, and all the garrison retired fully clothed, arms close at hand. Everyone waited for Montgomery and Arnold to make their move. Days passed, the defenders watching warily.

The bastions along Quebec's walls that protected the Upper Town had been improved and were manned. Two fences obstructed the route round the southern side of the rock into the Lower Town, along a path called Près de Ville. To block the rebels, should they attempt to come round the north side of the peninsula to enter the Lower Town from the suburb of Saint Roch, two barricades had been erected. The first stood near the entrance to Sault au Matelot Street, the second at the end of this street, where Rue de la Montagne, from the Upper Town, joined it. The houses along Sault au Matelot had been evacuated, except for one belonging to a merchant, Simon Fraser, which had two 3-pounder cannon and thirty men – Canadian militia and seamen led by Captains Chabot and Barnsfare and Volunteer John Coffin, a Loyalist from Boston. Carleton had appointed Lieutenant-Colonel Maclean his field commander for the coming battle.

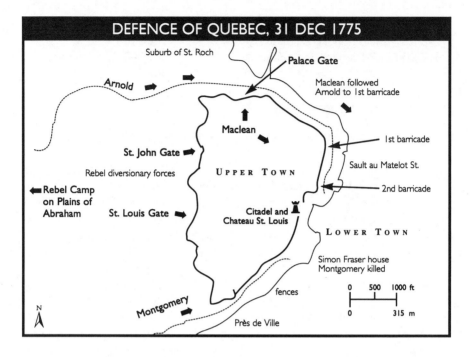

DEFENCE OF QUEBEC, 31 DEC 1775

Suburb of St. Roch

Palace Gate

Arnold

Maclean followed
Arnold to 1st barricade

Maclean

1st barricade

St. John Gate

Sault au Matelot St.

Rebel diversionary forces

UPPER TOWN

Rebel Camp
on Plains of
Abraham

2nd barricade

St. Louis Gate

Citadel and
Chateau St. Louis

LOWER TOWN

Simon Fraser house
Montgomery killed

fences

0   500   1000 ft

0   315 m

N

Montgomery

Près de Ville

In the rebel camp on the Plains of Abraham, Montgomery and Arnold planned a two-pronged attack. Montgomery would lead one force round the southern side of the rock, while his second-in-command took a larger body through Saint Roch by the northern route. The two commanders would meet inside the Lower Town, find a way into the Upper Town, and try to rush the defenders, catching them by surprise. While this was taking place, two small bands of rebels would keep up a lively fire near the Saint Jean and Saint Louis Gates, to distract the occupants and ensure that less strength would be thrown against the real striking forces.

The weather stayed fine; the nights were clear. Montgomery wished for falling snow or at least clouds to obscure his attack. He was getting edgy – many of his enlistments would expire on 1 January 1776. Before dawn on 31 December, in the nick of time, a blizzard raged; it interfered with visibility. Montgomery set out with 500 men for Près de Ville, and broke through the two fences without difficulty. Meanwhile, Arnold was leading his section of 700 men through St. Roch along the northern route past the rock. Capt. Thomas Ainslie, of the British Militia, recorded the next events:

> About 4 o'clock in the Morning Capt. Malcolm Fraser of the Royal Emigrants being on his rounds, saw many flashes of fire without hearing any reports; the sentries inform'd him that they had perceived them for some time on the heights of Abraham, the sentinels between Port Louis and Cape Diamond had seen fix'd lights like lamps on a street – the appearance being very uncommon

and the night favouring the designs of the enemy, Capt. Fraser order'd the Guards and pickets on the ramparts to stand to their arms. The drums beat, the bells rang the alarm, and in a few minutes the whole Garrison was under arms – even old men of seventy were forward to oppose the attackers.

The men Fraser had spotted were Arnold's. Montgomery's furtive approach along the south side of the rock was still undetected, but not for long.

When Montgomery's force was in front of Simon Fraser's house overlooking Près de Ville, the occupants released a hail of grapeshot from the two 3-pounder guns. Montgomery was killed, and two dozen rebels died with him. The others turned and fled helter-skelter. At approximately the same time, Arnold's vanguard reached the edge of the Lower Town, under steady fire from the ramparts above. On they crawled, stumbling in the oblivion created by the swirling snow, carrying scaling ladders to the first barricade in Sault au Matelot. Here Arnold fell, wounded below the knee, and was helped away by two of his men. Col. Daniel Morgan took command. This six-foot-four giant from the Kentucky Valley, who led a corps of frontier riflemen in fringed shirts, had been vehemently anti-British since receiving 500 lashes for striking a regular officer during Braddock's campaign of 1755. Brashly, Morgan, and his riflemen smashed through the first barricade. They halted farther up the street, waiting for the artillery to be brought forward. Soon chaos reigned, both within and outside Sault au Matelot. Some of the rebels following became lost; others retreated at the sight of wounded men trying to escape. In the Upper Town, Maclean had the situation well in hand. The defenders knew better than to take seriously the small groups of rebels firing near the Saint Jean and Saint Louis Gates. Maclean ordered a body of troops to march down Rue de la Montagne to reinforce the second barricade. Next, he sent 200 more out of the Palace Gate to march to the rear of the American position in Sault au Matelot. Both detachments included men of his own regiment.

Daniel Morgan's men attempted to mount the second barricade, but Capt. John Nairne, Royal Highland Emigrants, and some of his men wrested a scaling ladder from the rebels and used it to enter the second story of a house. After chasing out some rebels who had taken shelter on the ground floor, they began firing upon the men trapped in the street below. Then the troops who had left the Upper Town by the Palace Gate closed in, bottling up Morgan and some 400 others in Sault au Matelot. They sought refuge in houses when their line of retreat was cut off. In tears, Morgan handed his sword to a black-robed priest, rather than surrender it to a hated redcoat.

Rebel losses included some 400 captured, forty-two wounded (but safely back in camp), and thirty killed. Arnold later counted 700 survivors, but many rebels were not accounted for by either side. Ainslie put the number captured at 426, including forty-four wounded officers and men. Maclean

Lieut.-Col. Allan Maclean, the commander of the Royal Highland Emigrants. Maclean was an ardent Jacobite, but he served the British army loyally and commanded the battle for Quebec.

reported finding twenty more bodies once the snow had melted in the spring.

Maclean's casualties were light. Carleton reported one captain of the navy killed, and five rank and file wounded, of whom two later died. The captured rebel officers were housed in the seminary, and after a short stay at the monastery and the college of the Recollects the men were sent to the Dauphin Gaol. Carleton decided to gamble. He allowed captives of British birth to recant and enlist in the Royal Highland Emigrants. Maclean agreed, for he was anxious to complete one battalion. In all, ninety-four men joined, most of them Irish. Later, Maclean discovered that some were trying to desert, and Carleton ordered the suspects to turn in their uniforms and arms. The more blatant turncoats found themselves in the holds of ships in the harbour.

In the meantime, the rebels lingered in their encampment on the Plains of Abraham, except for the wounded Benedict Arnold who was moved to Montreal where he assumed command. On 6 May the *Surprise,* the first British ship of the spring fleet, sailed into the harbour, bringing with it a detachment of reinforcements. Now, Carleton had the resources to chase the small army of rebels from the neighbourhood. Carleton and Maclean led a sortie outside the city gates and the rebels offered no resistance. In their flight, Ainslie wrote, they abandoned most of their belongings: "they left cannon, mortars, field pieces, muskets and even their cloaths behind them. As we pursued them we found the road strew'd with arms, cartridges, cloaths, bread, port &cc." Maclean noted that his regiment partook of a meal laid out for the officers, who were interrupted by the sudden appearance of his vanguard. He then waxed caustic over the way Carleton was behaving, treating the rebels leniently despite the damage they had caused and deliberately refusing to pursue them. Had the second-in-command had his way, Montreal might have been cleared of its nest of rebels days sooner. When they reached Trois-Rivières, Carleton heard that Gen. John Burgoyne and the Baron von Riedesel had reached Quebec on 1 June, with the rest of the reinforcements of British, and German, regulars. (All were troops of George III, who was Elector of Hanover as well as King.) Carleton went off to greet his colleagues, leaving Maclean in command of the troops.

While Maclean remained at Trois-Rivières, the rebels withdrew as far as Sorel and encamped with reinforcements that had arrived there. During the winter, what the Continental Congress called the Army of the St. Lawrence had received 4,000 fresh troops, who were posted to Montreal, Fort Saint Jean, Sorel, Berthier, and The Cedars Rapids. The westernmost detachment had already suffered defeat. British regulars, Loyalists and Canadian volunteers, and a party of natives from Fort Niagara, had all gathered at Fort Oswegatchie (Ogdensburg, New York). Led by Capt. George Forster, the commandant at Oswegatchie, they descended the St. Lawrence, and on 20 May laid siege to the rebel position at The Cedars. Forster's men took 400 captives and negotiated the exchange of prisoners captured at Fort St. Jean, and with Col. Prescott at Sorel the previous November.

This news should have spurred Carleton to close in while the rebels at Montreal were off balance, but neither Carleton, nor Burgoyne, the new arrival, were in a rush. Soldiers who had been cooped up in transports at sea were not yet fit for duty, and provisions had to be moved up the St. Lawrence. At Sorel, rumours circulating among the rebels suggested that Maclean had only 300 men with him. Gen. John Sullivan, in command at Sorel and hoping to retake Quebec, ordered an attack on Maclean's position. Unknown to Sullivan, the Highlander had just been joined by Lieut.-Col. Simon Fraser of the 24th Regiment and four fresh battalions. On occasion, Canadians had helped the rebels, but Fraser and Maclean were in an area where they were loyal.

Sullivan, who was unaware of the situation, sent Brig. William Thompson forward with 2,000 men. Thompson landed eleven kilometres (seven miles) above Trois-Rivières. An accommodating Canadian agreed to guide the rebels

Mary Beacock Fryer

Royal Highland Emigrants. Men in uniforms of the 1770s re-enact battles of the period, in this instance at Fort Wellington, Prescott, Ontario, in 1975.

to Maclean's camp. Instead of taking the road, he led them into a swamp, through which they floundered to the point of exhaustion. Emerging from the swamp into a large field they confronted Fraser's men, drawn up in battle formation. A militia officer, Captain Landron, had seen the rebels landing and had hastened to inform Maclean. Thompson's rebels broke and fled, but Fraser's men captured 200 of them, including their leader. The survivors escaped back into the swamp. On 14 June, Carleton returned to Trois-Rivières, accompanied by General Burgoyne, the Baron von Riedesel, and enough British and German regulars to bring his expedition to 8,000 men.

Carleton divided his army into two sections. Burgoyne and Fraser landed with 4,000 troops at Sorel, which they found deserted. Sullivan had advance warning of the fleet's approach, and was hustling his demoralized force in boats up the Richelieu, making the most of a twenty-four-hour head start. He had 2,500 effectives; the rest were wounded or suffering from smallpox.

While Burgoyne followed Sullivan, Carleton sailed on with Maclean, von Riedesel, and the remaining 4,000 troops to deal with Benedict Arnold's rebels in Montreal. An aide warned Arnold of Carleton's impending arrival, and, like Sullivan he wasted no time. In four hours the rebels had left the city and were heading for Fort Saint Jean, and the loyal militia was preparing to welcome Carleton. By 17 June the governor was in Montreal, while Sullivan and Arnold, who had joined forces at Saint Jean, were withdrawing towards Lake Champlain.

By that stage in the campaign, Maclean's battalion stood at 400 men, and in another year it would be close to full strength. Maclean was looking forward to leading the regiment when General Burgoyne set out for New York State in the spring 1777. To his dismay, Burgoyne decided the Royal Highland Emigrants would remain behind as part of the Canadian garrison: "I propose Maclean's corps, because I very much apprehend desertion from such parts of it as are composed of Americans, should they come near the enemy ... In Canada, whatsoever may be their disposition, it is not easy to effect it."

Maclean fumed: Burgoyne had not stated the true reason for his decision. As a member of Parliament before the war, Burgoyne had spoken in the House of Commons against secret activities of Jacobites in London; one he had named specifically was Allan Maclean. Burgoyne was more alarmed at the thought of a regiment of kilted Jacobites than at enemy Americans, as Maclean well knew.

Maclean's regiment was promoted to the British establishment in 1778 as the 84th Foot. The first battalion, which he commanded, served in Canada. A second battalion, raised in Nova Scotia, served there and in the southern campaign. Maclean's commission allowed him five battalions, an allowance which proved to be overly optimistic. He had planned to raise his third battalion among North Carolina Highlanders. From Boston, before he set out to find recruits in Canada, he sent two of his officers south. The royal governor of North Carolina, Josiah Martin, purloined Maclean's officers, promoted them, and ordered them to raise the North Carolina Highlanders. Marching towards the coast in February 1776, on a rumour that a British army was coming by sea, the Highlanders were ambushed at Moore's Creek Bridge and decimated. Maclean's hopes for a third battalion were dashed, and he was enraged over the shady tactics of Governor Martin. After the war, the second battalion settled in New Brunswick, and those of the first who were not residents of Canada found new homes in what is now Ontario.

VIII

The Battle and Occupation of Little York (Toronto), 26 April–8 May 1813

The conflict known as the War of 1812 commenced on 18 June 1812 with the declaration by the United States of war on Great Britain. Americans maintain that it was a war nobody really won. However, since their intent was to capture Canada, to stop the British from blockading European ports and removing British-born men from their ships, and to defeat the tribes of the old Northwest, they lost the war because they failed in all three objectives. Yet American historians can point to mitigating circumstances. Strategically, the way to take Canada was to concentrate strength on one area, such as Kingston, the naval base for Lake Ontario. With Upper Canada cut off, moving on Montreal might have seemed a straightforward operation, especially at a time when both Canadas were weakly defended. Because so many troops were committed elsewhere, British officers operating against the Americans from Upper Canada were starved for regulars, professional soldiers; instead they had to depend on militiamen, part-time citizen soldiers with little training, except for flank companies that drilled more frequently. The factor that made an enormous difference was the native peoples, especially those in territory claimed by the United States.

The Americans were already at war against the natives along the northwest frontier, where warriors had banded together to curb the spread of westward settlement. While a major cause of the war was maritime rights, the United States also sought to punish Britain for her support of the native tribes. Thus, the Americans felt that they had to throw some weight against the interior and against the British bases, particularly Sandwich (Windsor) and Niagara, both important headquarters for the British Indian Department.

In the first year of the war, therefore, the Americans reinforced Detroit, only to have it fall, on 16 August 1812, to an inferior British-Canadian army dashingly led by Maj.-Gen. Isaac Brock, commander of the forces in Upper Canada, and the Shawnee warrior Tecumseh. Barely two months later, on 13 October, Brock was killed in action as he led troops against an American force at Queenston Heights, above Fort George on the Niagara Peninsula. (He was knighted posthumously for his success at Detroit.)

Brock's second-in-command, Maj.-Gen. Roger Sheaffe, succeeded in defeating this force, and taking more prisoners than he had troops. For this service Sheaffe was knighted; his performance at Muddy York was less distinguished, although that was quite understandable. Sheaffe was in York when the Americans struck, for a meeting of the legislature, but he was planning to proceed to Niagara, a more likely site for an attack. En route he had stopped to inspect Kingston, where, intelligence informed him, an attack was also expected.

Strategists in Washington, D.C., informed the commanding officers on the scene that they should attack Kingston, with its main naval base that gave sanctuary to the little Provincial Marine. The commanders in question were Maj.-Gen. Henry Dearborn, a veteran of the American Revolution, now sixty-two, overweight, and cautious, and Commodore Isaac Chauncey, United States Navy, the commander of the American fleets on the Great Lakes. In October 1812, Chauncey was dispatched to Sackets Harbor to create a naval base as a counterweight to Kingston. Chauncey, too, was cautious; he was still unnerved after he had tried to attack Kingston in November and been chased away. Dearborn and Chauncey suggested attacking Little York, because they knew that the British had started a second naval base there, and that York was poorly defended. They learned that the armed schooner *Prince Regent* was wintering at York, and under construction on the stocks was an even more ambitious vessel, the frigate *Sir Isaac Brock*. With an armament of thirty guns, the *Brock* would be the largest vessel on the lakes and could keep the American fleet bottled up in Sackets Harbor. Despite secrecy on the part of the Americans, more rumours of the planned attack had easily reached General Sheaffe at York. Rather than risk having the *Prince Regent* caught in the harbour, he ordered the schooner to sail for Kingston to join the other ships of the Provincial Marine.

The politicians had a special motive for agreeing with Dearborn and Chauncey. After the American reverses of 1812, they needed a victory. Capturing weak York would be the success needed to raise their country's morale. The population within York numbered about 600; the greater York area scarcely held 1,000 souls. The town, on its grid plan, began less than 100 yards (98.4 metres) west of the Don River (bounded by Jarvis, Front, Ontario, and Duchess Streets, although a new area was developing towards Yonge Street). Along with the houses stood the two-brick, one-storey Parliament Buildings, with a blockhouse beside them; to the east, facing the market square, was a building that could double as a barracks. From these barracks, soldiers were close enough to keep watch on the Don River bridge, the only route into town from the east. They knew that the town was safe from an attack by the

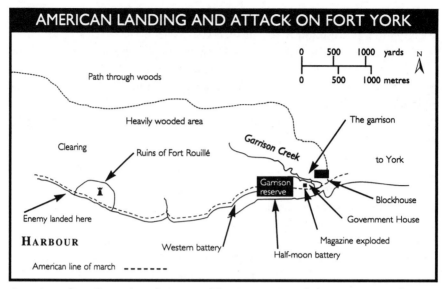

AMERICAN LANDING AND ATTACK ON FORT YORK

American fleet from that direction. The Easter Gap did not exist until 1858 when, during a storm, lashing waves broke through what had been a peninsula, turned it into an island, and created the second opening into the harbour.

The *Sir Isaac Brock* was in a small boatyard at the foot of present-day University Avenue. York's main defences lay farther west, close to the only opening into the harbour at that time, at Gibraltar Point on the tip of the peninsula, and ashore opposite it. Here the first lieutenant-governor, John Graves Simcoe, had started a fortified site on the west side of Garrison Creek. In 1800 the garrison moved to the east side of the creek. It consisted of huts that served as a barracks, and a blockhouse on the waterfront. Before his death, General Brock had been reinforcing Simcoe's old position on the west side of the creek, a site later called Fort York. Here stood Government House, a wooden structure, and a large powder magazine for the storage of surplus powder until it should be needed at Niagara. A palisade surrounded the garrison on the east side of Garrison Creek; a ditch and an earth rampart protected the area around Government House. Beyond lay the garrison reserve, which had been cleared of woods as a "field of fire" to ensure that no enemy could sneak up on the palisade. West of Garrison Creek were three gun batteries, one at Government House, one at the semi-circular Half Moon Battery west of it, and the last at the westernmost point on the garrison reserve, the Western Battery (at the foot of Strachan Avenue). A fourth battery stood east of the creek near the blockhouse.

The heaviest guns were at the Western Battery – two 18-pounders, ones that Simcoe had probably moved from the derelict Forts Haldimand and Oswegatchie (now in New York State). Neither had trunnions, and they were mounted on improvised carriages. Two efficient 12-pounders were mounted at Government House Battery, however General Sheaffe had another 12-pounder and two 6-pounders. He did not say where they were placed, but apparently no guns were allocated to the Half Moon Battery.

Sheaffe's defence force consisted of some 750 men: the flank companies of the 3rd York Militia, back home after the victory at Queenston Heights; one company of the Glengarry Light Infantry; two companies of the Royal Newfoundland Regiment (the latter two units were regulars raised in the provinces); Mississauga and Ojibway natives estimated at between forty-five and 100 strong; and some dock workers and civilian volunteers. Sheaffe would depend on the best professional soldiers he had on hand: two well-trained companies of the 8th (King's) Regiment of Foot. A battalion company was commanded by Capt. J.H. Eustace, and a grenadier company was led by Capt. Neale McNeale. The light company of the 8th was marching from Kingston at the time.

Against Sheaffe's meagre resources, the American force was 1,700 strong, almost all regulars: the 6th, 15th, and 16th United States Infantry; detachments of the 14th and 21st Infantry; two companies of light artillerymen; some volunteers; and Maj. Benjamin Forsyth's corps of riflemen. (Forsyth's men had wrought two recent American successes – raids on weakly defended Gananoque in September 1812 and on Brockville in February 1813. Both were cowardly attacks, however, not battles that one could brag about.) Although elderly Dearborn was in charge, the land force would be commanded by the energetic, thirty-four-year-old Brig.-Gen. Zebulon Pike (who had once attempted to scale the peak in Colorado that today bears his name). For the landing site, Pike had selected a clearing, possibly around the remains of Fort Rouillé, which had been built as a trading post by the French, but the exact site is unknown.

The American flagship was the *Madison*, a corvette completed at Sackets Harbor the previous November. She was followed by the brig *Oneida*, the large schooner *Julia*, and a dozen small converted schooners, all top-heavy with armaments. The *Madison* was armed with twenty-four 32-pounder carronades, which were shorter and lighter than conventional 32-pounders but accurate only for short distances. The vessels were accompanied by several bateaux, which served as landing craft.

The Battle: 27 April 1813

Watchers spotted the American fleet off the Scarborough Bluffs on the afternoon of Monday, 26 April. It had sailed from Sackets Harbor the day before, after being delayed several days by contrary winds. Amongst great excitement, the inhabitants speculated on where the enemy would effect a landing. Sheaffe suspected that the Americans would choose the clearing around old Fort Rouillé, west of the garrison reserve, but he could not be certain. He assumed that his best defence would be to concentrate his small force at the fortified site on both sides of Garrison Creek, and move through the woods to avoid becoming a target for the guns aboard the American fleet. He could not afford to leave the east exposed, however, so he stationed Captain Eustace's company and some of the 3rd York Militia under Lieut.-Col. William Chewett (who was also the surveyor general) at the building on the market square, to keep watch over the flimsy Don River bridge. Sheaffe sent Lieut. Ely Playter, two militiamen, and some natives to patrol east of the town in case of an attempted landing there.

Among York's notables was the recently arrived rector of St. James' Church, Rev. Dr. John Strachan, a keen patriot who longed to play an effective role. Awakened at four on the morning of 27 April, Strachan rode out to see the excitement for himself. Another who watched with alarm was John Beikie, Sheriff of the Home District; by the early light of dawn he could see the fleet off the lighthouse at Gibraltar Point. With a spyglass, Dr. Strachan observed men in the blue uniforms of the United States Infantry already climbing down into the bateaux that would carry them to shore. Sheaffe, meanwhile, was sending forward Maj. James Givins, an officer in the Indian Department, with a party of native warriors to take up a position near Fort Rouillé; they readied themselves to impede the landing force. Sheaffe ordered Maj.-Gen. Aeneas Shaw, the adjutant-general, to lead a patrol through the woods in support of Givins and the natives. Instead, Shaw persuaded the Glengarries to come with him. He then took a longer route than Sheaffe intended and would arrive too late to reinforce the warriors, the only group attempting to oppose the American landing.

According to the historian Col. C.P. Stacey, Sheaffe should have sent some of the 8th Regiment as the vanguard. Carl Benn, curator of Fort York and author of his own book on the battle, contends that the Glengarry Light Infantrymen were a suitable choice. Light infantry usually made up the vanguard.

The American fleet had been moving in a stiff wind from the east, which carried it farther west than Chauncey wanted. The bateaux, too, were swept westwards, and unable to make shore at the Fort Rouillé clearing. The troops had to land, on a wide front, somewhere along the site of the now-defunct Sunnyside amusement park, beyond the Exhibition grounds.

By eight o'clock, Maj. Forsyth's riflemen, uniformed in green, approached the shore in two large bateaux. The small American schooners moved in close to provide covering fire. Sheaffe had not attempted to move his two 6-pounders to the clearing, probably because of the difficulty of getting them through the woods, but the natives' marksmanship was so accurate that Forsyth ordered his men to lie on their oars and shoot back. Gen. Pike was still on the *Madison*, but he was firing for action. He ordered the rest of the force into bateaux, and posi-

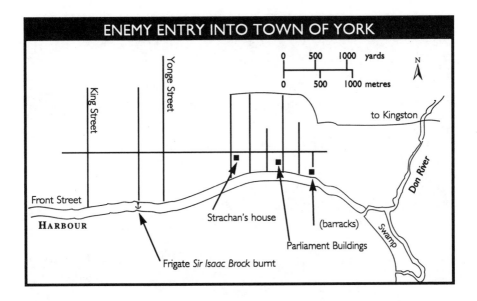

ENEMY ENTRY INTO TOWN OF YORK

King Street

Yonge Street

0   500   1000   yards

0   500   1000 metres

N

to Kingston

Don River

Front Street

HARBOUR

Strachan's house

(barracks)

Parliament Buildings

Swamp

Frigate *Sir Isaac Brock* burnt

tioned himself in the lead boat. Pike and three companies of the American 15th Regiment landed and were covered by Forsyth's men, who had also gained the shore. The men of the 15th, Pike in the lead, climbed a steep bank and took a commanding position on the high ground.

At that moment, Captain McNeale and his grenadiers arrived on the scene, and he ordered a bayonet charge. Pike's aide-de-camp, Lieut. Donald Fraser, remembered that the charge caused the Americans to retire briefly. The fierce thrust carried some of McNeale's men right to the beach. One American officer was bayonetted as he stepped from a bateau, but more troops landed and the grenadiers were soon overwhelmed. The survivors speedily retreated towards York. Behind them, Captain McNeale lay among the dead. Sheriff Beikie and his son Donald survived, but the body of another volunteer, Donald McLean, Clerk of the House of Assembly, lay with the dead grenadiers.

By eight o'clock, General Sheaffe, at Fort York, had been informed of the site of the enemy landing. Knowing that the threat would not be from the east, he ordered Captain Eustace and Lieutenant-Colonel Chewett to leave the market square and come west to reinforce the fort. Eustace obeyed, reaching Sheaffe by nine o'clock, but Chewett and his militia failed to appear.

At that point reports became confused. Sheaffe sent Eustace's company, the Glengarries, and more militia into the action, while the Americans continued to land from their boats. Pike's entire force was not ashore until ten o'clock. He formed his men in a clearing while the rest of Sheaffe's force was fleeing, pell-mell, for their defences. Many crowded into the Western Battery, where the 18-pounders were being loaded to reply to Chauncey's fleet, which

Death of Gen. Zebulon Pike. The mortally wounded Pike was taken aboard Dearborn's flagship to die after the powder magazine exploded.

was then approaching the gap north of Gibraltar point that formed the entrance to the harbour. Beside the gun was a small, open powder magazine. What happened next is unclear, but a spark, probably from the portfire about to be used to fire the guns, leapt into the magazine, which exploded with a tremendous blast. The effect was devastating to the many men crowded together. Nearly twenty were killed instantly, and others were seriously injured. Captain McNeale's grenadier company was decimated. One 18-pounder was out of action, but the other, now mounted on a platform, was able to fire high enough to threaten the American schooners attempting to gain the harbour.

Sheaffe, meanwhile, was moving from this battery to the Half Moon, keeping a demeanour of coolness that Strachan branded as lack of leadership. By eleven o'clock, Pike had landed his artillery, and his army began to advance from the clearing on a path that hugged the lakeshore. The British-Canadian force could do little to check Pike's advance. Some accounts reported that the Western Battery was stocked only with roundshot, effective only when firing at ships to destroy sails and rigging. It lacked, however, grape- or canister shot, which would have been successful against advancing footsoldiers. The defenders abandoned this battery and headed for the palisade. At twelve-thirty, Pike's men occupied the battery and moved on to the Half Moon battery, mere sod with no guns.

When the Americans were about "sixty rods" (300 metres) from the palisade, the Government House Battery opened fire with round shot and canister. Pike ordered his troops to "lie close" until his artillery could be brought forward to respond. The Government House Battery was soon silenced, and Pike stood hopefully, waiting for the white flag to run up inside the palisade in place of the Royal Standard. But Pike, who had seemed so close to success and a citation from Congress, was in for a shock.

Sheaffe had resolved to let York fall, but he would not surrender his regulars, not while the road lay open towards Kingston. The local militia and volunteers could conduct the surrender ceremony – he would be as far away as possible beforehand. He ordered the large powder magazine near Government House blown up, to keep it out of American hands and to do as much damage as possible. He assigned Sergeant Marshall (given name not mentioned) to this task. Pike was at the head of his brigade, interrogating a captured Canadian militia sergeant. Lieut. Ely Playter, who had brought some of the 3rd York Militia to the fort, went to the barracks on the east side of Garrison Creek to retrieve a coat before joining the other militia for a withdrawal towards the town. He was so close that he was lucky to survive after Sergeant Marshall lit the fuse and ran.

One of the spectators, a boy named Patrick Finan, later wrote of the blast, "as it rose, in a most majestic manner, it assumed the shape of a vast balloon." It must have been almost like the mushroom cloud of a nuclear blast. Until the great Halifax explosion of the First World War, it was likely the biggest explosion in Canadian history. Flying debris and the crashing of huge stones and timber did appalling damage to the American side. Pike himself was mortally wounded, his back and ribs crushed, and he was rushed aboard the *Madison* to die. At the time, thirty-eight Americans were killed and 222 were wounded; some of those men died later. All told, the Americans sustained some 320 casualties in the taking of the fort and palisade east of Garrison Creek. This was a 20 percent casualty rate; in other words, the American force had been decimated twice over, and the survivors were furious – taking York had been far too costly. To make matters worse, Sheaffe and his regulars had departed, the *Prince Regent* had escaped, and the Canadians were then setting fire to the *Sir Isaac Brock,* the ship Chauncey hoped to finish building and add to his fleet.

The time was now two o'clock in the afternoon. The Battle of Little York was over; the surrender arrangements, and revenge, had yet to begin. At that point, some of Chewett's own company of the 3rd York Militia arrived at Fort York, and the lieutenant-colonel soon followed. From his reading of the reports, Carl Benn concluded that Chewett had disobeyed Sheaffe's order of 8:00 a.m. to come at once to the fort. Benn found no satisfactory reason why Chewett had taken six hours to come; after all, Captain Eustace had reached Sheaffe by nine.

The Occupation: 27 April to 1 May

With Sheaffe gone, Chewett, assisted by Maj. William Allan, his second-in-command, sought to arrange surrender terms. He soon found an eager Dr. John Strachan at his elbow, volunteering to help in the negotiations, furious at the departure of the regulars, and accusing Sheaffe of coldness and heartlessness.

General Dearborn was in no mood to be generous, not after losing so many men *and* General Pike. He allowed only the militia officers to go home on parole for the night. All other captured soldiers were confined in the garrison blockhouse; the wounded were left untended. On the morning of the 28th, waving a copy of the proposed articles of capitulation that had been drafted by Chewett and Allan, an enraged Dr. Strachan sought out Dearborn. He found the American commander emerging from the boat that had brought him ashore from the *Madison,* where he had his quarters. Immediately Strachan offered his church as a temporary hospital for the wounded. Dearborn ordered him away, and when the clergyman tried to follow, Dearborn ordered him to stop. Strachan, refusing to be put off, bearded Commodore Chauncey: "Is this a new mode of treating people clothed in a public character?" the clergyman enquired. "I have had the honor of transacting business with greater men without meeting with any indignity."

Furthermore, Strachan declared, if Dearborn intended to wait until his soldiers had pillaged the town before ratifying the terms of capitulation, there would be no capitulation. The Americans might "do their worst," but they could never claim to have respected property after they had stolen it. At that, a chastened Dearborn accompanied Strachan to the garrison, and, with Chauncey, ratified the terms. The militia officers were at once paroled; then, with Strachan close by, the sick and wounded were moved to St. James' Church or to homes, and all ranks were paroled.

Some pillaging did take place. Extant claims for compensation made by twenty-three residents list belongings stolen, and damage to houses and other property. Most looters were Americans, but one Canadian also was named. Another whose house was pillaged was Major Givins – Dearborn maintained that he could not protect a man who had commanded natives, although he did try to stop other looters. Chauncey, too, disapproved of looting, and he ordered that books removed from the public library be returned. Penelope Beikie, wife of Sheriff John Beikie, believed that only the homes of people who had left town had been damaged. "I kept my Castle, when all the rest had fled; and it was well for us I did so – our little property was saved by that means."

No one reported a case of murder, but some claimed that rapes had occurred. What has lingered most in memory is the burning of Government House, the Parliament Buildings, government offices and storehouses, and the town blockhouse. After all, destroying military buildings was understandable, but putting Government House to the torch was less so. Later, Dearborn would

Mary Beacock Fryer

The restored and rebuilt Fort York stands in the heart of the City of Toronto. The CN Tower intrudes, as do many other features of the urban scene.

claim that Canadians had burned the buildings after his force had left York, a version given credence because the enemy had released the inmates of the jail. One reason claimed for torching the Parliament Buildings was the discovery of a scalp, which some Americans claimed had hung above the provincial mace. It was likely found in a drawer, however, placed there by a civil servant who was disgusted that it had been sent to the legislature. Both trophies were removed from the legislative chamber, probably by a naval officer. (No one ever admitted to the burning of the buildings. No soldiers were observed in the area, but sailors might have been there, for they were not uniformed at that time.) Mace and scalp, along with the thirty-foot (9.6 metre) Royal Standard (probably from the flagstaff at the garrison), were taken home as the spoils of war. The Americans packed up and began going aboard their fleet on 1 May, right after burning Government House. By the 2nd they were ready to sail, but were delayed by contrary winds that kept the ships in the harbour until the 8th.

Another American force returned and occupied York from 31 July until 2 August 1813. This time, because no British troops were present, no battle occurred. Legend relates that the men left town and the women placated their visitors with cups of tea. The invaders burned a storehouse at Gibraltar Point and the barracks. (They had likely spared it in the earlier attack in anticipation of using it during a later occupation.)

In the aftermath, Strachan wrote a pamphlet that strongly criticized General Sheaffe's performance, and sent it to a friend in Lower Canada. Strachan hinted that if the commander of forces, Sir George Prevost, would consider sacking Sheaffe, the pamphlet need never be published. Prevost did relieve Sheaffe of command in Upper Canada, but no such demotion befell Lieut.-Col. William Chewett of the 3rd York Militia. For his part in the capitulation articles he became a hero, even though he had certainly not attended to Sheaffe's orders, and in a small way had actually contributed to the defeat at Fort York.

At Westminster, in November 1814, an opposition member of Parliament objected to the burning of certain buildings when a British force attacked Washington. Nicholas Vansittart, then Chancellor of the Exchequer, cited a report that Major Allan had written to General Sheaffe. The Americans, Vansittart declared, had destroyed a capital, "for be it remembered that York was the capital of Upper Canada." In the House of Lords, Prime Minister Lord Liverpool declared that the destruction in Washington was in retaliation for what the Americans had done to York.

After 1816, the brick walls of the Parliament Buildings were restored, and for a time they served as a barracks until they were demolished as redundant. The Royal Standard captured at Government House was placed in the Naval Academy at Annapolis. In 1934, while on a goodwill visit to Toronto on the occasion of the city's centenary, President Franklin Roosevelt returned the mace, which now reposes at Fort York. The restoration of the fort began shortly after the April attack. The defences were strong enough, by 1814, to drive off an American squadron. Today, seven of the buildings at Fort York had their origins in 1812, the largest group of British army buildings from that era in the country.

The Battle of Little York was a trivial incident, with relatively little damage and loss of life, except for the American intruders. Yet it had a disastrous effect on the naval war on Lake Erie. At the time of the American attack, an irreplaceable stockpile of armaments and equipment intended for the British fleet on the upper lakes was stored at York, waiting until it could be moved on to Amherstburg. This material was captured by the Americans or destroyed by the British, in order to keep it out of enemy hands. Because of this loss, the British squadron was defeated at the Battle of Lake Erie on 10 September. This reverse led to the retreat that ended with the Battle of Moraviantown that October. Dearborn and Chauncey had come looking for a cheap victory, but their success had an effect far beyond their sanguine expectations.

IX

Fort Astoria, 1813–1846

The boundary between Canada and the United States through the Rocky Mountains had not been established when the War of 1812 began. Britain claimed, with some justification, that the Columbia River should be the dividing line between her colonies and the Americans. Britons and Canadians, who were mainly involved in the fur trade, had been more active than the Americans in the lands that now form the States of Washington and Oregon.

One American did have a fur trading post, on the south side of the Columbia River, seven kilometres (4.2 miles) upriver from the Pacific Ocean. The post belonged to the fur magnate John Jacob Astor (1763–1848), who emigrated from his birthplace, Waldorf, Germany, and founded the famous Anglo-American family. He opened his post, Fort Astoria, in 1811, as the headquarters of his new Pacific Fur Company. His employees were nearly all Canadians who had worked for the Montreal-based North West Company.

Astor expected that Fort Astoria would become the hub of a network of fur posts in the region, but the war that broke out in June 1812 altered his plans. His manager at the fort was Duncan McDougall, an old Nor'wester. Word of the outbreak of war did not reach Fort Astoria until 15 January 1813, when an employee, Donald McKenzie, who had seen a copy of President Madison's declaration while in Spokane, arrived with the news.

Astor's Canadian employees were torn. In the dead of winter, returning to Canadian civilization, thousands of miles to the east, was out of the question. The only sensible course was to wait and see what would happen next. Perhaps a British warship would come and blockade the mouth of the Columbia, asserting the mother country's claim to the territory west of the Rockies. But no British ship appeared.

On 11 April, men at Fort Astoria beheld two freight canoes – one flying the Union Jack – descending the last bit of the Columbia to the fort. Nineteen Canadian voyageurs paddled to the shore, and out leapt John George McTavish and Joseph Laroque, Nor'westers and the leaders of the tiny expedition. They had come to await the arrival of their Company ship, the *Isaac Todd*, expected by the summer. The ship did not come, however, and the Nor'westers departed late in August. In September, John George McTavish,

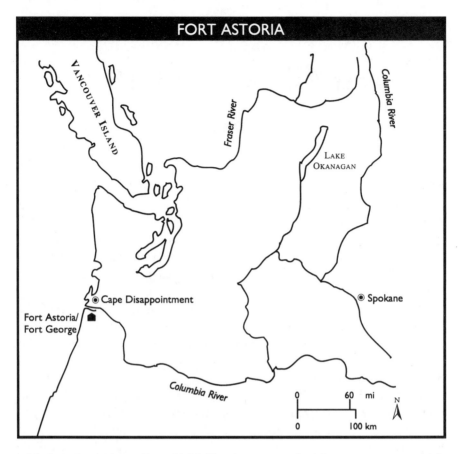

FORT ASTORIA

with Astor's employee Donald McKenzie, appeared with many canoes, which were loaded with furs.

McTavish gave Duncan McDougall, Astor's manager, a letter from one of their Company's partners, informing him that the *Isaac Todd,* escorted by the armed frigate *Phoebe,* had sailed from England in March with letters of marque and an order to capture Astoria. The little post was, they asserted, an American colony and therefore the enemy. The Astorians could probably have overpowered the Nor'westers – the fort had a cannon and the outsiders had only small arms. But the thought of the frigate *Phoebe* which was quite alarming.

When the Nor'westers suggested that Duncan McDougall let them purchase the fort, McDougall agreed. It seemed to be the best alternative to an attack by well-trained men of the Royal Navy. The Nor'westers agreed to pay the back wages that Astor owed the employees, and to provide food and passage to any who wished to return to Canada by land. Most agreed to stay on doing their usual jobs, however. The few Americans who had settled in the neighbourhood were shocked when the Nor'westers hauled down the Stars and Stripes and ran up the Union Jack. The frigate *Phoebe* never did appear, but on

30 November a vessel came downstream, round Cape Disappointment, causing more than a little consternation. What if she should turn out to be an American warship? But the new arrival was a sloop, HMS *Racoon*. The 26-gunner, commanded by Captain William Black, R.N., had come to capture Fort Astoria and carried a Nor'wester partner, John McDonald.

Black was shocked to discover that Astoria was already a British possession, and that it had not been earned through honourable combat but by unseemly purchase! He and his men would not therefore be eligible for the prize money that went with capture. Nevertheless, the occasion called for some ceremony. On 13 December, Black came ashore, with an officer of marines and an escort of soldiers and sailors, to be entertained at a formal dinner by partner McDonald. Black ran up another Union Jack on a special new flagpole on the little square inside the stockade, smashed a bottle of wine on the pole, and proclaimed that "Fort George" was now the property of His Majesty King George III.

Fort George/Astoria remained in British-Canadian hands until the Oregon Boundary Treaty of 15 June 1846, when the line between Canada and the United States was set at the 49th parallel all the way to the Pacific. Vancouver Island was given to Canada, however. An election slogan of the American Democratic Party in 1844 had been "fifty-four forty or fight!" The party claimed that the United States had every right to the entire Pacific coast to Alaska. Rather than send an expensive expedition to fight for the Columbia River boundary, Britain agreed to partition Columbia.

John Jacob Astor tried to have his fort returned. In 1814, he persuaded James Monroe, then the Secretary of War, to ask the peace commissioners to insist on the restoration of his fort. The fort had been bought not captured, however, and so it did not qualify for return on the same basis as Fort Niagara, Michilimackinac, or other American possessions that were in British hands when the Treaty of Ghent was signed on 24 December 1814. Fort George/Astoria thus remained a Nor'wester post until the Company amalgamated with the Hudson's Bay Company in 1821. The Bay men withdrew after the ratification of the Oregon Boundary Treaty of 1846.

X

The Battle of Crysler's Farm, 11 November 1813

The site of Crysler's Farm was obliterated during the construction of the St. Lawrence Seaway in the 1950s. Today, on the shore of man-made Lake St. Lawrence, stands Crysler's Farm Battlefield Park, where a plaque informs visitors of the events that took place nearby that were part of an American attempt to capture Montreal. Five weeks after the disastrous defeat near Moraviantown, Crysler's Farm was a rousing victory.

The Americans were emboldened after the reverses in the western portion of Upper Canada. Now they wanted to cut off the province, but just how that was to be done was uncertain. Some debaters favoured capturing Kingston, the lifeline to the heart of the province. Others wanted to drive straight for Montreal, to take control of much more territory. Still others suggested a two-stage approach: take Kingston first, and then attack Montreal. The northern states now had a new commander-in-chief, Maj.-Gen. James Wilkinson (1757–1825). His predecessor, Maj.-Gen. Henry Dearborn (1757–1829), had recently resigned.

Wilkinson, a resident of the Kentucky valley, was an unsavoury character, a one-time double agent who negotiated with the Spanish to obtain their protection for Kentucky, which was not yet a state. None of the American officers had much respect for him, but certain politicians were his friends. After the Americans' success at the Battle of Moraviantown, the bulk of their army was concentrated at Fort George on the Niagara peninsula, at Sackets Harbor on Lake Ontario, and at Burlington, Vermont, on Lake Champlain. The secretary of war was John Armstrong, who proposed a two-pronged attack: from Lake Champlain and from Sackets Harbor. Maj.-Gen. Wade Hampton, the commander in Vermont, would lead an army towards Montreal along the Châteauguay River. Wilkinson would order troops to leave Fort George and Sackets Harbor to rendezvous at Grenadier Island (the American island near the entrance to the St. Lawrence, not the larger Canadian one of the same name downstream below Gananoque). The two armies would meet at Saint Regis for the drive on Montreal. There were two catches, however. First, no order had been issued as to whether Wilkinson should take Kingston first or move directly on Montreal. Second, like most of his fellow-officers, Hampton loathed Wilkinson.

On 20 August 1813, Wilkinson came to Sackets Harbor to examine the situation, then moved on to Fort George to arrange troop movements from there. He was back in Sackets Harbor by 2 October, but was so ill that he was hardly competent to command. In the meantime, Secretary of War Armstrong had been at Sackets Harbor, and had made many of the arrangements. Spies were quick to inform the British commanders at Kingston of the activities on the American side of Lake Ontario – a massive army was gathering. The Kingston garrison was the 89th Regiment. Maj.-Gen. Baron Francis de Rottenburg (1757–1832), administrator and commander of forces in Upper Canada, dispatched the 104th and 49th Regiments from Burlington Bay and York to reinforce Kingston. The 49th was Brock's old regiment, nicknamed the "Green Tigers," the latter for their efficiency and the former for the green facings on their coats. The naval commander at Kingston was Capt. Sir James Yeo, R.N. Wilkinson's second-in-command was Maj.-Gen. Morgan Lewis, and his naval commander at Sackets Harbor was Commodore Isaac Chauncey.

On 17 October, Wilkinson left Sackets Harbor for the Grenadier Island rendezvous. When the fleet from Fort George arrived, together with the troops from Sackets Harbor, his army was 8,000 strong – fourteen regiments of infantry, two of dragoons, and three of artillery. The troops would travel in more than 300 bateaux and other craft suitable for shooting the rapids of the St. Lawrence. Twelve gunboats would protect the American flotilla.

The task of pursuing the Americans fell to Lieut.-Col. Joseph Morrison (1783–1826), the commander of the 89th Regiment, stationed at Kingston. Morrison had been born in New York City. His father was a deputy com-missary-general in the British army during the American Revolution. Morrison's troops would travel aboard the armed sloops *Lord Beresford* and *Sir Sidney Smith*, protected by seven gunboats. The little fleet was commanded by Capt. William Mulcaster, R.N. Both Morrison and Mulcaster were com-petent professionals, although Morrison had never, before Crysler's Farm, commanded troops in the field. He could depend on two able assistants, his second-in-command, Lieut.-Col. John Harvey, the deputy adjutant-general, and Lieut.-Col. Charles Plenderleath of the 49th Regiment.

Wilkinson got off to a bad start. His expedition set out later than he had anticipated, and horrendous autumn storms had destroyed some boats and damaged many others as they attempted to reach Grenadier Island. As well, Wilkinson was very ill, and chaos ruled on the island. Rain poured down, spoiling provisions and turning bread mouldy. Liquor brought along for med-icinal purposes was stolen and many of the men were often drunk. Vast stores had been lost when boats were wrecked. The Americans were not ready to depart from Grenadier Island until 28 October, very late for such a campaign.

They set off in four divisions, with Brig.-Gen. Jacob Brown in the lead and Brigs. John Boyd, Robert Swartout, and Leonard Covington following with their divisions. All would play crucial roles in the coming drama. The weather had now turned to a glorious Indian summer, but as yet Wilkinson had not decided whether to move on Kingston first or go directly to join Hampton at Saint Regis. Commodore Chauncey had been left in the dark until the 30th over what role his ships would play. Wilkinson then told him to guard the entrance to the St. Lawrence, to prevent pursuit by the British from Kingston. At last, Wilkinson had decided to make straight for Montreal.

Chauncey's order came too late, however. Captain Mulcaster and his gunboats had run down the north channel of the St. Lawrence, crossed to the south, and fired on Brigadier Brown's first division. Mulcaster then hurried back to Kingston with word that Wilkinson's flotilla was heading towards Montreal. Lieutenant-Colonel Morrison prepared to follow the Americans with 450 men from his own 89th Regiment, 160 from Brock's 49th, now much reduced from campaigning, and 20 militia artillerymen with two 6-pounder guns. Morrison, just thirty years old, was about to command his first battle.

All four of Wilkinson's brigades reached French Creek (Clayton, New York) by 3 November, and did not set out again until early on the 5th. Wilkinson, too ill to give directions, was unnerved by Captain Mulcaster's attack on Brown's brigade. Morgan Lewis, Wilkinson's second-in-command, was also ill. Later that day they passed through the Brockville Narrows, where islands gave some concealment from watchers on the Canadian shore. When the fleet reached Morristown, opposite Brockville, Wilkinson decided not to pass Prescott with his loaded boats. British regulars and Canadian militia had already built a blockhouse (the first Fort Wellington) and the river was narrower and free of islands. Wilkinson arranged for wagons to carry supplies by road along the American side while his troops marched. Crews would float the empty boats past Prescott during the night. He sent a proclamation across to the Canadians, to reassure them that their property would be respected, and in the hope of reducing opposition. But he was wasting his time: the numerous United Empire (U.E.) Loyalists knew better than to trust him. They, and other settlers, persisted in firing off their muskets and rifles as the Americans attempted to pass downriver.

By 7 November, a clear day, the British were stationing sharpshooters and the odd cannon along the north shore, manned by angry militia. That day, Lieut.-Col. Winfield Scott (1786–1866), left in command of the Americans holding Fort George, arrived on horseback. After Secretary Armstrong granted him a leave of absence, he rode through the woods to experience the fun of bursting shells and flying musket balls. To put a stop to Canadian activity, Wilkinson dispatched Brig. Leonard Covington with 1,200 of his best troops to clear the north shore. Commanding the rearguard of this expedition was

Artist's impression of the battle, from a mural at Crysler's Farm Battlefield Park near Morrisburg, Ontario. The field is partly obscured by blue smoke, as happened after a volley or cannon had been fired.

Capt. Benjamin Forsyth, a man that local Canadians already detested – with his corps of riflemen, Forsyth had raided Gananoque in September 1812 and Brockville in February 1813.

In the meantime, Canadian farmers were happily spreading alarming rumours that further unnerved Wilkinson. Captain Mulcaster was supposed to be at Prescott with many ships, 1,000 crack regulars, and bands of natives. On the 8th, Wilkinson ordered Brig. Jacob Brown to assemble some field guns and 2,500 men and take command of Covington's land forces that were attempting to clear the north shore. Wilkinson did not wish to attempt to shoot the Long Sault Rapids while the river was under Canadian fire. Accompanying Brown were Brig. John Boyd, an adventurer whom Brown despised, and Brig. Robert Swartout. By 10 November, the American flotilla was below Cook's Point, some three kilometres (two miles) above the Long Sault. Brown went aboard Wilkinson's boat to ask for orders, but the commander and General Lewis were both too ill to speak with him. Brown then set out to clear snipers near the road to Cornwall. By nightfall, Brown and Boyd were worrying, with good cause, about what might be happening to their rear.

Morrison's force had reached Prescott on the 9th, enlarged by 240 extra men – two flank companies of the 49th, some Canadian Fencibles, and three companies of grey-uniformed Canadian Voltigeurs. The latter two groups were Canadian regular regiments.

With a few militia dragoons to serve as couriers and another 6-pounder gun, Morrison's little army now comprised about 900 men, three field guns, and eight gunboats. The schooners *Beresford* and *Smith* returned to Kingston; they could not pass down the rapids safely and so were of no further use. Morrison proceeded downstream to the farm of John Crysler, where he set up his headquarters in the Crysler house. Thirty Mohawks from nearby St. Regis joined him and went out scouting through the woods in search of American reconnaissance patrols. The American force under Brown, Covington, Swartout, and Boyd, 3,700 strong, was a short distance to the east. Morrison was expecting further reinforcements to be sent from Kingston, while the four American brigadiers were wondering when the rest of Wilkinson's army would cross the river to support them.

On the morning of the 11th, a native fired on an American patrol. Brown and Boyd thought they were about to be attacked, and so sent a report to General Wilkinson asking for instructions. A courier returned with orders for Boyd, with Covington and Swartout's brigade to form a rear guard of 2,000 troops and move westwards in three columns on the British-Canadian position at Crysler's farm.

Americans under the command of Lieut.-Col. Eleazer Ripley of Swartout's brigade had little difficulty breaking up the Voltigeurs' line of

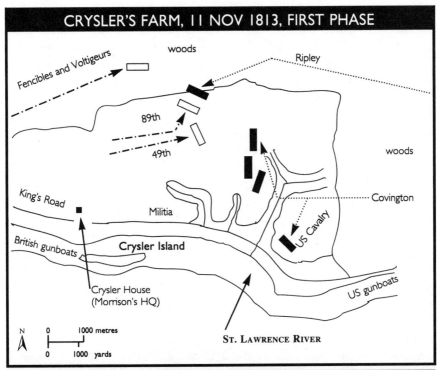

CRYSLER'S FARM, 11 NOV 1813, FIRST PHASE

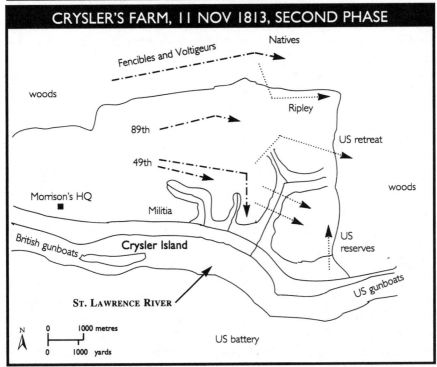

CRYSLER'S FARM, 11 NOV 1813, SECOND PHASE

skirmish, but the British soldiers of the 49th and 89th were in the right place for the training they had received. Morrison had chosen his spot with care, an open stubble field in front of his troops, and gullies ahead in which men from Fort Wellington and the artillery waited by their field guns. The right flank was protected by Mulcaster's gunboats on the river; the left flank was sheltered by a nearly impenetrable swamp that concealed native warriors and Voltigeurs. The men of the 89th were positioned next to the swamp, waiting in short, staggered rows known as echelon formation, from which they could close up or wheel about. The seasoned 49th had lined up on their right. The 89th were in their red tunics but, in the miserable weather, those of the 49th were concealed under their grey greatcoats.

What followed was a battle in the style usually fought on the open fields of Europe. The concentrated musket volleys worked with devastating effect – this was not the sort of woodland shootout at which the Americans were proficient. During the revolution they had poked fun at the British formations, especially when the skirmishing was in the forests of northern New York where volleys did little damage. Here Morrison, Harvey, and Plenderleath seized the advantage, forcing the Americans to face the thin red line, even though the 49th showed grey.

The invaders came on, Covington confident that many of Morrison's men were mere militia. The men of the 89th stood firm as wave after wave of Americans flung themselves against them. Brock's old 49th held their ground and dispersed a charge of American dragoons. The enemy then concentrated on the left flank, hoping to turn it, but the 89th wheeled round to face the attackers and the line held. By late afternoon the light company of the 89th had seized an American field gun. Soon the enemy broke and began fleeing haphazardly from the field. The Battle of Crysler's Farm was over, and Brigadier Covington lay dead where men of the 49th had shot him.

Morrison reported his casualties as 22 killed, 148 wounded, and 9 missing. Boyd's losses were 102 killed, 237 wounded, and 100 taken prisoner. One local man who distinguished himself was Capt. Reubin Sherwood U.E., who commanded a company of guides along the river. British officers recorded little about the achievements of the militia, but Sherwood was later decorated for some act of distinction.

While Brigadier Boyd was taking the trouncing from Morrison's men, Brigadier Brown and his advance guard of 1,700 men chased away the Canadian defenders of a bridge over a creek. The road to Cornwall lay open. Brown sent word that the rest of the army should join him, but when Wilkinson received a report of the decisive defeat of Boyd and the rear guard, he ordered Brown and his advance guard to withdraw. Brown soon crossed the St. Lawrence and rejoined Wilkinson's main army. By that time word had arrived of the defeat, on 26 October, of Maj.-Gen. Wade Hampton's

G.R.D. Fryer

Fort Wellington as it appears today.

Americans on the Châteauguay River, and of his withdrawal back into New York State. After a council of war, the desperately ill Wilkinson decided not to try to proceed, now that Hampton would not be at Saint Regis to support him. Wilkinson ordered a site on the Salmon River at French Mills, New York, fortified for a winter camp. He named it Fort Covington, after his dead brigadier.

The 1813 season ended with the burning of Newark (Niagara-on-the-Lake) and Queenston on 10 December, the British capture of Fort Niagara, and the American evacuation of Fort George. The war would last another year, during which Wilkinson lost the command of the northern army and went off to Texas. His successor was Jacob Brown, promoted to major-general, while Eleazer Ripley moved up from lieutenant-colonel to brigadier-general. Lieut.-Col. Joseph Morrison, the victor of Crysler's Farm, continued to serve along the St. Lawrence until the spring of 1814, when he was ordered to Kingston. From there, he received instructions to take his now-seasoned 89th Regiment to the Niagara frontier for the summer campaign there.

XI

The Battle of Moraviantown (The Thames), 5 October 1813

Moraviantown is on the Delaware Nation's reserve, south of the Thames River, sixteen kilometres (ten miles) upstream from Thamesville. Refugee Delaware natives came into Canada after the American Revolution, and in 1792 they settled along the north bank of the Thames. They named their village Fairfield. The settlement extended inland as far as the present village of Bothwell. This group of Delawares was Christian, converted by Moravian missionaries who accompanied them. Following the Battle of Moraviantown, victorious American troops laid waste to the neighbourhood and destroyed the settlement. The Delawares rebuilt their village south of the Thames in 1815, and named it New Fairfield, later changed to Moraviantown. The original reserve was larger, encompassing land north of the Thames, but in 1826 the Delawares sold 25,000 acres (about 10,000 hectares). The population was then 184.

Three sites are relevant to the battle. A marker on the north side of Highway 2, across the river from Moraviantown, indicates the original site of Fairfield village. The battlefield, with a marker and picnic site, is about three kilometres (two miles) downstream, north of the highway and closer to Thamesville. At Bothwell, eight kilometres (five miles) northeast, is the Fairfield Museum, which commemorates the Moravian missionaries. All three locations, and a plaque to New Fairfield in front of the church in Moraviantown, help piece together the events of October 1813.

By August 1813, the United States had taken control of Lake Erie at the naval battle off Put-in-Bay. Capt. Oliver Perry, United States Navy, defeated a wounded Capt. Robert Barclay, Royal Navy, a veteran who had lost an arm at Trafalgar. Land opponents were Maj.-Gen. Henry Procter, in command of British and Canadian troops holding Detroit; his native ally, the legendary Shawnee leader Tecumseh, who had been instrumental in the surrender of Detroit to the late Major-General Brock; and Maj.-Gen. William Henry Harrison, the governor of Indiana Territory. Harrison was approaching Detroit with an army of American regulars and militia. With the British fleet knocked out, Procter's position had become untenable. He was short of supplies, his troops were in rags, and he saw no choice but to withdraw up the Thames River. A major contributing factor to Perry's success over Barclay was the destruction of naval stores at York in April that had been intended for the Lake Erie fleet.

One of the younger participants was John Richardson, member of a distinguished Amherstburg family. His father, Robert, had been assistant surgeon to Governor Simcoe's Queen's Rangers (1791–1802 era). Dr. Richardson had married Madeleine Askin, a daughter of Col. John Askin, the wealthy Detroit merchant. John was bilingual, as was his mother, whose mother was French. He was born at Queenston in October 1796; the family relocated at Amherstburg after the Queen's Rangers were disbanded in 1802. Robert became the garrison surgeon at Fort Amherstburg (now Malden), as well as a district court judge. John's education was cut short by the war – he joined the 41st Regiment as a gentleman volunteer at the age of fifteen. He was delighted by this turn of events because he was able to escape from a sadistic schoolmaster – complaints to a stern father had fallen on deaf ears, but patriotism won out. John would later serve overseas as a lieutenant in the 8th Regiment. Later still, he wrote a poem, *Tecumseh* (about a man he knew well) and, among other writings, the novels *Escarté* and *The Canadian Brothers*, and a play *Wacousta* (about Pontiac, an acquaintance of his mother's).

The Battle of Moraviantown, or the Thames, was a British disaster, a result of Procter's slowness and, to some extent, the attitude of the native warriors who accompanied his army. Tecumseh, who failed to grasp the implications of the American hold on Lake Erie, saw no reason to sacrifice Detroit when the enemy was not at hand. Nor did the Shawnee leader, or others in the confederacy he led, realize that a cumbersome column of about 900 soldiers, with artillery, could not simply vanish into the forest or live off the land. Some of the warriors were Tecumseh's Shawnee followers; others were content to serve for rations. After some disagreement, many agreed to stay with Procter, who assured them that he would find, along the Thames, a suitable spot to do battle. Some of the other natives drifted away from their encampment on nearby Bois Blanc Island.

On 24 September, Procter commenced his withdrawal, burning anything of value at Detroit and moving his troops, the 1st and part of the 2nd battalions of the 41st Regiment, across the Detroit River to Fort Amherstburg. The women and children, among them Procter's wife and daughter, went ahead in wagons. By the 26th, Procter was destroying everything of use to the enemy at Amherstburg and collecting all available horses, and Perry's fleet was entering the Detroit River. Procter continued his withdrawal, reaching Sandwich on the 27th. Some of his meagre supplies were piled in wagons, others in small boats. John Richardson, now sixteen, who had come through Brock's capture of Detroit and the actions at Frenchtown, Fort Meigs, and Fort Miami,

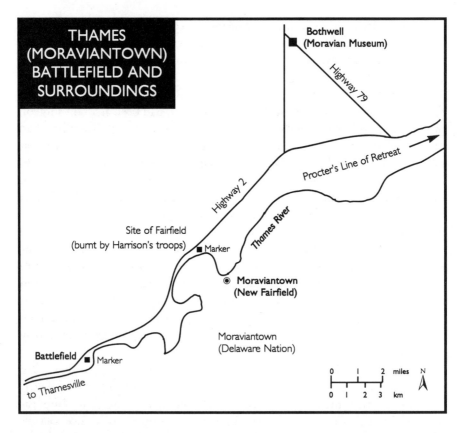

THAMES
(MORAVIANTOWN)
BATTLEFIELD AND
SURROUNDINGS

Bothwell
(Moravian Museum)

Highway 79

Procter's Line of Retreat

Highway 2

Thames River

Site of Fairfield
(burnt by Harrison's troops) ■ Marker

⦿ Moraviantown
(New Fairfield)

Moraviantown
(Delaware Nation)

Battlefield ■ Marker

to Thamesville

0   1   2 miles   N
0 1 2 3 km

marched disconsolately along with the 41st. Procter proceeded along the
north bank of the Thames River, aware by now that Harrison would not be
far behind him.

Harrison had some 3,000 troops, regulars and militia, but felt hampered
because he lacked horses and, thanks to Procter, could not commandeer any
locally. At Detroit Harrison left a large garrison, in case the natives returned.
Keenest among his troops were Kentucky volunteers led by the state governor,
Isaac Shelby, who viewed not only the natives' lands but Canada, too, as
the rightful property of the United States. Harrison's mobility improved
when another Kentuckian, Lieut.-Col. Richard Johnson, joined him with
500 mounted riflemen. By 2 October, the American vanguard, under Johnson, was at the mouth of the Thames, where he met Perry's gunboats. They
started up the river on the 3rd. Serving Harrison as a scout was a former resident, Matthew Dolsen, a rebel during the revolution who had come to the
Thames Valley in quest of cheap land. When war broke out, he defected to
Detroit and joined the enemy. (This was Bad Matthew Dolsen; Good
Matthew Dolsen, U.E. Loyalist, had died that August at his farm near Dover,
a spot the local people called Dolsen's.)

Procter had his second-in-command, Lieut.-Col. Augustus Warburton, scout for a suitable place to make a stand against Harrison. He ordered some earthworks at Dover, but hoped to move the main body of troops to a defensive site beyond the Delaware village of Fairfield. Near Chatham, Procter's men burned and sank three gunboats, hoping to impede Perry's progress, but the commander failed to order bridges removed, which would have slowed down Harrison's ground force. Communication was poor. Procter, who had temporarily gone ahead to check on his family, had promised Tecumseh that he would make his stand at Chatham; when the Shawnee arrived and found no fortifications, he was furious.

Harrison's vanguard advanced, and on the 5th Richard Johnson captured two British gunboats loaded with ammunition. Procter, now about three kilometres (two miles) from Fairfield, was searching for a defensive site from which his rear guard could protect his slow-moving column. But time had run out. Proctor deployed all his troops across the road, in two lines, the second some hundred metres (328 feet) behind the first. He wanted his soldiers shoulder to

The Moravian village, at first called New Fairfield, was rebuilt after the original Fairfield was destroyed by Harrison's troops.

shoulder, the traditional way, to improve firepower, but, rather than lose native support, he yielded to Tecumseh's demand for an open formation. Shoulder to shoulder, Tecumseh insisted, the redcoats would form one large target. The position might have been strong had Procter's men had time to cut trees for abatis. Tecumseh was pleased that the site was wooded, for he thought that trees would be an obstacle to the enemy advance. The north bank of the Thames protected Procter's left flank, and along his right flank lay a stretch of swamp. Tecumseh left his white pony behind and led his people into the swamp, where they concealed themselves. Procter had one 6-pounder field gun – sheer bluff, since no ammunition fitted it.

Harrison wanted to send his mounted riflemen into the swamp, frontier-style. Horses could quickly scatter the natives. Johnson, however, recommended riding straight at Procter's centre, because his mounted men were accustomed to racing among trees. The charge began, and Procter's front line fired a ragged volley before dissolving in disarray. The second line repeated the action and collapsed in disorder. Having sown confusion, Johnson left the surrender to the foot soldiers and ordered his riders into the swamp. They met with strong opposition, until Tecumseh himself was slain. His followers fought on, while those less committed fled. When the surviving warriors were forced to abandon the swamp, they had to leave thirty-three corpses behind. (Natives usually went to lengths to remove their dead to avoid mutilations.) Tecumseh's body was rumoured to have been among those found, but it was never identified.

Procter and 246 of his officers and ranks escaped, formed small groups, and with the women and children reached safety at the head of Lake Ontario with the reserve troops stationed above Burlington Bay. Of the rest, twenty-eight officers and 606 men were killed or captured; American losses were seven killed and twenty-two wounded. Harrison decided that his lines of supply were too extended and that a withdrawal to Detroit would be prudent. On learning that Harrison would not be coming on, the British commanders abandoned a plan to withdraw their protection from York and Burlington Bay and attempt to hold only Kingston.

John Richardson was among the prisoners. He had fought in three nasty skirmishes, shot and killed a mounted rifleman, and watched a Delaware warrior strike a wounded Kentuckian with a tomahawk and lift his scalp. He managed to escape from a party of mounted riflemen led by Lieut.-Col. James Johnson (Lieut.-Col. Richard Johnson's brother). As he ran, John caught a glimpse of many captured redcoats before crossing in front of some other American cavalry bearing down on him. He shoved his musket under some soft mud and surrendered to Gov. Isaac Shelby, a man he considered vulgar. (To Richardson, Americans were uncivilized, a few blood relations excepted.)

National Archives of Canada, C-319

Tecumseh, the Shawnee war leader, formed a confederacy to curb white settlement.

All the captives were to march up the Maumee River; however, one of Richardson's Askin aunts was married to an American, Elijah Brush, who interceded for him. He was sent instead to Put-in-Bay, where his father, also a prisoner, was tending to the wounded Capt. Robert Barclay. By the spring of 1814, John was in Frankfort, Kentucky, where most of the British prisoners were being held. The officers were on parole. Earlier, some of them had been confined in irons, following a report that British-born American citizens had been unfairly prosecuted in England, a misery John Richardson did not share. Soon the officers in Frankfort were allowed to return to Canada, if they could pay their way. With relatives to help out, John was able to reach home, although the last day he spent in Frankford was disconcerting. During his stay he had charmed a responsive widow old enough to be his mother. Her usual boyfriend tried to attack him at knife-point, and John fled for his life to his lodgings in a local tavern.

Procter returned to Montreal. A year later, he faced a court-martial over his conduct of the campaign. He was found guilty of negligence and poor judgment, and was suspended from duty and pay for six months. He died in England in 1822.

In Detroit, on 14 October 1813, Major-General Harrison signed an armistice with the native tribes and accepted women and children as hostages for the good conduct of the warriors. A serious consequence of the defeat on the Thames was the abasement of the natives in the northwest. Their lands could now be overrun by American settlers. Over time, these self-sufficient people would be pushed westwards, their descendants ultimately forced to subsist on reserves far from the ancestral homelands.

XII

The Battle of Lundy's Lane, 25 July 1814

I n the portrait section of the Smithsonian Institution in Washington, D.C., is a bust of Gen. Winfield Scott. Below the name is the addition, "the Victor of Lundy's Lane," a claim that many Canadians would dispute.

Three sites figured prominently in the Battle of Lundy's Lane. The Lane originally ran westwards at right angles to the Niagara River and swung south after it intersected with Portage Road, coming to an end near the Falls. A church and a cemetery with a monument today occupy the site on the hill. Lundy's Lane extends eastwards from the Queen Elizabeth Way interchange and today ends at Highway 8 (Portage Road, originally built to carry traffic around the Falls from the lower landing at Queenston to the terminus at Chippewa). Growth of the former Chippewa village has obscured another important site, at the Chippewa (now Welland) River. A tangible related place is restored Fort Erie, where the Niagara campaign of 1814 came to an explosive end.

Some of the characters from the Crysler's Farm incident reappear, while others are new. Lieut.-Gen. Gordon Drummond (1772–1854) had superceded Francis de Rottenburg as administrator and commander-of-forces in Upper Canada. Drummond was born in Quebec City. His father was an agent for a British firm, a deputy paymaster-general, and a legislative councillor. In command of the regulars and militia west of Kingston was Maj.-Gen. Phineas Riall (1775–1850); like many British officers Riall was Anglo-Irish.

On the American side, Jacob Brown, apparently a well-known smuggler of Sackets Harbor, had been promoted to major-general. Brown would command what turned out to be the final attempt to recapture the Niagara peninsula. His three brigadier-generals were Eleazer Wheelock Ripley (a battalion commander at Crysler's Farm); Winfield Scott, the enthusiastic sightseer with Wilkinson; and Congressman and notable "war hawk" Peter Porter, commander of the New York militia.

For Britain, the military situation had improved. On 11 April, Napoleon abdicated and then went into exile on the Island of Elba. The governor-general of the Canadas, Sir George Prevost, soon received word that reinforcements were heading for Quebec and that he would be able to put thousands more regulars into the field. In the first wave would come the 4th Battalion 1st Foot (Royal Scots), Nova Scotia Fencibles from Newfoundland, the 90th Foot from the West Indies, and the 1st battalions of the 6th and 82nd Regiments from Bordeaux. Twelve more regiments and three companies of artillery from the Duke of Wellington's army would not be far behind.

For his expedition against the Niagara frontier, Maj.-Gen. Jacob Brown managed to round up 5,000 regulars and volunteers. Winfield Scott had 1,319 officers and men in his brigade; Eleazer Ripley had 992. Peter Porter commanded 728 Pennsylvanians, 440 New Yorkers, 56 Canadian volunteers and 500–600 native warriors. The others in Brown's force were 327 artillery-men and some light dragoons. For months, Winfield Scott had been drilling the regulars at Buffalo, and thus they were far superior to those who had served in the 1813 campaign. Because of a shortage of blue cloth issued for American infantry regiments, Scott's men were uniformed in grey, and they looked deceptively like militia.

By 2 July, Riall's force was distributed widely. The 90th Foot, not yet at Montreal, was intended for Niagara; 600 "effectives" of the 41st Foot occupied Fort Niagara; 1,500 of the 1st Royal Scots and the 100th Foot were posted between Forts George and Erie, with a small garrison encamped at Chippewa; a detachment of the 19th Light Dragoons and the flank companies of the Lincoln Militia were also along the Niagara River; 500 of the 103rd were in reserve at Twelve Mile Creek or Burlington Bay; and 1,000 of the 8th Foot and the Glengarry Fencibles were at York. Drummond wanted to hold Fort Niagara, which the British had captured the season before, in order to control the harbour.

Both sides expected their naval squadrons on Lake Ontario to bring rein-forcements and supplies. The Americans would have the edge when two huge new ships, the *Superior* and the *Mohawk*, nearly ready at Sackets Harbor, could join Commodore Chauncey's fleet. The British naval commander, Sir James Yeo, awaited the *St. Lawrence*, under construction at Kingston. When ready it would have an armament heavier than Nelson's *Victory*, no mean feat for a Lake Ontario shipyard.

Brown resolved to by-pass the British holding Fort Niagara, and to make his strike above the Falls, hoping in time to move north to meet Chauncey's fleet near Fort George. On 3 July, Winfield Scott landed his brigade below Fort Erie, while Eleazer Ripley took his men ashore above the fort. When natives moved to cover the rear, the garrison of one company of British regu-lars and twelve gunners surrendered. By that time, Major-General Riall had decided to reinforce the garrison at Chippewa. He rode there himself at the head of five companies of Royal Scots, while from York the 300 effectives of the long-serving 8th Foot, all that were fit for duty, would soon join him.

Lieut.-Col. Thomas Pearson led the flank companies of the 100th, some militia and natives, forward, in order to counter any move towards him from the south. Riall was unaware that Fort Erie had already fallen, and assumed that a rumoured approaching American force would be a small detachment. He followed with his regulars over the bridge at the Chippewa River to take up a position south of the village. He would be joined there shortly by the men of the 8th Regiment.

The next day, on 4 July, on Major-General Brown's orders, Winfield Scott was leading his brigade north from Fort Erie, followed by Ripley's. Porter had set off to clear snipers from the woods. As Scott neared the Chippewa River, he beheld Riall's men drawn up on the far side. Because the river was too deep to ford, the only way to engage Riall was to cross the sole bridge. Instead, Scott withdrew some three kilometres (two miles) south over a bridge that spanned Street's Creek, near Daniel Street's mills and farm. By the 5th, Jacob Brown was ready to launch an attack before Riall could receive any more reinforcements. After some stragglers joined him, his striking force was again 5,000 strong to Riall's 2,000, counting the natives. Peter Porter crossed Street's Creek with his Pennsylvanians and the natives, but soon found, to his dismay, that Riall's force had erected a gun battery on his side of the Chippewa River. He retreated back over Street's Creek, where Scott's brigade waited.

By that day, the 5th, the 8th Regiment had reached Riall, who advanced towards Street's Creek with 1,500 men and some field guns. Riall was confident that most of the Americans were still investing Fort Erie. The land between the creek and the Chippewa was open plain along the Niagara River, with enclosing forest 1,000 metres (3,280 feet) inland. At 5:00 p.m., Brown ordered Winfield Scott to deploy three battalions on the plain beyond Street's Creek. After some artillery fire from his field guns, Riall sent the 8th Regiment to the right, and ordered the Royal Scots and the 100th to charge Scott's grey-clad front. Only when the grey line came on with discipline and steadiness did Riall exclaim, with an oath, "Why, those are regulars!"

His casualties mounted as his own side stood up to the concentrated firing from Scott's field guns and musketry. Riall withdrew his troops back across the Chippewa River, and had the natives in his rear guard destroy the bridge. Riall was not outnumbered – Ripley's and Porter's brigades were not yet on the scene. But Scott's musket and artillery fire had been too accurate. When Riall counted his casualties, he found 148 killed and 321 wounded; Brown's losses were 60 killed and 268 wounded. Brown and Scott had won the Battle of Chippewa, but Lundy's Lane, twenty days in the future, would be the critical test.

Ripley and Porter caught up with Scott, and the three brigades occupied Riall's recently vacated army camp at Chippewa. On the 7th, to forestall the superior American force from circling round and attacking his rear, Riall fell

Harper's Weekly, 16 June, 1866.

An interpretation of the battle published in 1866.

back to Fort George. Jacob Brown followed after him, occupied Queenston, and began fortifying the Heights. Brown hoped that Commodore Chauncey's squadron would arrive shortly from Sackets Harbor with reinforcements and supplies so that he could lay siege to Forts George and Niagara.

At that point, Lieut.-Gen. Gordon Drummond was about to take personal command. He ordered his Volunteer Incorporated Militia Battalion of Upper Canada, which included the well-trained flank companies from many militia regiments, and Lieut.-Col. Joseph Morrison and his 89th Regiment, from Kingston to York. Others being shunted westwards were the flank companies of the 104th, also at York, and five companies of Canadian Fencibles from Lower Canada to Kingston. By 12 July, the 6th, 82nd, and 90th had reached Montreal, all bound for Upper Canada. Drummond reached York on the evening of 22 July. Following was Dr. William "Tiger" Dunlop, then an assistant surgeon in the 89th; he was ranked as a lowly subaltern. Travelling with a fellow subaltern, they found that all the horses were held in reserve for senior officers. Dunlop posed as a general, his friend as his aide-de-camp (A.D.C.). Thus, outwitting military bureaucracy, they received good horses and travelled to York in comfort.

By the 24th, Jacob Brown had withdrawn from Queenston to Chippewa. His force was depleted to 2,644 effectives, and the day before he had received a letter from Sackets Harbor informing him that Commodore Chauncey's squadron was still there – he could not expect supplies or fresh troops. He decided instead to bring supplies from a depot at Fort Schlosser, on the New York side of the Niagara River opposite Niagara Falls. Once Brown and his detachment had left for Fort Erie, Riall advanced from Fort George. His vanguard of 1,000 took up a defensive position five kilometres (three miles) above

Chippewa, on a hill where Lundy's Lane joined Portage Road. For about one-and-a-half kilometres (one mile) inland from the Falls the country was open cropland, but a fringe of woodland bordered the Niagara River. The vanguard was in position at 7:00 a.m. on Monday 25 July.

Early that morning, General Drummond, Lieutenant-Colonel Morrison with his 89th, and some York Militia reached Fort George. Riall was near Lundy's Lane with 1,500 men and four field guns. Morrison at once departed with 800 men to support Riall – his 89th, detachments of Royal Scots and the 8th Regiment, and the light company of the 41st. They reached Riall in the afternoon. Marching from Twelve Mile Creek to reinforce them was Lieut.-Col. Hercules Scott, of the 103rd Regiment, with 1,200 men and two 6-pounder guns.

Jacob Brown was suspicious that the British at Fort George might cross the river and attack his depot at Fort Schlosser. To ensure that attention would focus on Canadian soil, he decided to create a diversion to distract his enemy, by attacking Queenston. He ordered Winfield Scott to begin to advance from Chippewa with his brigade, now 1,072, all ranks. Scott reached Lundy's Lane towards 6:00 p.m., and ordered his men from marching column into battle line. Finding Riall's position at the hill, and unwilling to risk being attacked before he could form columns for a retreat, Scott resolved to advance immediately without waiting for Ripley and Porter to support him.

Even before he saw Scott's brigade moving from column into battle line, Riall thought that Brown's entire army was upon him, and he ordered a

Fort George, as it would have looked at the time of the battle, from Fort Niagara on the New York side of the Niagara River.

Metro Toronto Reference Library, John Ross Robertson Collection

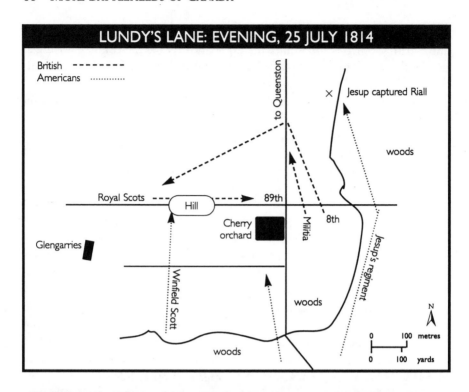

LUNDY'S LANE: EVENING, 25 JULY 1814

British ----------
Americans ....

Jesup captured Riall

woods

Royal Scots ----   Hill   ----▶ 89th

Cherry orchard

8th

Militia

Jesup's regiment

Glengarries

Winfield Scott

woods

woods

N

0 ___ 100 metres
0 ___ 100 yards

to Queenston

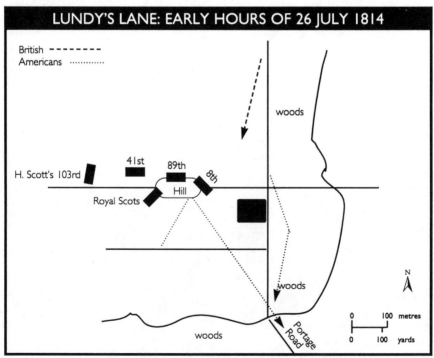

LUNDY'S LANE: EARLY HOURS OF 26 JULY 1814

British ----------
Americans ....

woods

H. Scott's 103rd   41st   89th   8th
              Royal Scots   Hill

woods

woods

Portage Road

N

0 ___ 100 metres
0 ___ 100 yards

withdrawal. Fortunately, Gordon Drummond was on the scene, having ridden from Queenston, and he countermanded the order. There were now 1,600 troops on the south-facing side of the hill at Lundy's Lane, with more at outposts or coming. The Glengarries were on the right, some Royal Scots, the 89th, and the light company of the 41st were high on the slope in the centre. In front of them the artillerymen had set up two 24-pounder guns near the crest, two 6-pounders, and some rockets, the latter the invention, in 1805, of Sir William Congreve, an artillery officer. One company of the 8th, the 19th Light Dragoons and the Incorporated Militia Battalion were on the left beside Portage Road.

Scott's brigade struck at 7:00 p.m., and Maj. Thomas Jesup and his 25th Infantry Regiment succeeded in driving back Riall's left flank. A stream of men in the American right flank flowed north through woods along the bank of the Niagara River. Drummond's centre held firm, and in near hand-to-hand combat drove Scott's centre back. Riall was badly wounded. In the gathering gloom his stretcher bearers carried him into the midst of Jesup's men on the American right, who claimed him as their prisoner.

On the battle raged. At 8.30 p.m. Jacob Brown arrived with Ripley and his brigade, by which time Scott's was reduced to 600 effectives. Ripley's men succeeded in pushing Drummond's back, but Hercules Scott arrived with his 103rd Regiment and the other fresh troops from Twelve Mile Creek and the sides were again more evenly matched. The fight went on in total darkness, illuminated only by flashes from musket and cannon, and "the rockets' red glare" that Francis Scott Key would watch near Baltimore in September. Peter Porter finally arrived with his brigade and mixed in among the rest. By midnight, both Winfield Scott and Jacob Brown had been wounded, and Ripley, now in command, ordered a withdrawal to Chippewa. They left unopposed by British and Canadian troops too exhausted to offer pursuit. Many were too dazed to notice the Americans leaving.

The casualty count was appalling, the bloodiest encounter in the entire two-year conflict. American losses stood at 173 killed, 571 wounded, and 117 missing. The horrified Drummond counted his at 84 regulars killed, 559 wounded, and 193 missing. His militia losses were 142 in the incorporated battalion and 20 from the Lincoln and York detachments. Morrison of the 89th was wounded, Riall, who would lose an arm, was among the 42 prisoners that Drummond reported.

Inasmuch as they were in command of the gory field, the British and Canadians could count themselves the winners of a tactical victory. Drummond had more reinforcements to call upon, but Brown had none. If any American deserved credit for his performance that day, it was the conservative Eleazer Ripley, who conducted a successful withdrawal, first to Chippewa. He ordered Street's mills burnt and all supplies and guns his men could not carry dumped in the Niagara River. He wanted to keep going all the way to Fort Schlosser and safety, but the wounded Brown resolved to keep a bridgehead by holding Fort Erie. Winfield Scott is not so much the "victor of Lundy's Lane," therefore, as the man who may have lost the battle, because he launched his attack before the other brigades could support him.

Drummond was determined not to follow until his troops had revived and reinforcements were at hand. He did not begin investing Fort Erie until 3 August, although he set up headquarters halfway between Chippewa and the fort on the 1st. In the interval, Brown had had his men build a fortified camp beside Fort Erie. By now the *Mohawk* and the *Superior* were afloat, and Commodore Chauncey had seized control of Lake Ontario. Drummond was cut off from any lake-borne supplies, but he went ahead and had his troops digging defensive lines and preparing a camp closer to Fort Erie. By 13 August he had begun bombarding the fort with six field guns. On the 15th he moved his troops out of their lines and attempted an assault, but was repulsed with heavy losses. At dawn a stockpile of ammunition blew up, and many of Drummond's terrified men ran away. All told, he lost 906 men to the Americans' 84.

Throughout the stalemate, during which British forces burned Washington (23–25 August) and raided Baltimore (12–15 September), skirmishing continued around Fort Erie. On 17 September the Americans attempted a breakout. They left the fort and attacked Drummond's lines, but were driven back. Drummond's losses were 609 men; the Americans lost 511. Drummond now felt obliged to withdraw to Chippewa.

Finally, the mighty ship *St. Lawrence* was rigged and sailing – 60 metres (197 feet) at the waterline, 112 guns, and room for a crew of 1,000. She had proudly led Yeo's squadron to the waters off Fort George by 20 October. As soon as spies warned him that the *St. Lawrence* was about to leave Kingston, Chauncey ran his squadron into Sackets Harbor and refused to challenge Yeo. Although 4,000 reinforcements had crossed over to Fort Erie, now that Chauncey could not help, Brown and the other senior officers decided to abandon the campaign. They began moving men and equipment across the Niagara River, and on 5 November they blew up Fort Erie. Tiger Dunlop, leaving Chippewa to tend the wounded being forwarded to York, remembered that his regiment was 500 strong before Lundy's Lane. Outside Fort Erie it had been reduced to sixty able-bodied rank and file, commanded by a captain, with two senior lieutenants carrying the colours, "and myself marching in rear – voilà. His Majesty's 89th Regiment of Foot."

The war ended with the signing of the Treaty of Ghent on 24 December 1814, which meant a return to the status quo, except for one oft-forgotten territorial change. The Americans had taken the British base on Carleton Island, at the head of the St. Lawrence, and they did not return it. Perhaps one

Yeo's great flagship *St. Lawrence*. Built at Kingston, it carried a heavier armament than Nelson's *Victory*, and was the largest sail-powered warship on Lake Ontario. The Americans were building a bigger one at Sackets Harbor when the war ended.

Metro Tororonto Reference Library, John Ross Robertson Collection

reason why Americans are convinced they won the war is because they decisively defeated the British at the Battle of New Orleans on 8 January 1815. By that time, however, Britain and the United States were officially at peace, and so the victory did not count.

The British regiments began to depart. They were required again in Europe after Napoleon's escape from Elba. Dunlop sailed with the 89th, which did not reach its destination until after Wellington's victory at Waterloo on 18 June 1815. In memory of Winfield Scott's brigade, cadets at the United States Military Academy at West Point adopted the grey for their uniforms. The colour has been in use there ever since.

In 1987, during an archaeological dig on the west side of Fort Erie (the site of the American camp), some thirty bodies were exhumed. Scraps of clothing and other artifacts identified twenty-eight of them as American soldiers. With due ceremony, a guard from the United States Army escorted flag-draped coffins containing the remains home, for interment with full military honours in the Bath National Cemetery, New York.

XIII

The Battle of Windsor,
4 December 1838

The drama of the Rebellions of 1837 and the infuriating border raids of 1838 have attracted considerable attention over the years. The rebellions in Upper Canada (Ontario) were mere scuffles; the attacks on such places as Windmill Point near Prescott and on Pelee Island were much more serious. Apart from minor annoyances, the raid on Windsor in December 1838 was the last threatening incursion following the rebellions. The site of the battle in Windsor, then a tiny village, was the orchard belonging to François Baby, a former member of the Legislative Assembly for Essex County. The Baby house in central Windsor, close to the Detroit River, is now a museum. The orchard lay to the west and south of the house.

A leading personality was Lieut.-Col. John Prince (1796–1870), commander of the 3rd Essex Militia Regiment. Prince was born in Hereford, England. A lawyer, he emigrated to Upper Canada in 1833. He purchased a lot on the Detroit River above Sandwich, then a larger and separate community from Windsor.

One cause of the rebellion in Upper Canada was the control of the government by a lieutenant-governor and his appointed council who dispensed patronage to friends. Opposed to this "Family Compact" and the Tories was the Reform Party, whose supporters wanted a government responsible to the electorate. The Reformers had won the election of 1834, but a newly appointed lieutenant-governor, Sir Francis Bond Head, arrived in 1836 and called another election. The Tories won a majority of seats, through rowdy tactics and behaviour that caused mounting tension. A weak economy, considerable unemployment, and a poor harvest in 1837 added to the unrest. Two local uprisings, William Lyon Mackenzie's on Toronto's Yonge Street, and Dr. Charles Duncombe's in the London District, were easily put down by the militia. The attacks on border communities by exiled Canadians – and American supporters calling themselves "Patriots" or "Hunters" – were more severe threats. The Hunters were members of secret societies called Hunters' Lodges. Some historians are content to style them Patriots, but since their

A view of Prescott in the 1870s. The windmill where the invaders took shelter in November 1838 had been converted into a lighthouse. Prisoners taken there and those taken at Windsor were tried at Kingston and London. Some were hanged; others were transported to a penal colony.

only common objective was the removal of the British from Canada, perhaps "republicans" is the more fitting title.

Throughout 1838, the Colonial Office in London sent a large reinforcement of British regular troops to Upper Canada. The lieutenant-governor who replaced Sir Francis Head was Sir George Arthur. He was concerned that many regulars would desert to the United States, for them the promised land, if they were stationed close to the border. Arthur formed a policy of accommodating the professional soldiers inland, but close enough to counterattack should the need arise. He stationed militia regiments at border points. For the Windsor border area, detachments of the 2nd and 3rd Essex Regiments were on guard. The nearest regulars were at Fort Malden, below Amherstburg, where the Detroit River was wider. At the time of the attack on Windsor, the regulars at Malden were the 34th Regiment of Foot, commanded by Lieut.-Col. Richard Airey. A twenty-eight-man detachment of the 2nd Essex Militia was on duty at a barracks in Windsor. Downstream at Sandwich, five kilometres (three miles) away, near Lieutenant-Colonel Prince's farm, part of the 3rd Essex had billets.

The leader of the republicans (misnamed Patriots) was "General" Lucius V. Bierce, who expected to gather about 400 followers at Detroit – he anticipated finding many willing troops from among legions of unemployed men in the town. His three division commanders were "Colonel" S.S. Coffinbury, a

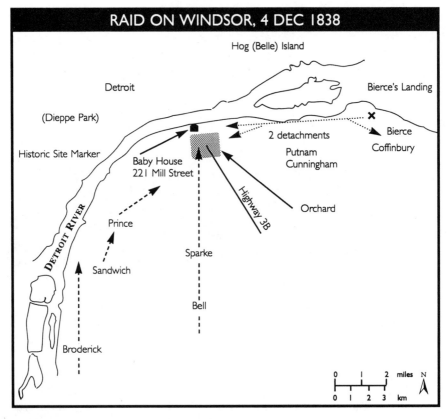

RAID ON WINDSOR, 4 DEC 1838

Hog (Belle) Island

Detroit

Bierce's Landing

(Dieppe Park)

Historic Site Marker

Baby House
221 Mill Street

2 detachments

Putnam
Cunningham

Bierce

Coffinbury

DETROIT RIVER

Prince

Sandwich

Sparke

Bell

Broderick

Highway 3B

Orchard

0   1   2 miles N
0 1 2 3   km

newspaper editor from Mansfield, Ohio, and Cornelius Cunningham and William Putnam, both Canadian exiles from the London District. Making lukewarm attempts to prevent border crossings was Gen. Hugh Brady, commander of the Northwestern Military Department of the United States Army.

On the night of 3 December, General Bierce and some 250 to 300 men took over the American steamer *Champlain* that was plying the Detroit River. Bierce's supporters had numbered 400, but since he had done everything he could to avoid crossing the river, some 100 had drifted away. He was finally shamed into bringing over the remaining men. At 2:00 a.m. on the 4th they landed at a farm some five kilometres (three miles) above Windsor. According to one version, the steamer left so that no one could desert, and the men marched to the village. Sgt. Frederick Walsh commanded the detachment of the 2nd Essex. His men resisted the attackers until they were out of ammunition; they then tried to withdraw but could not get clear. The invaders began setting fire to the barracks and the occupants tried to escape. In the fracas, according to Thomas Robinson of the militia, two of Walsh's men were killed.

The burning embers used to ignite the barracks reportedly came from the fireplace of a Black man named Mills. One version claims that Mills shouted

"God save the Queen!" or something similar, and was shot dead. Two adjacent houses burned with the barracks. Bierce's men also burned the steamer *Thames,* which was docked nearby. While a messenger was galloping to Sandwich to alert Lieutenant-Colonel Prince, Bierce read a proclamation, calling on Canadians to rise up, that bore the signature of William, a son of Samuel Lount (who had been hanged for his part in the rising at Toronto). William Lount was the "military secretary" of the Hunters in the west. After he finished reading the proclamation, Bierce, like Gilbert and Sullivan's Duke of Plaza Toro, proceeded to lead his troops from behind. With thirty men, probably those under fellow American Colonel Coffinbury, he retired close to the point where they had landed.

Of the other two detachments, one had reached the centre of the village, while the other, of about 150 men, had gone beyond to the Baby farm by the time the first militia soldiers entered Windsor. They were forty men of Capt. John Frederick Sparke's Provincial Volunteer Militia, as well as Capt. John Bell's company of the Kent militia. Close behind them marched three companies of the 3rd Essex Regiment. These five companies fought the Battle of Windsor. Sparke's well-drilled men had red tunics with which, thus far, very few of the militia had been issued. The battle flowed through the Baby orchard until the accurate fire from Sparke's men sent the invaders reeling. Part of the Essex militia flanked the enemy and caught him in its crossfire.

At that point a militia officer, with Dr. John Hume, assistant surgeon to the 3rd Essex, came rushing up from Sandwich to help. Finding Bierce's second detachment in the village, the two men ran, but the enemy hunted Dr. Hume down and killed him with axe and bayonet. Then Lieutenant-Colonel Prince rode in from Sandwich, "dressed in a fustian shooting coat and fur cap" rather than a uniform, and leading reinforcements of his regiment. He later stated that his entire force amounted to only 130 men. Uncertain of the enemy's strength or location, he ordered a retreat towards Sandwich. Before he set out he had sent a courier to Fort Malden, because he felt he needed the support of the closest regulars.

Prince was livid over the murder of his close friend, Dr. Hume, and furious with American officials who had not done enough to prevent the rogues crossing the Detroit River. To make a statement he ordered four prisoners summarily shot.

At about 11:00 a.m. Capt. Edward Broderick joined Prince with 100 men of the 34th Regiment, a field gun and artillerymen under Lieut. Dionysius Airy (a brother of Richard, the lieutenant-colonel of the 34th), and some fifty natives under George Ironside, a native agent. The regulars, militia, and natives then set out for Windsor looking for fleeing republicans. During the pursuit, forty-four were taken prisoner. Prince had one more man summarily executed, and reported that twenty-one of the enemy had been killed.

John Prince as a young man, from a miniature.

Bierce and the thirty others who had stayed a safe distance to the rear retreated to the shore where they had landed, stole some canoes and boats, and made it safely to Hog Island (now Belle Island, Michigan). According to one account the American steamer *Erie,* sent by Gen. Hugh Brady from Detroit, nearly caught them. Another version claims that the *Erie* did in fact take into custody some of those trying to escape. Meanwhile, the regulars came close to catching up with them. One of the officers who kept a diary recorded that they spotted half a dozen "rebels" pulling off in a boat:

> The field piece was immediately unlimbered and pointed against it. The range was a long one, about 1000 yards and the boat not far from the shore of Hogg [*sic*] Island. Airey however managed to get 5 shots at it before the men could gain the woods, all of the balls struck close to the boat and one of them, the third, took away a man's arm, who was conveyed on board the U.S. steamer *Erie* which had during the whole of the morning been cruising in the river to prevent the rebels taking refuge in the American territory.

Among the forty-four captives were Cornelius Cunningham and William Putnam, as well as two of Dr. Duncombe's rebels, Paul Bedford of Norwich and Joshua Doan of Yarmouth. All were taken to Amherstburg by the regulars and sent on to London for trial. Lieutenant-Governor Arthur ordered a regular officer at Chatham to investigate the cold-blooded killings of the five prisoners, cautioning him to get "the information required in a manner, the least calculated to wound Lieutenant-Colonel Prince's feelings, which I wish to avoid." Prince's action had the wholehearted approval of the local people, and Arthur hesitated to prosecute their hero.

Arthur hurried to Windsor for a first-hand report, and to arrange to have more companies of regulars stationed at Sandwich, despite the danger of desertions. He resolved to deal harshly with the men captured on Canadian soil as a result of border infractions. All would face military court-martial, and eleven who were captured near Prescott in November were hanged at Kingston. Among the six who were executed in London were Cornelius Cunningham, William Putnam, Paul Bedford, and Joshua Doan. Some ninety men taken on various raids went to the penal colony in Van Diemen's Land (Tasmania).

By the close of 1838, regulars in Upper Canada numbered 5,000, all ranks — eight-and-one-half regiments, two squadrons of dragoon guards, and some artillerymen.

The Baby House stands close to the site of the battle. It is now a museum.

Mary Beacock Fryer

To investigate the unrest and make recommendations to remedy the situation, a new governor-general, Lord Durham, had arrived in Quebec in June. Because he felt that the home government did not give him the support he required, he returned to England in November, and wrote his famous report. He recommended uniting Upper and Lower Canada, and granting them responsible government. The union came into being in 1841; responsible government was delayed until 1846.

Between 1838 and 1840, minor incidents continued. British and American ships fired on each other in the St. Lawrence; an Orange parade was cancelled in Cobourg; and vigilance foiled an attempted raid on Cobourg. Even Brock's monument on Queenston Heights was dynamited, in April 1840.

In 1843 some rebels received pardons. Mackenzie himself was pardoned in a general amnesty in 1849. He returned to Toronto and won a seat in the assembly in 1851. Before his successful election, Mackenzie visited the Parliamentary Library, then in Montreal. John Prince, an M.L.A., was there to attend the session. On 28 February 1849, Prince wrote in his diary, "I turned William Lyon Mackenzie, the Traitor, out of the Library." Prince lived down Arthur's displeasure, and later moved to Sault Sainte Marie. He was elected to the legislative council in 1856.

XIV

The Red River Expedition, 1870

R ed River in 1870 was not a battle fought by opposing sides – it was a battle against terrain and elements on the difficult journey to Winnipeg. Even today, this journey will challenge hardy canoeists. One can also traverse some of the area by car, canoeing for short distances. A site worth visiting is restored Lower Fort Garry, north of Winnipeg. The remains of Fort Garry, sometimes called Upper Fort Garry, a site that features so prominently in the Riel legend, are in the heart of the modern city of Winnipeg.

One reason for including this expedition is because so many of the important characters in subsequent battles were present. Garnet Wolseley, the leader of the expedition, was commander-in-chief of the British army during the South African War. Capt. Redvers Buller was the original commander-in-chief of the British army against the Boers, where he earned the nickname "Reverse Buller" for his many setbacks. Sam Steele, the archetypal Mountie, served in the Rebellion of 1885 and in South Africa. Acheson Irvine and William Herchmer, future Commissioners in the North West Mounted Police, were along in 1870 and held important posts in 1885. Like Steele, Herchmer also served in South Africa.

The cement that holds the three settings together – 1870, 1885, and South Africa, 1899–1900 – is William Dillon Otter, major of the Queen's Own Rifles in 1870, commander at Cut Knife Hill in 1885, and lieutenant-colonel commandant of the 1st Canadian Contingent at the Battle of Paardeberg in 1900. Otter did not join the Red River expedition, but was so zealous that he spent his holiday from his job with the Canada Company accompanying the troops part of the way. That Otter was one of the first Canadians to become a professional officer commanding Canadian troops is no surprise.

The expedition to Red River was deemed necessary by the government of Sir John A. Macdonald because of disturbances in the settlement at the forks of the Red and Assiniboine Rivers. Local French-speaking Métis and their supporters, led by Louis Riel, had formed a provisional government to treat with Ottawa. By 1869, the Hudson's Bay Company had completed negotiations to have the two-year-old Dominion of Canada purchase its vast territory of

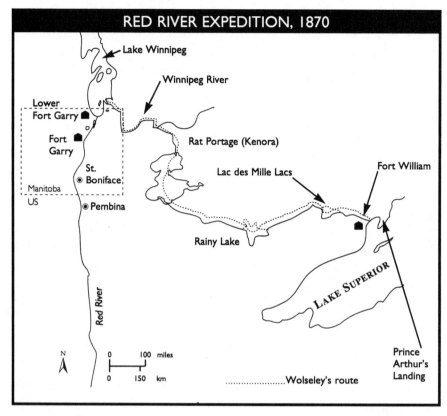

RED RIVER EXPEDITION, 1870

Lake Winnipeg

Winnipeg River

Lower Fort Garry

Fort Garry

Rat Portage (Kenora)

Fort William

St. Boniface

Lac des Mille Lacs

Manitoba

US

Pembina

Rainy Lake

LAKE SUPERIOR

Red River

N

0   100 miles

0   150   km

Wolseley's route

Prince Arthur's Landing

Rupert's Land for 300,000 pounds. Already, settlers from central Canada were moving to the vicinity of a fledgling Winnipeg, however, and parties of surveyors had begun laying out townships. The mixed-blood population had not been consulted adequately, and people were alarmed that their claims to the lands they occupied might be invalidated. By 2 November, Riel had set up headquarters in Fort Garry, a Hudson's Bay Company post.

In December, a national council of Métis drew up a list of conditions for annexation: the right to elect their own legislature, and an assurance that French and English would be official languages and that Métis customs would be respected. In the meantime, the Dominion government chose William McDougall as the first lieutenant-governor of the new territory. When McDougall, who travelled through the United States, was stopped at the border above Pembina by armed Métis, Macdonald dispatched Donald Alexander Smith, the senior Hudson's Bay Company officer on hand, to negotiate a peaceful transfer of the settlement to Canada.

On 12 May 1870, the government in Ottawa passed the Manitoba Act, which incorporated most of the Métis's demands. It came into effect on 15 July, and Manitoba entered the Dominion as the fifth province. There was a catch, however.

Riel had permitted the execution, by firing squad, of Thomas Scott, a recent settler and Orangeman. This so inflamed the Orangemen of Ontario that Macdonald deemed some conciliatory action to be necessary. He ordered that an expedition prepare to go to Red River, in order to quell any further disturbances there, and to depose Riel's illegally established provisional government. Col. Garnet Wolseley, the commander, was also the quartermaster-general. A British regular officer, Wolseley came from an Anglo-Irish family. He arrived in Canada with reinforcements sent in the wake of the *Trent* affair of 1861. The removal of two Confederate agents from the British steamer *Trent* by a Union vessel had aroused Northern opinion against Canada.

Wolseley was in a hurry to reach Red River. The British government had resolved to withdraw all regular troops from Canada in 1871, which meant that professional soldiers accompanying him would have to return to central Canada before winter. His force was composed of a few engineers and gunners, some 250 regular soldiers of the 60th Regiment and their commander, Lieut.-Col. Randle Joseph Feilden, and two battalions of militia. Macdonald decided that one battalion could come from Ontario, but the other must be raised in Quebec, to demonstrate that he was not necessarily catering to Orange opinion. These were the 1st (Ontario) Rifles, commanded by Lieut.-Col. Samuel Peters Jarvis of Toronto, and the 2nd (Quebec) Rifles under Lieut.-Col. Louis Adolphe Casault. Each battalion consisted of 21 officers and 350 ranks divided into five companies. The senior major of the Ontario Rifles was Griffiths Wainwright, and of the Quebec Rifles the anglophone Acheson Irvine. The latter appointment confirmed a lack of enthusiasm among Quebec francophones. Some other officers and many in the ranks were from English-speaking Quebec families.

William Herchmer was a captain in the Ontario Rifles. Samuel Steele, of Medonte Township, signed on as private, although he had a commission in the 35th "The Simcoe Foresters." The prime minister's son, Hugh John Macdonald, was an ensign in the Ontario Rifles. Fred Denison, of Toronto, was an A.D.C. to Wolseley, who would call upon his services for the Nile Expedition of 1884 (which failed to relieve Khartoum).

The convenient way to Red River was by train through Chicago to St. Cloud, the railway terminus, and from there by wagon and boat. This route was out of the question, however, for a British expedition bent on occupying an area towards which many Americans were casting expansionist eyes. The troops would travel by an all-Canadian route north of the Great Lakes. That meant crossing nearly 1,000 kilometres (600 miles) of wilderness where the waterways were the highways, and where a rudimentary start had begun on constructing a road.

The construction contract from the Canadian government had been won by Simon Dawson, a surveyor who had explored the area west of Fort William.

In 1857 he proposed a part-water, part-road route by way of Dog and Shebandowan Lakes. Some work began the next year, but construction on the section from Fort William towards Shebandowan Lake did not start until 1869, when the government knew it would be taking over Rupert's Land. In January 1870, Dawson received government permission to enlarge his work force. By May, the road reached Shebandowan Lake, and some work had been completed on portages leading to Lac des Milles Lacs.

The road would do for troops on foot, but wagons might be too heavy for the new surface. Dawson also helped find horses and hired teamsters and voyageurs, many of them native, to serve as boatmen and guides. Much work would have to be done by the troops – setting up depots, moving supplies – before they faced the task of carrying loads along portages. Boats had to be constructed, and at portages they would be slid along on parallel logs called skids, or hauled up steep slopes where steps were cut for the men carrying loads, tumplines placed across their foreheads. Wagons built at Markham, Ontario, accompanied the troops. The expedition left Toronto early in May, in time for the peak of the black-fly and mosquito season.

Wolseley's force went by train to Collingwood. The first instalment to arrive boarded the steamers *Algoma* and *Chicora*, which made for the canal at Sault Ste. Marie. It was on the American side, but American use of the Welland Canal during the Civil War had set a precedent. The *Algoma* passed through, but an inspector delayed the *Chicora* until the British ambassador in Washington convinced President Grant that no military equipment would be on board; it was carried alongside, out of sight of the inspector. Three other steamers followed the *Chicora* and helped move men, provisions and equipment to Fort William. (This fort has been rebuilt and is open to the public. It stands on a site a few kilometres downstream from the original.)

Wolseley reached Fort William on the morning of 25 May, and he named the spot where the steamers docked Prince Arthur's Landing, after Queen Victoria's son, who was then in Canada serving with the Royal Engineers. By that time, Dawson's road had reached Shebandowan Lake, but Wolseley resolved to move his men by water as far as possible. The local red marl clay would form a quagmire in wet weather.

Rain was not a problem at the beginning. Drought had left the country tinder dry, and a forest fire had destroyed timber that had been cut for bridges and culverts. The men had to rebuild parts of the road and replace burnt-out shanties. The base camp at Fort William was comfortable, and the locally produced food was good. But Canadian-made boots were of poor quality, and the insects were a painful nuisance. For part of the time, soldiers practised rowing, in preparation for the journey ahead.

National Archives of Canada, 138791, photo by Notman of Montreal ca. 1860–70

Col. J. Garnet Wolseley (later 1st Viscount Wolseley) commanded the expedition to Red River.

Wolseley established a series of advance depots. The first was at a wooden bridge over the Kaministiquia River, thirty-four kilometres (twenty miles) from Fort William, where the men built a redoubt in case any Fenians known to be lurking around Duluth appeared. From there on the going was more difficult, the country hilly and rough. Rain now slowed down the troops' efforts. The senior British officer in Canada, Lieut.-Gen. James Lindsay, who arrived in June to inspect the works, remarked that a spade was as vital to an infantryman as his rifle.

When he found that a wagon could hold only one boat at a time, Wolseley wanted more than ever to move mostly by water. By 4 June, the first boats had been hauled up above Kakabeka Falls, on the Kaministikwia River, and launched. Capt. John Young of the 60th Regiment, with thirty of his regulars and twelve voyageurs as boatmen and guides, was the first to depart for Matawin Bridge, nineteen kilometres (twelve miles) away. The militia would not set out until the last of the regulars had left. Wolseley placed his faith in his professional troops, and intended to ensure that they drew the lion's share of the credit.

The 150 boats required were oared and each carried a square sail. Some were planked, but most were clinker-built. In the former the planks did not overlap, as they did in the latter. Each boat was about ten metres (thirty-two feet) long and two metres (seven feet) wide. Three canoes had native paddlers. Although Wolseley had his own gig, he preferred the canoes. The native leader was Ignace Montour, a very experienced voyageur from one of the Mohawk reserves.

The boats moved in brigades of fifty men; each boat carried ten to twelve men and two or three voyageurs to serve as bowmen and steermen. All told, there were twenty-one brigades. On 5 July Wolseley moved his headquarters to Matawin Bridge, which the first brigade had passed on 14 June. Dawson was perturbed at the condition of the boats. In places the water had been too shallow, and damaged boats required repairs before proceeding. He regretted that Wolseley had not brought more wagons from Collingwood. Sam Steele, who later wrote a book about his life, found moving the heavy boats along the portages a nightmare requiring all the strength each man possessed. Carrying loads where skids had been laid was awkward, but removing them and putting them back for the next boat meant lost time. On the 14th, Wolseley moved his headquarters to Ward's Landing, at McNeil's Bay on Shebandowan Lake. In the meantime, behind him, all through July, men were working in relays, on the road, carrying freight, and boating.

On 16 July, St. Swithun's Day, the first brigade left for Fort Garry, commanded by Capt. Redvers Buller. McNeil's Bay was 180 kilometres (110 miles) from Fort William, which left nearly 785 kilometres (470 miles) to traverse to Fort Garry. Each brigade of boats carried camping equipment and sixty days' provisions. Dawson sent voyageurs ahead to lay the skids for the first portage. Captain Buller found, when he reached the portage to

Kashabowie Lake, that he had to wait for voyageur guides to catch up with his brigade.

The militia followed once all the regulars were on their way. Wolseley was now far ahead; he had left after the second brigade of regulars set out. With the Ontario Rifles came eager Maj. William Otter, and his commanding officer in the Queen's Own Rifles, Lieut.-Col. Charles T. Gillmor. At Shebandowan Lake, their holiday time nearly over, they had to turn back. Otter recalled later that they had not found the journey arduous – but then, as guests, they probably were not required to work.

The last brigade of militia left McNeil's Bay on 2 August. By that time, the first brigade of regulars was about 240 kilometres (144 miles) ahead, but there had been jam-ups. Sam Steele thought Lieutenant-Colonel Feilden was too cautious about overworking his men. Since Feilden rode in the first brigade with Buller, everyone else had to wait.

At most portages the troops dragged the boats to dry ground. Some men were harnessed to towlines, others moved along each side to keep the boat on the skids. Those who could be spared carried boxes or barrels. The portage to Kashabowie Lake was easy, but beyond the lake, at the drainage divide between streams flowing to Hudson Bay and those flowing to Lake Superior, the men had to struggle up a steep hill. While Wolseley was at this portage, a canoe from Red River arrived carrying a letter from Donald Smith – all "was quiet around Fort Garry," Wolseley read the message with scepticism. He had his own agent travelling through the United States, and he expected to find the agent at Fort Francis.

From the drainage divide onwards, the men would have a somewhat easier time. Until this stage they had to fight the current while rowing; now they would be riding downstream to the Red River itself. Lac des Milles Lacs was very confusing, for it had so many islands that officers required compasses to find their way. The next hurdle was a very steep hill at the portage to Baril Lake, thirty-two kilometres (nineteen miles) from the drainage divide. The name might relate to the barrel-shape of the hill, but Sam Steele claimed that a fur trader, fearing a barrel of rum he carried might be stolen by other traders, had his men bury it, and put up a wooden marker inscribed "A la Mémoire de Monsieur Baril."

Men doing hard physical work required enormous meals. Overworked cooks had little time for sleep. Food was the "pork, beans and hardtack" of a contemporary song, and dried potatoes and apples were made palatable by soaking them.

The next serious challenge was Deux Rivières Portage, below Pickerel Lake, one of the most difficult along the route. Here the troops had to climb a rock so steep that an advance party had built a ladder, and had cut steps around the side of the hill for the men carrying loads. Boats were hauled up the ladder by crews working from above; anyone below would be at risk if a rope should give way. Beyond lay Sturgeon Lake, a delightful place where natives speared huge fish that the officers ate with relish as they praised the roe. As well as sturgeon, the lake yielded pike, pickerel, and maskinonge, a relief from the provisions that the men carried with them. A large canoe brought Wemyss Simpson, M.P. for Algoma, here. He had been sent by Ottawa to persuade the local natives not to oppose Wolseley's troops. Simpson explained that the white men did not covet their land; they merely wanted to pass through.

At the west end of the lake were four sets of rapids. Four men and two guides took each boat down the first while the rest of the men walked; at the second set the men carried the cargoes, and at the third and fourth everyone rode. Wolseley had instructions nailed to a tree for later brigades. Number six company, Ontario Rifles, cleared these rapids at 9:30 on the morning of 6 August, and left the date and time carved on a barrel stave that they set in a tree.

From Lac La Croix, Wolseley had the choice of two routes, one by the Maligne River, the other through Namekan Lake. Both led into Rainy Lake. Wolseley chose the second – rapids in the Maligne River were more dangerous. Around Namekan he noticed poison ivy, as well as succulent blueberries. He reached the Hudson's Bay post of Fort Francis on the morning of 4 August, and found a few single-storeyed buildings on the west bank of Rainy River below a high waterfall. To his delight the postmaster offered him a chair and his bedroom. While he was enjoying the fort's fresh cabbages, he met his agent, Lieut. William Francis Butler, who had come by canoe from Fort Garry in twelve days. Although Butler had tried to keep his presence there a secret, he received an invitation from Louis Riel to come to the fort. When Riel queried his furtive conduct, Butler told the leader of the provisional government about alarming reports he heard while travelling through the United States that implied he would be in danger at Red River.

When the expedition was ready to move on, Wolseley left Number Seven Company, Ontario Rifles, as a garrison for Fort Francis. Before he set out, a messenger arrived from Fort Garry, urging Wolseley to hurry, and to take the new road that ran from North West Angle (in Rainy Lake) direct to Fort Garry. Disenchanted with all the roads he had already used, Wolseley decided to go by water, along the Winnipeg River that drained a series of lakes into Lake Winnipeg, a route that had become a highway since La Vérendrye's travels. It is quite picturesque, as it drops 106 metres (348 feet) over a distance of 262 kilometres (158 miles). Wolseley found the ride exciting. By this time the men, including the sturdy Redvers Buller, were in fine condition and did not tire as quickly. Sam Steele remarked that Buller "always took at least 200 lbs, sometimes 300 lbs."

The Métis leader Louis Riel.

The toughest portage was Grand Décharge, around Slave Falls. While the first brigades were descending the portage, Wolseley went by canoe to the rear. On his return he met some of the Ontario Rifles on 18 August at Slave Falls. From there, Wolseley pushed ahead to catch up with the regulars at Fort Alexander, the Hudson's Bay Company post close to the exit into Lake Winnipeg. He thought he would wait there until all the militia arrived before proceeding up the Red River to Fort Garry.

After Grand Décharge, fourteen portages remained. Most were easy, for they were short; water levels were low, which tamed the rapids. Wolseley reached Fort Alexander on Saturday, 20 August. Waiting for him were all his regulars – men of the 60th Regiment, his gunners, and engineers, who had been received by Donald A. Smith. Wolseley sent a messenger to Fort Francis to tell Number Seven Company of the Ontario Rifles to leave for Fort Garry. They were to try out the new road from the north west arm of Rainy Lake direct to Fort Garry. By now, excited that he was so close, Wolseley decided not to wait for the militia, and to press on with his professionals. If there was to be a fight, he did not want any credit to go to amateurs.

After church parade on Sunday, the regulars left in fifty boats down the last bit of the Winnipeg River and camped on sandy Elk Island in Lake Winnipeg. On Monday the 22nd the boats moved in two lines into the shallow Red River with its low, reedy banks, the men rowing against a light current. In the lead boat were Lieut. William Butler and one of the controllers, alert to anything that might arouse suspicions. The troops encountered a band of Swampy Cree, but no one appeared to know what was happening at Fort Garry.

Wolseley sent a message to Lower Fort Garry, downriver from the other fort. William Flett, a Hudson's Bay Company officer, replied that Riel was still in Fort Garry. The men of the 60th were sparring for a fight as they bivouacked on the night of the 22nd. They rose at 3:30 a.m. on the 23rd and at 8:00 a.m. were served breakfast at the lower fort before continuing. A mounted intelligence officer scouted forward, and Wolseley landed one company of the 60th to march between the river and the road that ran parallel to it, to keep 400 metres (1,300 feet) ahead of the boats, and to act as skirmishers. They had orders to hold anyone they found, in order to forestall warning the occupants of Fort Garry.

As dusk approached, Wolseley decided to camp for the night, and to enter Fort Garry by daylight. From a distance, a mounted Louis Riel observed the soldiers' preparations. Rain began to fall, until by dawn the men were huddled in misery. Meanwhile, the men of the 60th in the advance party had detained several people and purloined mules, carts, and more than enough horses to call themselves mounted rifles. This was fine for men used to horses, but one bugler was bucked off by a nag unaccustomed to the racket. By the 24th, most of the officers were mounted, but the rain had not let up. The day turned out

Mary Beacock Fryer

A "Voyageur" poses outside the stockade of the rebuilt Fort William,
5 September 1993. Inside the fort are exhibits depicting life during the fur trade.

to be an anticlimax – when the men landed, they marched into an empty fort.
Riel had crossed the border, temporarily. Some of his supporters had gone
with him, and others were at home or in hiding. There would be no fight, no
battle honours for the 60th.

Wolseley let them have a holiday after the long, fatiguing march. The regulars behaved, but the civilians on the expedition, and many locals, went on a
riotous drinking binge. Wolseley was loath to keep order when he lacked the
authority, however. He had hoped to be appointed lieutenant-governor to succeed the disgruntled William Mcdougall, but the government chose instead a
Nova Scotian, Adams Archibald, who was some days' travel from Fort Garry.
He had only reached Fort Francis on 23 August, the day before Wolseley's
troops entered Fort Garry. When Archibald drew near on 2 September, most
of the militia had reached their destination. Wolseley sent a guard of the
Ontario Rifles to escort Archibald, and organized a parade and salute by his
gunners.

By that time, some of the regulars had already left. On 29 August, two
companies of the 60th, uniforms now faded and threadbare, had begun retrac-
ing their way down the Red River and Lake Winnipeg, bound for central
Canada, a black bear as their mascot. By 10 September, all the regulars had
gone and Wolseley took his leave of Archibald. The weather was fine, and the

black-flies and mosquitoes had vanished. All the regulars had reached their former bases by late October. The militia remained to garrison both Fort Garrys for the winter and to maintain an outpost north of Pembina. Wolseley's successor was Lieut.-Col. Samuel P. Jarvis, of the Ontario Rifles. His predecessor had stationed this regiment at Fort Garry and the Quebec Rifles at Lower Fort Garry, an undiplomatic move since the francophones in the latter regiment would have been more compatible with most of the Métis.

In the spring of 1871, the discharged militia set off for home, or remained to settle. Each veteran was entitled to 160 acres (65 hectares) for his services. Lieutenant-Governor Archibald formed provisional companies from among men who were willing to re-enlist for a second year, and placed them under the command of Maj. Acheson Irvine, formerly of the Quebec Rifles. One of his captains was William Herchmer.

Manitoba had a minor brush with the Fenians in October 1871, when a small body of Irishmen, veterans from the Union army during the American Civil War, crossed the border and occupied the Hudson's Bay post north of Pembina. This generated a flurry of excitement in the Red River settlement. Lieutenant-Governor Archibald appealed to the Métis for support, and Louis Riel, now living quietly on his farm at St. Vital, south of St. Boniface, approved. Major Irvine mustered 200 of his active militia, and joined by volunteers numbering nearly 300, set out on 6 December, a cold, wet day. With them went 200 Métis, including Riel and another Métis leader, Ambroise Lépine. The expedition was not needed, however; American troops had crossed from Pembina on the 5th, rounded up the Fenians, and escorted them home.

This action prompted Ottawa to add 200 militia to the garrison at Red River. Their commander was Maj. Thomas Stott, of the 42nd Brockville Infantry Battalion, who had been a captain in the Ontario Rifles. *The Volunteer Review*, a newspaper for the military, reported that Stott's force reached Deux Rivières Portage on 1 November, and hoped to be at Fort Garry by the 12th. The report informed readers that Maj. Acheson Irvine was a son of Colonel Irvine, principal A.D.C. to many governors-general.

Louis Riel remained at home until 1875. Twice he was elected member of Parliament representing Provencher – on 22 January 1874, and on 4 February 1875, but was expelled from the House of Commons both times. In an effort to dispose of what seemed to be a worrisome threat, on the 24th, just days after his second election, Riel was declared an outlaw and banished from Canada for five years. He eventually made his way to Montana, where he supported his family by teaching school, until the call sounded again for the founder of Manitoba to lead his people.

XV

Whiskey Fort,
A Non-Battle Site, 1874

Although Alberta is fortunate enough to be decidedly short of battlefields, some less-than-scrupulous Americans once set up posts to sell "firewater" to unsuspecting natives. The most important of a dozen "whiskey forts" was Whoop-Up. This restored site is at the south end of Indian Battle Park in Lethbridge, on the low, slip-off slope at a bend on the east side of the Oldman River. The park itself commemorates a days-long fight between Cree and Blackfoot in 1870; inside the fort is a display recounting this battle. The original fort probably stood closer to the junction of the Oldman and St. Mary rivers. Above Indian Battle Park are gullied, steep banks typical of many prairie rivers, rising to the level of the city and spreading out over the grassy flatlands.

The original Fort Whoop-Up, date of construction deliberately opaque, was a group of log cabins, encircled by a flimsy wooden stockade. It was the work of two partners, J.J. Healy and A.B. Hamilton. In 1870, a group of inebriated natives turned on the villains responsible and burned down the shabby premises. Healy and Hamilton rebuilt, this time for strength. They had no intention of backing off from so lucrative an operation.

By 1874, Whoop-Up had bastions at the four corners of a stout, loopholed stockade, a small cannon and one howitzer, and square-timbered buildings. It was also native-proof. Iron bars extended across the chimney tops so that the natives could not simply drop in. Instead, they had to feed their buffalo hides and other pelts into a grating beside heavy oak gates that to them remained closed. Through the grating a trader would hand out a tin cup of "rotgut," possibly raw alcohol dyed brown with tea.

In 1873, the Canadian government established the North West Mounted Police in order to ensure peace, order, and good government on the prairies. The work of one group of policemen under orders to eliminate Whoop-Up and all the other whiskey trading posts, has become the great legend of the prairies, mixing fact with fancy, thus.

On 9 October 1874, Assistant Commissioner James Macleod rode near the fort with 150 policemen and two 9-pounder field guns. With his troop he had ridden the 1,600 kilometres (1,000 miles) from Red River to deal with

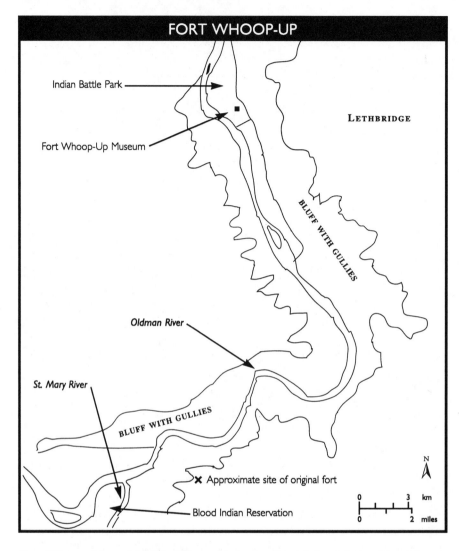

FORT WHOOP-UP

Indian Battle Park

LETHBRIDGE

Fort Whoop-Up Museum

BLUFF WITH GULLIES

Oldman River

St. Mary River

BLUFF WITH GULLIES

X Approximate site of original fort

Blood Indian Reservation

N

0   3   km

0   2   miles

Fort Whoop-Up and build a Mountie post in the vicinity. Macleod's guide was Jerry Potts, the legendary scout and son of a Scottish fur-trader father and a Blackfoot mother.

Stopping high up the bank of the Oldman River, overlooking the stockade on the flat below, Macleod trained his guns. Leaving his police, their mounts, and the guns close to the rim of the valley, Macleod went ahead to parley with the occupants of Whoop-Up. He pressed his horse forward and it picked its way carefully down the loose sand of a gully and trotted forward over the flat. Macleod hoped that, by holding a discussion with the traders, he would be able to avoid a shooting war. He was less than enchanted by the sight of the Stars and Stripes flying over Whoop-Up, well north of the 49th parallel. Macleod reached the oak gates unopposed, dismounted, and knocked.

After some delay the gate swung open, and there stood a tall, distinguished, gentlemanly individual, David Akers, who, Macleod soon learned, had been a Confederate officer during the American Civil War. Not a drop of whiskey was to be found in the fort, however – someone had tipped off the traders. Akers invited Macleod and his officers to dine on buffalo steaks, served by two native women, who were apparently his close friends. Afterwards, Macleod enquired whether he could purchase the fort, to be used as the new post. But Akers declined. Macleod had the manpower to insist, but that was not the Mountie way. So goes the legend; Macleod's reports tell a different story.

Through a lightly falling snowstorm, Jerry Potts led the Mounties thirty-three kilometres (twenty miles) up the Oldman River, past its junction with the St. Mary River, to a large grove of cottonwood trees that could provide both shelter from the snow and wood for the barracks. The police built Fort Macleod on an island. After the fort was inundated during spring floods, they rebuilt it on the site of the present, restored fort, now open to the public. From this site Macleod dispensed justice, sitting as the magistrate and levying fines. He sent out parties of police to confiscate furs and liquor wherever they found it. Leif Crozier led some of the parties, with Jerry Potts as his scout. Macleod reported, in October, that he had received word of some concealed liquor "which I expect to get hold of, and only hope I may be able to get hold of the owners too."

This could be the incident on which the legend was based. He did eliminate Whoop-Up and other whiskey posts, which marked the beginning of the Mounties' firm war on the whiskey traders in the Northwest.

Fort Whoop-Up

Glenbow Museum, NA 550-18

XVI

Cut Knife Creek and Hill, 2 May 1885

F rom Battleford, Saskatchewan, the Cut Knife Creek and Hill battlefield is not difficult to locate. Follow the Yellowhead Highway (Number 16) towards Lloydminster, about fifty kilometres (thirty miles) to Paynton, a tiny hamlet punctuated by grain elevators. Turn south on an unpaved road, which leads through the Poundmaker Reserve, for about twenty kilometres (twelve miles). Just past the fairground is a narrow road upwards to the right, which leads to markers on the Cut Knife battlefield. (If you miss that turn, take the next one to the right, which also leads to the markers.) Farther south above the road is Cut Knife Hill; the battle took place on the hill that has the markers.

In 1884, Louis Riel left Montana, at the call of the Métis who were living along both branches of the Saskatchewan River. Led by Riel, they had won a great concession from Canada at their Red River settlement in 1870. Because of their concerns, the postage stamp–shaped province of Manitoba had entered the Canadian Confederation. Métis who had rebelled were promised pardons and the right to the lands they claimed, but many felt threatened by the influx of settlers from central Canada. Few were comfortable in an area where their traditional mode of life – a blend of subsistence farming, fur trading and buffalo hunting – was no longer compatible. Some remained and adapted to more intensive farming; others moved west and north, in search of a place where they could resume the old ways.

By 1884, they again felt threatened by the advance of settlement. In June, Gabriel Dumont and three others arrived at St. Peter's Mission School, where Riel was teaching native and Métis boys, and asked him to return to lead another "protest" against the Canadian government. Riel left with them for the main Métis community at Batoche.

New factors had now come into play. Buffalo had all but vanished from the plains because of excessive slaughtering for their hides, and natives, now confined to reserves, were as discontented as the Métis over the destruction of their most important source of food. In contrast to 1870, at this second Métis uprising some natives joined their relatives of mixed blood. Another difference was the presence in the Northwest of a police force, authorized by an Act of Parliament on 23 May 1873 – the first detachment of the North West Mounted Police (NWMP) had set out for Fort Garry, Manitoba, in October. As well, communications with the Northwest had improved – the transcontinental railway extended beyond Calgary, except for some gaps north of Lake Superior, and police posts and the larger settlements were linked by telegraph.

An early warning of trouble came from Superintendent Leif Crozier at Fort Carlton, a North West Mounted Police post some fifty kilometres (thirty miles) west of Batoche. On 11 March 1885, Crozier informed Ottawa that rebellion was inevitable. By that time Riel had reached Batoche. On the 19th, as he had done at Red River, he proclaimed a provisional government, with himself as president. Gabriel Dumont was his adjutant-general. Two days later, Riel sent a party to demand the surrender of Crozier's post. On the 26th, Crozier and ninety-eight of his policemen and volunteers attacked Dumont at Duck Lake and were badly beaten. Crozier fled to Fort Carlton. Twelve of his force and five of Dumont's had been killed. Commissioner Acheson Irvine, NWMP, major of the Quebec Rifles in 1870 at Red River, hastened from Regina with ninety police to reinforce Fort Carlton. Then, not certain he could hold his position, he withdrew all his police down the North Saskatchewan River to Prince Albert, the largest settlement, a move considered bad judgment in some quarters.

Playing in the background to the Battle at Cut Knife was the attack, on 30 March, on Battleford by members of the band of the Cree Chief Poundmaker, who left their reserve around Cut Knife Creek. The Cree laid siege to the town. The inhabitants, Métis and white, took refuge in Fort Battleford, the police barracks. The warriors looted and burned many properties. On 2 April, Cree, under Wandering Spirit, attacked settlers at Frog Lake, killed nine of them, and took some prisoners. By that time the vanguard of an expeditionary force was already in the Northwest. Its spearhead was the 90th Winnipeg Rifles, the only militia regiment between Ontario and the Rockies.

The military situation was different than in 1870. The only garrison of British regulars in the country was at Halifax, and their purpose was to protect British naval interests, not defend Canada. The prevailing opinion in Canada held that, when an emergency arose, the government could call on eager volunteers to serve the national interest. One who disagreed was Lieut.-Col. William Otter, now the commander of the two-year-old Infantry School Corps, based at Stanley Barracks in Toronto. Otter was an anomaly, a professional soldier even though he was a militia officer, although he did command a permanent unit. He believed fervently in the existence of a well-trained Canadian permanent force. As adjutant of the Queen's Own Rifles at age twenty-two, he had seen what could happen to raw but enthusiastic volunteers at

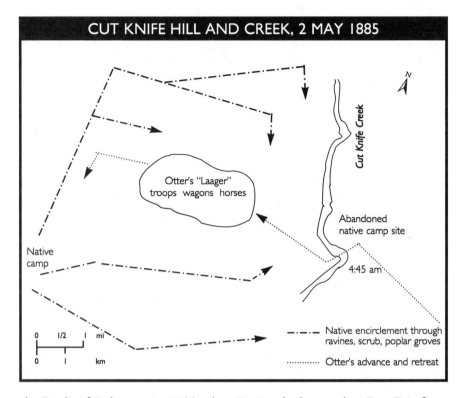

CUT KNIFE HILL AND CREEK, 2 MAY 1885

Otter's "Laager"
troops wagons horses

Cut Knife Creek

Abandoned
native camp site

Native
camp

4:45 am

0   1/2   1   mi

0   1   km

—·—·— Native encirclement through
ravines, scrub, poplar groves

············ Otter's advance and retreat

the Battle of Ridgeway in 1866, when Fenians had crossed to Fort Erie from Buffalo, New York. The invaders were seasoned veterans demobilized from the Union army, crack troops. At first, the Queen's Own managed the required steadiness, but they were no match for the Fenians and were soon dispersed in a tragic rout.

Pressure from Otter, and other like-minded civilians, had persuaded the government to establish Infantry and Cavalry companies and Artillery batteries, known as schools, in key locations. These formed the nucleus of a permanent force. By 1885, Infantry Schools had been set up in Toronto and London, Ontario, St. Jean, Quebec, and Fredericton, New Brunswick. Artillery Schools were at Quebec City and Kingston. A Cavalry School was also operating in Quebec. A Mounted Infantry School had started up in Winnipeg, which soon had an artillery battery.

The Canadian citizen-soldiers of the militia came under the command of a British regular soldier, the General Officer Commanding the Militia (GOC). In 1885, that officer was sixty-year-old Maj.-Gen. Frederick Dobson Middleton, who, like Garnet Wolseley, was of an Anglo-Irish military family. His last appointment had been as commandant of Sandhurst. The Minister of Militia and Defence, responsible for assembling Middleton's field force and equipping it, was the Hon. Joseph Philippe René Adolphe Caron. Originally,

Middleton planned one powerful thrust on Batoche, with his entire force of nearly 2,000 men, some of them local, but most from central Canada. While the journey to Winnipeg was easier than Wolseley's, four gaps – in all 140 kilometres (84 miles) – in the railway line through northern Ontario had to be bridged by sleighs and marches through deep snow and bitter cold. That hardship was for the troops only, however. Middleton travelled, unchallenged, by train through the United States and reached Winnipeg on 27 March.

The first contingent of 600 troops from the east left Toronto on the 30th and arrived in Winnipeg on 7 April. Meanwhile, Middleton had hurried to Troy, the nearest point on the railway line to the trouble spots. A detachment of the 90th Winnipeg Rifles had preceded him, and he took with him the rest of the regiment and the Winnipeg Field Battery. In Ottawa, Caron ordered the dispatch of some of the permanent force and quotas from the better militia battalions – the Queen's Own Rifles and the 10th Royal Grenadiers from Toronto, organized by Lieut.-Col. William Otter and Lieut.-Col. Henry Gasett, the 65th Mount Royal Rifles from Montreal, the 9th Voltigeurs from Quebec City, the Governor-General's Foot Guards from Ottawa, and the Midland Battalion, a composite unit of Ontario militia.

By 2 April, Middleton was at Qu'Appelle with 800 men, ready to march towards Batoche. His plans, however, had changed. Because of the clamour for protection from people around Edmonton, he sent orders for the 9th Voltigeurs and the 65th Mount Royal Rifles to continue to Calgary, to join an Alberta field force. He did not trust troops from Quebec, and he preferred not to have them in his main column. The Alberta field force came under the command of a local half-pay officer, Maj.-Gen. Thomas Bland Strange, who owned a horse ranch nearby. Middleton also arranged for the Winnipeg Light Infantry, a hastily raised new regiment, to be sent to Strange's force.

He ordered a further detachment of 550 men, under Lieut.-Col. William Otter, to go by train on to Swift Current. This column would lift the siege of Battleford 220 kilometres (132 miles) to the north, where despairing refugees were clamouring for relief. Otter's force consisted of 200 civilian teamsters, 50 men of the Governor-General's Foot Guards, 273 Queen's Own Rifles under Lieut.-Col. Augustus Miller, 50 red-coated soldiers of "C" Company, his own Toronto Infantry Schoolmen, about 50 Mounties led by William Herchmer (now Superintendent Herchmer, NWMP), and 100 artillerymen of "B" Battery, Kingston, under Maj. Charles Short, with two 9-pounder field guns. Two Gatling guns had arrived from the United States, with an American officer, Lieut. Arthur "Gatling" Howard, to demonstrate them. One was assigned to Otter's column, the other to Middleton's. All but the police would travel together. Herchmer would join Otter along the way. (The quota allowed the Queen's Own had been 250, but twenty-three extra volunteers had stowed away on the train out of Toronto, lured by the jingoism current at the time.

Some, determined not to miss the fun, found other ways to join up. In Toronto, George McAllister and three friends were not welcome in the Queen's Own. Like Middleton, they had travelled to Winnipeg by train through the United States but at their own expense, and found a welcome in the 90th Winnipeg Rifles, which was hungry for recruits.)

Middleton's instructions to Otter were deliberately vague; he did not want to be blamed if anything went wrong. Otter interpreted his "do not fear responsibility" as giving him a free hand. He reached Swift Current early on 12 April, where he expected that steamboats from Medicine Hat would carry his force to Clarke's Crossing, on the South Saskatchewan River. Water levels were so low that the steamers were stranded on the sand bars in the prairie river. On the 14th, Middleton ordered Otter to go by land, and he set out with wagons for the forty-kilometre (twenty-four mile) march to Saskatchewan Crossing, straight north. They arrived before nightfall, but the barge that was used as a ferry had sunk.

They had to wait for the Hudson's Bay Company steamer *Northcote* before they could cross. The steamer arrived, bringing Herchmer and his police. The crossing took three days, owing to high winds that hampered the ferry. By the 17th, the men had dragged the last wagon up the steep river bank to the prairie above, where Otter made camp. When the column set out on the 18th, the police led, clad in brown fatigues. Only half the police and six scouts were mounted; the rest rode in wagons or marched.

The 500 people stranded at Battleford were relieved that help was on the way. The natives bottling them up were not numerous, but they had intimidated the settlers by setting the prairie ablaze. Settlers had lit their own fires to prevent the natives using the brush as cover. Rumours were rife – another Cree chief, Big Bear, was thought to be coming to reinforce Poundmaker's braves. Otter's column was plodding along on the 18th, the day damp and cheerless, the track muddy. The men ran out of fuel; they could glean little wood to prepare warm food. Lieut. Richard Cassels, of the Queen's Own, wondered whether their biscuit ration was left over from Wolseley's expedition of 1870.

On the 21st, scouts from Battleford met refugees coming downriver from Fort Pitt, a NWMP post seventy kilometres (forty-two miles) to the north. Their leader was Inspector Francis Dickens, luckless son of Charles, the durable Victorian novelist. The next day, one of Herchmer's scouts brought word to Battleford that Otter was only a few miles off. His police, in advance of the marching column, had skirmished with some natives who were butchering a cow near the Eagle Hills. Late in the afternoon of the 23rd, Otter ordered the men to set up camp just thirteen kilometres (eight miles) from Battleford, to avoid approaching in the dark. With Otter so close, the natives decided to leave. As parting shots they set fire to Judge Charles Rouleau's house, and torched the Hudson's Bay Company warehouse on the south side

Montreal Witness 1885

Lieut.-Col. William Otter commanded the troops at Cut Knife and later the 1st Canadian Contingent in South Africa.

of the Battle River, which blew up because of the coal oil and gun powder in stock.

On the morning of the 24th, the men made camp at a one-time government house on the south bank of the Battle River, which they fortified and named Fort Otter. The troops then forded the river (the natives had destroyed the only bridge) to an enthusiastic reception by the liberated refugees. Otter had done what Middleton expected of him, but both his troops and the settlers wanted more. The soldiers wanted a fight, the locals, revenge. News arrived of Middleton's indecisive engagement with Gabriel Dumont at Fish Creek, to the south of Batoche, where eleven men had been killed and forty-eight wounded. Otter telegraphed Middleton for instructions on what to do next. Middleton wired that Otter should do what was necessary to defend Battleford – "You have sole command." Otter interpreted this as giving him authority to go after Poundmaker's warriors.

Mary Beacock Fryer

Poundmaker's grave on the Cut Knife battlefield. The monument is surrounded by a gravel circle that depicts the floor of a tepee. Poles forming the tepee frame had been removed for the winter when this photograph was taken on 4 October 1993. A cairn is visible in the background.

In search of support, Otter sent a wire outlining his plan of attack to Lieut.-Gov. Edgar Dewdney at the headquarters of the Northwest Territories Council in Regina. Dewdney approved, adding, "Herchmer knows the country to Poundmaker's reserve." He thought that the Sand Hills would be the most dangerous grounds, and that Otter should have reliable scouts. When Middleton ordered Otter to remain at Battleford, Otter resolved on a "scout" to begin on 30 April, but he wired Middleton for more definite instructions. Middleton told him only to reconnoitre at present, but by the time the telegram arrived Otter was on his way.

The night before Otter set out, natives who had been around Battleford sent a request to Big Bear to reinforce Poundmaker's band, and another to Riel asking for guns and ammunition. Otter left nearly half his force to garrison Battleford and set forth on patrol with 300 men – Mounties on horseback, gunners, Queen's Own, Foot Guards, and volunteers of the Battleford Rifles, plus fifty wagons, two 7-pounder cannon belonging to the police, and one Gatling gun. At dark they made a wagon-encircled "laager" (the troops had picked up expressions from veterans of the 1881 campaign against the Boers in South Africa). They rested until the moon was high, ate, and continued until dawn. By 7:00 a.m. on 1 May, Otter's column had covered thirty kilometres (eighteen miles), half the distance to Poundmaker's reserve. Again they stopped, dined, rested until nearly midnight, and marched, planning to surprise the natives at dawn. Their route lay between the meandering Battle River and the Eagle Hills Escarpment towards Cut Knife Creek near the centre of the reserve. At first they were moving through bush, wary of a surprise attack, but bush soon gave way to open prairie. Scouts had told Otter that the native camp lay on the east side of Cut Knife Creek.

At 4:00 a.m., they found a deserted camp, with marks on the ground for 200 tepees, and so assumed that the natives had learned of their approach and fled. They continued on to Cut Knife Creek. The creek was about eight metres (twenty-seven feet) wide, and half a metre (twenty inches) deep, flowing in broad meanders between steep banks of a gully some 260 metres (853 feet) wide between its crests. Beyond the creek, due west, lay Cut Knife Hill, and beyond the hill lay a longer, steep hill with a large, triangular-shaped open field spread over the crest that was flanked by poplar-choked ravines to south and north. Otter decided to cross the creek, climb the hill, have breakfast, and rest the horses before attempting to find the Cree. The men crossed in single file, police in the lead followed by the artillerymen and guns, the main body, and wagons in the rear. From the high western bank the scouts saw cattle on a hill to the south, but no sign of the natives.

Officers in front of the main body heard rifle fire ahead. Police on foot and gunners, serving as infantry and armed with rifles, who had moved over the crest of the hill, were shooting at natives in the ravine on the south side. They were joined by other artillerymen, who had galloped the three field guns up the hill. Diarist Lieut. Richard Cassels, of the Queen's Own, wondered whether they had fallen into a trap, but neither side was alert. The natives had not left the neighbourhood, but had moved their camp to a low area just beyond the brow of the hill. Native scouts were not aware of Otter's approach, but Otter's scouts ought to have found the native camp – although the Cree knew an attack was likely, their camp was unguarded. Only one man was awake when the first troops appeared on the hill. The natives who exchanged fire with the Mounties were not Crees but Stonies visiting Poundmaker's people. Puffs of black smoke arose as the artillerymen fired the two 7-pounders, and the Gatling gun began rattling on the tepees below and beyond the ravines.

In Poundmaker's camp as well were captives, among them Robert Jefferson, farm instructor and school teacher for the reserve. When he heard firing, he dressed and ran outside to find confusion as the men hurried the women and children to safety. Jefferson ran to Poundmaker's tent and found the chief draped in a patchwork quilt, which, he insisted, would make him invisible in battle; Poundmaker, the political leader, would not take charge of the defence: his war chief was the talented young Fine Day, who had commanded the braves at Battleford.

Back on the hill, amidst the firing, Otter deployed his troops, artillery, and police in front, and Toronto Infantry School Corps on the right, facing the ravine to the north. A dry gully separated these troops from the rear guard of the Battleford Rifles, some from all the corps, and the teamsters and wagons. The Queen's Own Rifles and Governor-General's Foot Guards moved to the edge of the ravine on the left. Capt. Robert Rutherford, of the Artillery, thought that if Otter had ordered his men to charge down the hill, they would have threatened to overwhelm the Cree, who might have surrendered to protect their families. But Otter decided to hold his place on the hill. Now the Stonies charged, fearing that Otter's guns might find the range of the camp. At this surprise attack, some of the soldiers fell back. Maj. Short rallied them and drove the Stonies into their ravine, killing three.

From that point on the Cree, now reinforcing the Stonies, had the strategic advantage, and made good use of the cover that the wooded ravines allowed. Each time the troops thought they had found where the natives were hiding and directed their fire at that spot, the war chief Fine Day would move them to other parts of the ravines, creating the impression that Otter was surrounded and outnumbered. Fine Day stood on a hill south of the field, where he could see the entire site, signalling orders to his warriors with a small mirror, a forerunner of the heliograph.

Four hours after the battle began, one of the 7-pounder guns collapsed, its carriage rotten. The trunnion on the other 7-pounder cracked, and every time it fired the barrel leapt up. The Gatling gun blazed away, doing little damage because its crew could not see where the natives were. After concentrating on the front for a time, the warriors fired from the left, and then not far from the rear, where the Battleford Rifles and some men from the other corps tried to disperse them. Capt. Rutherford turned the remaining functioning 7-pounder around to support them, and almost struck his own troops. Some of the Queen's Own moved into the ravine south of the field, but when they were not reinforced they returned to their original position. Fine Day now had Otter nearly encircled, and his men were drawing close to the gully that separated Otter's forward troops from those in the rear.

By 11:00 a.m., Otter realized that his position was hopeless; a withdrawal could be as dangerous as an advance, however. Militia remained in front and along the ravines to hold back the warriors while the Battleford Rifles and the artillerymen cleared a path to the rear. Capt. Rutherford moved the 7-pounder down to cover part of the line while others crossed Cut Knife Creek and took up commanding positions high on the banks. Once the teams were across, the troops began backing cautiously down the hill, police and infantry schoolmen in the rear. They were wary, but did not meet with any opposition. The last shot rang out at 12:15 p.m. After that, the warriors vanished.

Robert Jefferson, the prisoner among the Cree, reported that Poundmaker had taken charge from Fine Day. The warriors were right to defend their women and children, but a massacre of Otter's troops would do more harm than good. Respect for their political leader was such that the warriors obeyed. As a result, Otter got off scot-free, even though he had painted himself into a corner. His losses were eight killed and fourteen wounded. Newspapermen accompanying the so-called patrol reported that at least 100 natives had been killed; Robert Jefferson put Fine Day's losses at six killed and three wounded.

An hour after the last shot was fired, the disheartened troops began their march back to Battleford, leaving behind the very ammunition the warriors needed. They reached Fort Otter by ten o'clock that night, where reporters turned Otter's defeat into victory; Big Bear had been about to join Poundmaker (he was miles away); Otter's action had prevented Poundmaker from joining Big Bear; the scuffle proved that natives were no match for "regular" troops. The *Saskatchewan Herald* outdid itself, reporting Otter's march and return in barely thirty hours as "one that will live in history."

Two stern critics were the former NWMP Superintendent James Walsh and Archbishop Alexandre-Antoinin Taché. Otter should not have attacked unless he had a strong enough force to win a battle, hold his ground, and dictate terms, they said. They, and others, feared a larger native uprising. On 7 May, scouts sent by Otter were chased out of the Poundmaker Reserve. At that time, while Poundmaker wondered about seeking sanctuary among the Blackfoot, his warriors were preparing to take the entire camp to join Riel at Batoche, the very situation Middleton dreaded.

Middleton's column, including the 90th Winnipeg Rifles and Torontonians George McAllister and friends, reached Batoche on 9 May. On the 12th, when his men charged their rifle pits, the Métis fled. Gabriel Dumont reached the United States, but Riel surrendered to Middleton on the 15th. Middleton then moved his force to Battleford, where he gave Otter the dressing-down of his life. Poundmaker and 150 of his warriors surrendered to Middleton on the 23rd, but Big Bear remained at large. The last battle took place on 3 June, between Inspector Samuel Steele, NWMP, the private in the Ontario Rifles in 1870, and Big Bear's Cree at Frenchman's Butte on the North Saskatchewan River near Fort Pitt. Steele was leading the police vanguard of Maj.-Gen. Strange's column that had relieved Edmonton in May. Strange's force had been sweeping eastwards to meet Middleton's. Big Bear escaped from Frenchman's Butte, and Middleton organized four columns to hunt him down. None found him, but he surrendered at Fort Carlton on 2 July.

Among the men who paid the supreme penalty were Riel, hanged in Regina on 16 November, followed by Wandering Spirit and seven other natives outside Fort Battleford on the 27th. Poundmaker and Big Bear were each sentenced to three years in Stony Mountain Penitentiary. Poundmaker served one year and was released in April 1886, his health destroyed. He died four months later, in July on the Blackfoot Reserve, probably of tuberculosis. Big Bear was released in March 1887, and was also in poor health. He died on the Poundmaker Reserve in January 1888. Commissioner Irvine took the blame for certain defects in the Mounties' performance; the following year, William Herchmer replaced him. Many of the volunteers came home with souvenirs – George McAllister gleaned a beaded belt and a scabbard on the Batoche battlefield, and in due course he received his Canada General Service Medal.

The execution of Louis Riel had far-reaching effects. Quebecers embraced him as one of their own, and abandoned the Conservative Party for generations. Big Bear was revered as a remarkable leader of his people, while Poundmaker became the hero of the Battle of Cut Knife Creek. His forbearance had saved Lieut.-Col. William Otter's force.

In 1967, Poundmaker's remains were removed from the Blackfoot Reserve and reinterred on the Cut Knife battlefield. A monument of black marble marks the grave, a fitting resting place for the Cree chief.

XVII

Paardeberg, South Africa, 18–27 February 1900

Paardeberg was the first overseas battle in which Canadian troops participated. It was also a turning point in the South African (2nd Boer) War of 1889–1902. This was not the first time Canadians had served abroad. Nearly 400 volunteers followed Lieut.-Col. Frederick Denison on the Nile Expedition of 1884–85, but these volunteers were civilians. The Nile venture, commanded by Gen. Garnet Wolseley, went to relieve Gen. Charles G. Gordon at Khartoum. Voyageurs had served Wolseley well on the journey to Red River in 1870, and he knew their skills were what he required to ascend the Nile. The expedition neared Khartoum on 28 January 1885, only to learn that the city had fallen and that Gordon was dead.

The South African War was long, costly, and bloody: 22,000 Boers, 25,000 Britons, and 12,000 Africans lost their lives. In his book *The Boer War,* Thomas Pakenham pointed out that this was the first time since Wellington that a British army had fought against troops that wore boots. (He overlooked the presence of British troops at the Rebellions of 1837–38 and Red River in 1870; rebels and Métis were not barefooted.) The war in South Africa, as fought by the Boers, was a twentieth-century battle that the British, at Paardeberg, tried to fight in the old way. The foot soldier fared badly when confronted by mobile, mounted infantry. After observing the enemy in action, war correspondent Winston Churchill wrote that one mounted Boer rifleman on the veld was worth from three to five British regulars, an accurate assessment that did not endear him to Britons. The veld, open grassland with minor obstructions like "kopjes" (Afrikaans for heads), rocks, and rivers that meandered between steep-sided banks, held echoes of Cut Knife Creek. The veld (and the prairies) made ideal cavalry country, but until late in 1900 the British were chronically short of horses and depended heavily on conventional infantry.

Today, Paardeberg looks very much as it did in 1900. Now, as then, there is no large settlement. It is a minute hamlet, now spelled Perdeberg, in the shadow of steep Paardeberg Hill, which rises some 300 metres (1,000 feet) from the grassy veld. The battle site is west of this hamlet and hill. Below, to

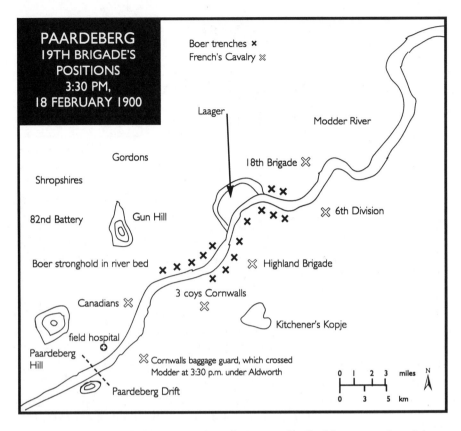

**PAARDEBERG
19TH BRIGADE'S
POSITIONS
3:30 PM,
18 FEBRUARY 1900**

Boer trenches ×
French's Cavalry ⊠

Laager

Modder River

Gordons

18th Brigade ⊠

Shropshires

× ×

82nd Battery   Gun Hill

× × ×   ⊠ 6th Division
×

Boer stronghold in river bed   × × ×   × ×
× ×   ⊠ Highland Brigade

Canadians ⊠

3 coys Cornwalls
⊠

field hospital
✛

Kitchener's Kopje

Paardeberg
Hill

⊠ Cornwalls baggage guard, which crossed
Modder at 3:30 p.m. under Aldworth

Paardeberg Drift

0 1 2 3 miles N
0   3   5 km

the south, the Modder River winds its way over the ford known as Paardeberg Drift. Rows of kopjes lie a few kilometres back from each bank of the river, forming a more unbroken line on the north side than on the south.

Many British officers serving in 1899 recalled their humiliating defeat during the 1st Boer War, on 27 February 1881 at Majuba Hill, Natal. The site lies southwest of Charlestown, close to the border with the Transvaal. A battle cry during the second war against the Boers was "Remember Majuba!"

In 1899, South Africa was divided into two self-governing British colonies, Natal and the Cape, the latter with a substantial Boer element, and two Boer republics, the Orange Free State, and the Transvaal. The Orange Free State was independent; the Transvaal was self-governing, except in matters of foreign policy. The gold rush to Witwatersrand that began in 1886 gave Britain an excuse to interfere in the Transvaal. Although Britons had flocked there, the government of President "Oom Paul" Kruger would permit only long-term resident males over forty to vote. With the foreign population increasing so rapidly, Kruger feared that the Boers would become a minority. The trouble started in the Transvaal, but President Marthinus Steyn, of the Orange Free State, supported Kruger. Boers originated the term "commando" for their individual armies, the name was later applied to military units trained for raids and assaults.

By September 1899, Britain had decided to send 10,000 reinforcements to Natal. The man chosen as commander-in-chief was Gen. Sir Redvers Buller, a captain at Red River in 1870, who would land at Cape Town on 31 October. Meanwhile, Kruger and Steyn were calling up their burghers, men who fought in everyday drab clothing. The Boers were well prepared. They had been shopping for arms for years – buying small-bore magazine rifles, Lee Metfords from Britain, and Mausers from Germany. Their modern artillery comprised 155 mm guns (Long Toms) from Creusot, France; 75 mm field guns and 120 mm howitzers from Krupp, Germany; and Maxim-Nordenfeldt 1-pounders (Pom Poms) from Britain. The Boers had equipped themselves with smokeless powder, a combination of nitric and sulphuric acid and cellulose developed in the 1860s. The British were still relying on black powder, of potassium nitrate, sulphur, and charcoal, that created blue smoke and revealed their whereabouts. Men who did not raise much smoke could be more invisible.

A Boer defensive site was the laager, wagons drawn into a circle and protected by trenches. On sturdy ponies they could strike and withdraw. British intelligence was weak; the open veld made reconnoitring dangerous, and the country was only sketchily mapped. They did have observation balloons, however, a help under the right weather conditions, as well as the heliograph. This instrument had two adjustable mirrors, so placed to reflect a beam of sunlight in any direction. A key-operated shutter interrupted the beam, to signal the dots and dashes of Morse code.

Paardeberg and the First Canadian Contingent

Early in October, Joseph Chamberlain, the colonial secretary, enquired of the government of Wilfrid Laurier whether Canada would supply some troops to South Africa. This placed the prime minister in a dilemma, caught between the French Canadians who wanted nothing to do with a British war and keen English Canadians, albeit a minority, who could not wait to lay down their lives for Queen Victoria. Laurier yielded to pressure from these "patriots."

On 12 October, his government authorized the creation of a Canadian contingent. (Henri Bourassa resigned his seat in protest on the 18th. Nevertheless, Laurier plunged ahead.) Command would go to Lieut.-Col. William Otter, the commander at Cut Knife and still a militia staff officer. The Infantry School Corps had now been absorbed to form the Royal Canadian Regiment. This battalion, the permanent force, remained at home, but a second one was created, of volunteers from all the militia regiments. It was called the 2nd (Special Service) Royal Canadian Regiment. Enlistment was for one year, and Canada would pay the troops until they reached South

Africa. After that time, Britain would assume the cost but, because British pay rates were lower than in the Canadian permanent force, Canada would provide a supplement. Otter's battalion was divided into eight companies. "A" Company was recruited in British Columbia and Manitoba, "B" Company in London, "C" in Toronto, the left half of "D" in Kingston and vicinity, the right half in Ottawa, "E" in Montreal, "F" in Quebec City, "G" in New Brunswick and Prince Edward Island, and "H" in Nova Scotia. Full strength for each company was 125 men. With officers and staff, the total complement was 1,029. Otter's two majors were Lawrence Buchan, of Toronto, and Oscar Pelletier, a son of Sen. Sir Charles Pelletier. (Not all French Canadians were as perturbed as Henri Bourassa; while "E" Company was nearly all anglophone, "F" Company was one-quarter francophone.)

After hasty preparations, the 2nd RCR embarked on 30 October from Quebec City aboard the *Sardinian*. With Otter sailed 41 officers and 962 other ranks. Support staff included four doctors, four nurses, three chaplains, (Anglican, Presbyterian, and Roman Catholic), war correspondents, and twenty-three supernumerary officers. Otter took exception to one of the latter, Lieut.-Col. Sam Hughes, of Lindsay. Hughes had expected an important command, and when none was offered he wangled permission to sail on the *Sardinian* in mufti. Once the ship left Canadian waters, Hughes appeared in uniform.

Otter ignored Hughes. He was far too busy training raw recruits any way he could on the crowded ship. The 2nd RCR landed at Cape Town on 29 November, where Otter discovered that he had khaki duck uniforms for only six of his eight companies. The smart-looking six marched up Adderley Street on the way to camp, while the embarrassing two went by back streets with the baggage. Serious training was delayed until the battalion reached Belmont, on the railway line about 1,000 kilometres (600 miles) northeast of Cape Town, an important depot and centre for the troops.

The 2nd RCR, destined for action at Paardeberg, represented only part of the Canadian war effort. A second contingent, two battalions (four squadrons) of Canadian Mounted Rifles, each of 370 men, and a brigade of artillery, in all 1,281 soldiers, sailed for Cape Town in relays beginning on 21 January 1900. The commander of the first battalion Canadian Mounted Rifles was Lieut.-Col. F.L. Lessard; of the 2nd it was Lieut.-Col. William Herchmer, veteran of Red River and Cut Knife, on leave from the North West Mounted Police. The commander of artillery was Lieut.-Col. C.W. Drury. The mounted riflemen, the most suitable for operations on the veld, were part of a brigade under Maj.-Gen. Edward Hutton, a former (unpopular and dismissed) General Officer Commanding the Canadian Militia. A third battalion of the RCR was recruited for Halifax, to release the regulars of the 100th Regiment for duty in South Africa.

In March, 537 more men left. They had been recruited by Donald A. Smith, the Hudson's Bay Company officer, now Lord Strathcona. This cavalry unit was commanded by Col. Samuel Steele, on leave from the NWMP, and known, naturally, as Strathcona's Horse. Steele and his men joined Sir Redvers Buller's oft-reversing field force in Natal. One year later, in March 1901, some Canadians went to join the South African Constabulary, and in April 1902 four more units of mounted rifles followed. The war ended only weeks later. Some men stayed on, serving in the South African Constabulary until 1906. Altogether, 7,364 Canadians served with the British army in South Africa.

While Otter was at Belmont, training and instilling the discipline he thought so necessary for success, the Boer commandos were roaming the countryside and laying siege to three British towns – Ladysmith, Kimberley, and Mafeking. Buller suffered three major defeats in his efforts to lift the siege of Ladysmith. Holed up at Kimberley was Cecil Rhodes, Prime Minister of the Cape until 1896 and now a partner in the huge diamond company, DeBeers Consolidated Mines Limited, and an instigator of the war. The beseiged Britons at Mafeking were commanded by Col. Robert Baden-Powell, later founder of the Boy Scout and Girl Guide movements.

The setting for Buller's third setback, on 24 January, was Spion Kop, outside Ladysmith, and probably the most dramatic battle site to visit – rural, tranquil, and sad. Author Thomas Pakenham declared that the commander of Buller's 5th Division, Lieut.-Gen. Sir Charles Warren, snatched defeat from the jaws of victory. Churchill was there, reporting events, and Mohandas Gandhi, the future Indian leader, was a stretcher bearer.

Because Buller was doing badly, Field-Marshal Frederick Lord Roberts had been appointed to supercede him as commander-in-chief, while Buller retained the Natal Field Force. Gen. Horace Lord Kitchener sailed with Roberts as chief-of-staff. The two reached Cape Town on 10 January 1900 and prepared to take charge.

At Belmont, the men of the 2nd RCR were training, doing outpost duty, and guarding the railway line. Many chafed under Otter's strictures, and all complained about the fact that they had been in South Africa for two months without seeing much action. Things were about to change. On 8 February, Roberts and Kitchener reached Belmont by train and summoned Otter. The 2nd RCR was to join the 19th Brigade under Maj.-Gen. Horace Smith-Dorrien. The other regiments in this brigade were the 1st Gordon Highlanders, 2nd Shropshire Light Infantry, and the Duke of Cornwall's Own Light Infantry. The 19th Brigade would be part of the 9th Division under Lieut.-Gen. Sir Henry Colville.

Roberts started a sweep to relieve Kimberley, by cutting the communications of Gen. Piet Cronje's Transvaal commandos, who were besieging the town. Roberts's strategy began with a march to the Modder River, sixty-seven

Paul Kruger, the president of the Transvaal Republic, was of German descent. (His forebears arrived in South Africa in 1725.) The majority of the Boers descended from Dutch families.

kilometres (forty miles) from Kimberley. Because of illness at Belmont, the 2nd RCR now had just thirty-one officers and 865 men fit for duty. They started their march on 13 February, a most taxing event, since they traversed the open grassland, bush, and thorn patches of the veld in high summer. The terrain was rough and broken by many kopjes. Poorly watered at best, the land was dry. The sandy soil rose in clouds of choking dust, stirred up by the wagon train and cattle the troops were driving to provide fresh beef in camp.

As the men marched in column, thirst plagued them. Water bottles could not hold enough to last the day. With lips and throats so parched, they could not swallow the ration of dry biscuit, and the salt beef they received made their thirst worse. At Ram Dam, on a tributary of the Riet River, they found only muddy water to drink. The rivers, Otter realized, were serious obstacles – the banks were incredibly steep. They reached Waterval Drift on the Riet River on 15 February. Downstream, Boers led by Christiaan DeWet staged a daring raid on Roberts's supply wagons, seizing a third of them and depriving the army of much biscuit and bully beef.

Early on 16 February, news arrived that Maj.-Gen. John French, commander of Roberts's cavalry, had relieved Kimberley. The day before, Cronje had perceived the threat French posed, and had withdrawn his force fifty kilometres (thirty miles) to the Modder, a tributary of the Riet. He had set up a laager east of Paardeberg Hill on the north bank in a wide gully stretching some three kilometres (two miles) and almost parallel to the river bed. Now some 5,000 Boers, a few of them women and children, and their livestock, were at the laager, and some were cutting trenches along both sides of the Modder to the west of the circle of wagons.

By the 17th, the 2nd RCR had reached Klip's Drift on the Riet River, about ten kilometres (six miles) below the spot where the Modder River flows into it. After a rest, they made a night march along the south side of the Modder At 5:00 a.m., they had reached Paardeberg Drift. The 19th Brigade had marched behind the 9th Highland Brigade, which was spread along the south bank of the river. On the 18th, a Sunday, Smith-Dorrien received orders to deploy the 19th Brigade. The Shropshires, Gordons, and 2nd RCR were to cross the Modder over Paardeberg Drift. The Cornwalls, under Lieut.-Col. William Aldworth, would remain on the south bank with the wagons and supplies. Otter sent "A" and "C" Companies forward, with "D" and "E" Companies in support. The other four companies were his reserves.

At high summer the water level should have been low, but the Boers had broken a dam. The men found that the water reached up to their armpits, and so the first half of the battalion marched in single file, clinging to a rope that the regulars had stretched across. The other half simply marched four abreast, arms linked. As they rose from the water, they found their khaki breeches bulging, filled with water trapped by their puttees. Some men cut their breeches to help shed the impeding weight.

By then, four brigades and four artillery batteries were closing in on Cronje's laager. Smith-Dorrien set up his own headquarters on Gun Hill, to the east of Paardeberg Hill, where he had an unobstructed view, and vowed to forego shaving until Cronje surrendered. The Gordons were to his northeast, the Shropshires and an artillery battery were around the base of Gun Hill. By 10:00 a.m., all eight companies of the 2nd RCR had crossed the Modder, and were moving east, close to the north bank and towards the Boer trenches that were dug along both sides of the river. At that stage, although the senior officer present was Lieut.-Gen. Thomas Kelly-Kenny, Kitchener seized command. Roberts was at Jacobsdal, on the Riet River – he had caught a chill.

Kitchener's plan was brutally simple – a frontal assault on Cronje's laager. Orders were slow to reach battalion commanders and the brigadiers. Smith-Dorrien had been told only where to deploy the brigade – Otter's sole order had been to station his battalion along the north bank. He did not even know where Smith-Dorrien was, but some RCRs under Capt. Clive Bell, an instructor with the RCR machine-gun section, had taken a gun and joined their brigade commander on Gun Hill. Bell saw it as the obvious spot to fire with effect. Suddenly, the RCRs along the river bank heard the rattle of Mausers. Some ran forward, others dropped and crawled along. None could see the source of the fire, which intensified. They were pinned down, compelled to shelter behind rocks, anthills, any cover. For Otter, crouching behind an anthill, this seemed another Cut Knife, the same meandering river, the same high banks, but with a more murderous fire and soaring casualties.

By noon, the men had no water left, but at 1:00 the sky opened and a deluge began, leaving them shivering in sopping clothes. Some Boer snipers had reached a gully on their left, and were taking a deadly toll. At 3:00 the sun returned and Otter crawled out, looking for Smith-Dorrien, but unable to find him, he crawled back to his lines. When a stretcher bearer was shot (one of several), the RCR's medical officer, Maj. Eugene Fiset, took the bearer's place. Chaplain Father O'Leary was moving over the field, exposing himself unstintingly.

At that point, French's cavalry arrived from Kimberley to join the encirclement of Cronje. One of the regiments under French's command was the 9th Lancers. (London-born trooper Robert Dyer had his first opportunity to meet Canadians; he would emigrate to Canada in 1910.)

Early that morning, 18 February, Kitchener surveyed the site of the battle from a hill south of the Modder that the men had christened "Kitchener's Kopje." By afternoon, dismayed at the apparent stalemate, the chief of staff plunged across the river and raced his horse about, furious that the troops seemed reluctant to tolerate heavy casualties. He ordered Colville, Smith-Dorrien's division commander, to send Lieutenant-Colonel Aldworth and half his Cornwalls to the north side of the Modder to get behind the Canadians and attack. By 4:00, Aldworth had crossed with three-and-a-half companies. He found Otter, heaped scorn on inexperienced colonials, demanded a bayonet charge, and issued the order. The Cornwalls obeyed, and the RCRs rose up, followed, and found themselves mixed in with some of the Highland Brigade that had crossed with the Cornwalls. Confusion reigned. Smith-Dorrien recalled:

At 5.15 p.m. I was horrified at seeing our troops on the right of my line rise and charge forward with a ringing cheer. I, at that time, believed that only Canadians were there; but … Lieut.-Col. Aldworth, D.S.O. … had been sent

Col. Samuel Steele, NWMP, commanded Strathcona's Horse in South Africa, and later a division of the South African Constabulary.

Glenbow Museum, NA 2382-2

over by a higher authority to charge the Boer position, and that the Canadians, who would not be left behind, had joined in.

To succeed, the men had to charge across 500 yards (457 metres) of open ground. The leaders managed 200 yards (183 metres) before diving for cover. The Boers were enfilading from the left. Otter withdrew most of his battalion to bivouac near the Modder, but some undertook hot, thirsty outpost duty. Others volunteered to stay until dark to collect the wounded and dead. Boer sniping continued until 10:00 p.m. At 2:00 a.m. on the 19th the last stretcher party returned. Otter's casualties were eighteen killed and sixty-four wounded, three mortally, in this futile action. Aldworth was among the dead. Smith-Dorrien arrived and congratulated Otter on the "steadiness and courage" of the RCR. Both were delighted by the actions of Private Hornibrook – unarmed, he had pretended to possess a concealed pistol, and captured one of Cronje's staff officers.

On the south side of the Modder, during the afternoon of Sunday the 18th, Gen. Christiaan DeWet, with from 300 to 600 Boers, stormed and captured Kitchener's Kopje, where the chief-of-staff had stood to survey the scene hours before.

By dawn that Monday, the 19th, the situation was more clear. British casualties were over 1,300, more than at any of Buller's reverses, while the Boers lost nearly 300. As well, most of the Boer horses and cattle had been killed during the artillery bombardment. Cronje asked Kitchener for a truce to bury his dead, but just then Roberts, informed of the disaster at Paardeberg, arrived by ambulance from Jacobsdal. Determined to force Cronje's surrender before other commandos could close in, Roberts declined the truce. He did consult his generals, however, and found that, Kitchener and Colville excepted, none favoured another frontal assault. Smith-Dorrien suggested a siege, trenching towards the Boer position during continued heavy bombardment, and Roberts approved the plan.

The Siege of the Boer Laager
The British army found that the Boers, in their trenches along the Modder, were nearly invulnerable. Only a direct hit could do any damage, but the bombardment of the laager was more effective. On the 20th, with the Gordons and the Shropshires on the right, the RCR manned a line north of the Modder, again suffering from thirst. Otter tried to send a water cart, but the Boers fired a Vickers-Maxim gun at it. During the day, four Canadians were wounded. On the next day, Gen. French's horsemen drove DeWet's Boers from Kitchener's Kopje. All the while, detachments from the RCR and the other units were digging trenches as fast as they could, hampered because the brigade was short of entrenching tools. Rations were short, because of DeWet's theft of the supply wagons.

The 22nd passed in much the same way as the 21st, except that chilling rain fell. Otter now had only one blanket for every two men, because so many blankets had been sent to field hospitals with the wounded. At one of these hospitals, Dr. Arthur Conan Doyle, who earned his knighthood in South Africa before he dreamed up Sherlock Holmes, was treating some of the injured Canadians.

The British trenches were traversed by earth banks, sandbagged and loopholed. Boer trenches, while much deeper, were not connected and had no parapets. Thus, the Boers could not move from one trench to another without exposing themselves, and their heads were visible when they fired. By the 25th, rain had turned the campsite of the RCR into a large pond. Worse, the Boers were pushing their dead animals out of the laager and floating them downstream. The stench was overwhelming. The only source of drinking water was the Modder, which now had a disagreeable, sweetish taste. Fatigue parties went to the water to push out corpses caught by branches and debris so that the current could carry them away.

On the 26th, Monday, the RCR relieved the Cornwalls in the trenches. "A" Company was ferried across the Modder, where it could protect the others by enfilade. The Canadians stood guard by day and dug trenches by night. The bombardment was appalling, louder than ever after four howitzers arrived by rail for Roberts's force. Conditions in the Boer laager were growing worse – food was low, filth and rotting carcasses were everywhere, and the dead and wounded men grew in number. Hope of relief from other commandos was fading. By evening, Smith-Dorrien had informed Roberts that the new trenches were close enough for a successful assault, and received permission to proceed at dawn on the 27th – Shrove Tuesday and the 19th anniversary of Majuba.

The only cover for the assault lay in a belt of bush 300 yards (275 metres) wide on the river bank. To the left lay open flat ground, and so the approach had to be close to the river as long as possible. In the evening, Smith-Dorrien deployed his brigade. Two hundred Gordons were split between the right and left trenches, "a-b" and "b-e" (see map on page 136). "A" Company was Otter's weakest one, and he left it to guard the camp. Six companies – 480 men – were arranged in two ranks: the rear one, of 240 men, would be in trench "e-f" and be equipped with entrenching tools, rifles slung, to dig advance trenches; the remaining half would form a front rank before the trench. Otter was in the centre, with Maj. Buchan to his left and Maj. Pelletier on the right. To the right of the RCRs were 30 Sappers with their Royal Engineer officers. Fifty Canadians of "A" Company were on the south side of the Modder in trench j, while the remaining RCRs were in reserve at trench "g." Behind trench "g" were the brigade's balloon section, stretcher bearers, and reinforcements from the Highland Brigade.

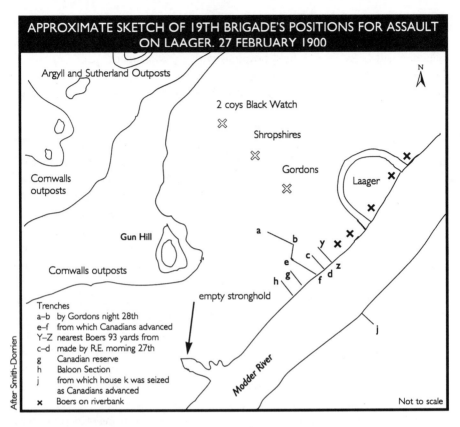

APPROXIMATE SKETCH OF 19TH BRIGADE'S POSITIONS FOR ASSAULT ON LAAGER. 27 FEBRUARY 1900

Argyll and Sutherland Outposts

2 coys Black Watch

Shropshires

Gordons

Laager

Cornwalls outposts

Gun Hill

Cornwalls outposts

empty stronghold

Modder River

Trenches
a–b by Gordons night 28th
e–f from which Canadians advanced
Y–Z nearest Boers 93 yards from
c–d made by R.E. morning 27th
g   Canadian reserve
h   Baloon Section
j   from which house k was seized
     as Canadians advanced
×   Boers on riverbank

After Smith-Dorrien

Not to scale

The men settled down into the crowded trenches at 10:30 to catch what sleep the cramped space allowed. They were awakened at 1:45 a.m., and by 2:15 the RCR had advanced, the men holding hands because of the difficulty of maintaining their line in the bushes. "H" Company was closest to the river bank. "G" and "F" Companies were on their left and were more exposed. Smith-Dorrien anticipated that they would require twenty-five minutes to get close enough for the assault, but he was too optimistic. When he did not hear anything, he assumed that the RCR had gone in the wrong direction and ordered a reinforcement. At 2:50, the Boers opened fire within sixty-one metres (200 feet) of the front rank. Some Canadians rushed, others returned the fire, some lying flat. The second rank was busily digging an advance trench; it was eighty-six metres (280 feet) from the Boer trenches, but on higher ground, and it looked straight into them. Canadians on the south bank were also digging a new forward trench.

By daylight, the Boers were close to enfilading the latter new trench. Smith-Dorrien signalled the troops at "j" trench to seize a house, "k." The confusion grew worse. The Canadians on the north bank thought they heard an order to retire and carry back the wounded. The companies to the left failed to enter the newly dug trench, to Otter's humiliation. One RCR was actually bayoneted by a Gordon sentry, which infuriated Otter. The other half of the front rank stayed, and by 5:00 a.m. most were in the new trench and able to open fire. Smith-Dorrien called on the Boers to surrender, although the laager was 400 to 500 yards (397–488 metres) behind the first of the Boer trenches.

A white handkerchief showed above the forward trench; others waved from rear trenches, and at last a white sheet floated above the laager. The troops were jubilant, especially the veterans of Majuba. Otter now counted his casualties of the day – six killed and twenty-one wounded, all from "G" and "F" Companies, the ones who had been in the most dangerous position. Major Pelletier had received a slight wound before the final action. Otter's total losses since those on 18 February were twelve killed and thirty-seven wounded. Boer losses on the 27th were seventy killed and less than 200 wounded. The British had 4,200 prisoners (several of them women), 5,000 rifles, and a large stock of ammunition. Cronje formally surrendered on the 28th, and more rejoicing followed when news arrived that Buller had relieved Ladysmith that same day.

Satisfied with the rightness of his judgment in rejecting the frontal assault before trenching, Smith-Dorrien rode to Gun Hill for the shave he had promised himself nine days before. The Boers left the trenches and mingled with their captors. Most were relieved that the fighting was at an end. The

A view of the veld south of the Modder River.

RCR was delighted to leave the vicinity of the stinking laager and move to a clean, sweet-smelling new campsite.

The RCR stayed with Roberts's army for the rest of the year-long tour of duty, although the battalion was not kept together as a unit. The army occupied Bloemfontein on 13 March, where the 2nd Canadian Contingent caught up with Roberts. Otter received a bullet in the neck in a minor skirmish at Israel Poort on 25 April, a small place thirty miles (fifty km) east of Bloemfontein. The wound was not serious, but alarmingly close to his jugular vein. Major Buchan took command for a month. A cavalry column relieved Mafeking on 17 May. Roberts's army took Johannesburg on the 31st, and Pretoria on 5 June. There, the RCRs joined the other battalions in a march past before Lord Roberts. By September part of the first contingent was on the way to Cape Town. Some of the men, under Major Pelletier, reached Halifax on 1 November. The rest, with Lieutenant-Colonel Otter, left Cape Town on 7 November and arrived in Southampton, England, on the 29th. The men moved on to Windsor and paraded before Queen Victoria. After much celebration, they sailed from Liverpool on 12 December and reached Halifax on the 23rd.

The 2nd Canadian Contingent returned home following its year of service. After serving with Buller in Natal, Lord Strathcona's Horse arrived in Halifax in March 1901. Soon afterwards, Col. Sam Steele left to command a detachment of the South African Constabulary in the Orange River country and did not return home until 1906. Trooper Robert Dyer resigned from the 9th Lancers in 1910 to take a job with Seagram's racing stable in Kitchener (then Berlin). He enlisted again in 1914. Dyer barely survived a gas attack, which deprived three young children of their father. He lived only nine months after he was demobilized and sent home.

Lieut.-Col. William Otter returned to his post at Stanley Barracks in Toronto. Eventually, he became a major-general and Sir William Otter, K.G.B.

Sam Hughes: Corollary/Conundrum

Every summer, over nearly seven decades, descendants of Abraham Beacock have gathered for a reunion in Blackstock, Ontario, to celebrate their kinship. For the Beacock family of Brockville, a star of the show in the 1930s was Annie, the wife of a distant cousin, Jim Beacock. Annie was a sister of Sir Sam Hughes. Hughes was a hero, the only distinguished Canadian in the family circle. What a shock it was to later learn that he was considered, in some quarters, to be a buffoon, a figure of controversy, the vociferous defender of the Ross rifle who made many enemies. In South Africa, despite Otter's poor opinion, the man who believed that volunteers would always perform better than any permanent force, was indeed the swashbuckler. Rejected by Otter, he

Margaret Dyer Downing

Trooper Robert Dyer and friends of the 9th Lancers. Dyer is stretched out in front, on the right. The Lancers were at Paardeberg. After Dyer resigned, he emigrated to Canada to work at Seagram's racing stable in Kitchener (Berlin). He re-enlisted in 1914, and was disabled by a gas attack. He lived only nine months after he was reunited with his wife and children.

operated as an irregular. His superiors were often outraged, but the men under him liked his daring and his breezy friendliness, so different from the aloof stance of British professional officers. Hughes was critical of most of these officers, and made no bones about declaring that British generals were only good at filling hospitals.

After the *Sardinian* docked at Cape Town on 29 November 1899, and Otter had marched off with the 2nd RCR, Sam Hughes went hunting for a military role. He had hoped to command one of the battalions of rifles in the 2nd Contingent, but Lessard and Herchmer were chosen instead. Sam Steele offered him a captaincy in Lord Strathcona's Horse, which Hughes haughtily rejected.

In late February, as Roberts's army was pushing northeast, some Boers living in the Cape near the Orange River, west of Roberts's line of march, took up arms. From March until mid-May, a mixed force of infantry and mounted troops under Brig.-Gen. Herbert Settle was operating in the northwest of Cape Province, protecting Roberts's flanks. Settle accepted Hughes, who justified the confidence by demonstrating a flair for scouting.

Settle's force swung as far west as the border of German West Africa (Namibia), searching for Boer commandos, seizing munitions, and foraging. Hughes led a mounted detachment that was usually well ahead of the main body. Settle occupied Prieska first, then Kenhart, and, on 27 March, Upington. Here Hughes showed his daring coolness. He was advancing with part of his detachment, but decided that they were too slow. He dashed ahead with his interpreter and five others, covering 317 kilometres (185 miles) in two days, exchanging shots with Boers as they flashed by. At Upington he decided not to wait for the rest of his detachment to catch up. He how had nine mounted men – two of them Boer prisoners – and he hitched two teams to a cart, to resemble a field gun. Raising a great dust that suggested a much stronger force, he surprised a Boer rear guard, galloped through Upington, and captured the town. Then, fearing a counterattack, he rashly armed twenty Blacks (who would have been shot at once had the Boers returned in force). Luckily for Hughes, and the Blacks, the intimidated Boers stayed away. The next day, while waiting for Settle to arrive, Hughes and two men went from farm to farm searching for arms and foraging. A favourite trick was to surprise Boer families while they were at prayer. Afterwards, he would apologize, and at times even give them some of his own money.

Once Roberts was too far away for Cape Boers to threaten him, Hughes was assigned to Lieut.-Gen. Sir Charles Warren, the loser of Spion Kop and about as popular with top British brass as Hughes was with Otter. Warren's force, 2,000 strong, went to pacify the country near Botswana and to secure the towns of Douglas, Campbell, and Griguatown. Boers under Gen. Piet De Villiers were inciting their fellows to rise. Again, Hughes was with the vanguard, and his detachment was the first to enter Douglas. On 29 May, Warren ordered camp set up at Faber's farm, outside Campbell. It was a vulnerable site, open and surrounded by hills. At dawn on 1 June, 600 Boers swooped down from the hills. Hughes rallied a few men, stormed a kraal where most of the horses were confined, and drove some Boers upslope. Other officers repeated the action, although the Boers captured many horses before they made off beyond the hills. Before Warren took action to move out, the Boers counterattacked, killing twenty-three men and wounding thirty-two. Hughes was furious over the site Warren had chosen, and enraged when the general whitewashed his report to Roberts.

The Boers fled Campbell without offering resistance; the next objective was Griguatown. On 7 June, Warren sent Hughes ahead with a detachment, warning him not to attempt to occupy the town unless he was certain the Boers would not fight back. Hughes ignored the caution, and rode almost unopposed into Griguatown. Warren then sent him off with eighteen men to locate De Villiers's laager, reputed to be near Kururman, where, Warren understood, many Boers were ready to capitulate. Again, he ordered Hughes only to find the laager, and leave its capture to the entire force. But this time Hughes was even bolder. He concealed his men, rode into the laager alone, and demanded surrender. The Boers were negotiating with him when a messenger arrived with a report that Roberts was under attack. Hughes bluffed again, saying that the British had already captured the Boers responsible for the attack. Most of the Boers in the laager agreed to surrender, but fifty, including De Villiers, escaped after dark. Hughes had 220 prisoners, many horses, ammunition, rifles, and other supplies, but Warren was furious when he arrived. Hughes had disobeyed orders, and as a result De Villiers, the prize, had eluded him.

He dismissed Hughes at once, who went to Cape Town hoping for another assignment. A month later, Roberts ordered him to leave South Africa. From Cape Town he had been sending scathing reports to both Canadian and local newspapers. Back home, he never admitted he might have been at fault, and he clung to his belief in the superiority of untrained volunteers over regulars. Some politicians believed him, or were simply aware of his popularity with voters. He was made Minister of Militia and Defence under Prime Minister Sir Robert Borden at the outset of the First World War and dubbed Sir Sam Hughes, K.G.B., in 1915.

XVIII
Hong Kong, 1941

O n Christmas Day, 1941, the British garrison at Hong Kong surrendered to a larger Japanese invading force. Among the prisoners of war were the survivors of two Canadian battalions, the first Canadians to go into action in World War II. According to widely held hindsight, the nearly 2,000 officers and men should never have been dispatched to Hong Kong. Sending them was political expediency. At the time, however, there seemed a rationale; only later did it prove to be based on false premises.

The fault lay in underestimating the qualities of the Japanese fighting men. When the War Office at Whitehall, London, asked Canada for a reinforcement for Hong Kong, Prime Minister Mackenzie King's government acquiesced. Winston Churchill, prime minister of Great Britain since May 1940, at one time maintained that Hong Kong was indefensible and ought to be evacuated. Others, less realistic, disagreed, and later Churchill sided with them.

The reinforcement, they argued, would show the Japanese that Britain had resolved to hold Hong Kong and deter them from attacking. It would also reassure the Chinese commander-in-chief, Gen. Chiang Kai-shek, whose country had been overrun, that Britain would not desert his cause. Besides, abandoning the colony without a fight would undermine American authority in the Philippines.

The British Crown colony of Hong Kong comprises three areas. Hong Kong Island was ceded to Britain in 1842, and the Kowloon peninsula in 1860, as a result of two opium wars. In 1898, Britain leased the New Territories for ninety-nine years (due to expire on 1 July 1997, when all three areas revert to China). Most of the flat land lies in the New Territories; the Kowloon area and the Island of Hong Kong are mountainous. Victoria, the capital, occupies the main north coastal stretch on the Island. To repel an attack implied using strong positions in gaps and passes and near the peaks of rugged hills.

Both the governor, Sir Mark Young, and the commander-in-chief, Maj.-Gen. Christopher M. Maltby, were new to the colony. Maltby, who had long served in India, had come in July to succeed Canadian-born Maj.-Gen. Edward Grasett, while Young had settled into Government House, in Victoria,

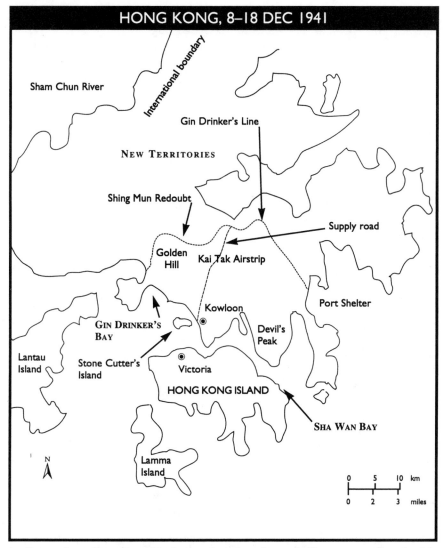

HONG KONG, 8–18 DEC 1941

Sham Chun River

International boundary

Gin Drinker's Line

NEW TERRITORIES

Shing Mun Redoubt

Supply road

Golden Hill

Kai Tak Airstrip

Port Shelter

Kowloon

GIN DRINKER'S BAY

Devil's Peak

Lantau Island

Stone Cutter's Island

Victoria

HONG KONG ISLAND

SHA WAN BAY

Lamma Island

N

0   5   10   km

0   2   3   miles

in September. Grasett, returning to London through Ottawa, conferred with Maj.-Gen. Henry D.G. Crerar, chief of the General Staff (they had been cadets together at R.M.C. Kingston). Grasett tried to persuade his old friend of the need to reinforce Hong Kong. In London he convinced the War Office, which led to the approach to Mackenzie King's government. Canada agreed to pledge two battalions of infantry. The remaining question was, which ones?

Col. John K. Lawson was the director of military training. He had assessed the twenty-six battalions of the Canadian Army and classified them according to their readiness for combat. "A" Class was the most prepared; "B" was second best, but "C" he deemed not recommended for operations. Yet the two infantry battalions assigned to Hong Kong were the Winnipeg Grenadiers and the Royal Rifles of Canada both from "C" Class. Senior officers wanted to keep "A" and "B" Class battalions for service in England.

Commander of the Grenadiers, headquarters Winnipeg, was Lieut.-Col. John L.F. Sutcliffe; commander of the Royal Rifles, from Quebec City, was Lieut.-Col. William Home. The senior battalion majors were George Trist and John H. Price. Colonel Lawson, promoted brigadier-general, was the commander of the whole contingent. His senior administrative officer was Col. Pat Hennessey. All were veterans of combat in World War I. One battalion would represent the west and another the east, especially a Quebec regiment – one-quarter of the men in the Royal Rifles were French-speaking.

When the decision was taken to send these battalions, both were on garrison duty outside the country. The Winnipeg Grenadiers were in Jamaica, and the Royal Rifles were in Newfoundland (which was not then part of Canada). After they were recalled, little time was available for training, something few politicians thought necessary – their duties in Hong Kong would be similar to those they had performed already. Since, supposedly, no attack was imminent, there would be plenty of time to bring the battalions to combat fitness after they reached the colony.

Before the Canadians arrived, the Hong Kong garrison had four battalions of regular troops. The 1st Battalion, Middlesex, a machine-gun regiment, and the 2nd Battalion Royal Scots, an infantry unit, were from Britain. The others were infantry regiments from India: the 5th Battalion, 7th Rajputs, and the 2nd Battalion, 14th Punjabis. Supporting the regulars was the 2,000-strong Hong Kong Volunteer Defence Corps, led by a retired British officer, Col. H.B. Rose.

The Winnipeg Grenadiers and the Royal Rifles of Canada arrived home from Jamaica and Newfoundland in September and October 1941. As both were below strength, 436 new recruits had to be enlisted. Some were sixteen- and seventeen-year-olds who must have lied about their ages. According to one officer the new enlistments were "the sweepings of the depots," men no other unit wanted.

Not all the soldiers to be sent were that inexperienced. John Stroud, now an active leader of the Ontario Chapter, Hong Kong Veterans' Association, had enlisted in the Toronto Scottish in June 1940. He attended the Machine Gun Training Centre at Valcartier, Quebec, and had also learned to drive a bren-gun carrier before he was part of a detachment of 150 men from his regiment who were sent to Newfoundland. When he heard that the Royal Rifles might be slated for duty overseas, he swapped places with a man in that regiment. The 150 men of the Toronto Scottish had been on guard duty at Cape Spear, where some had died falling off a cliff in thick fog. If a man had to lay down his life for his country, it should be in combat. Stroud found himself back at Valcartier waiting impatiently while the Rifles received some basic training.

HONG KONG ISLAND, 18–25 DEC 1941

Tanaka's 229th

Shoji's 230th

Doi's 228th

Kowloon

Lei U Mun Channel

Victoria

Sai Wan Bay
(cemetery)

Jardine's
Lookout

Mount
Butler

Mount Nicholson

West Brigade:
(Lawson/Rose)
2 coys Middlesex, Punjabis,
Most Rajputs, Punjabis,
Royal Scots, Winnipeg
Grenadiers, Hong Kong
volunteers

Wong Nei Chong Gap

Aberdeen

Bennet's
Hill

Tai Tam Gap

Hotel

REPULSE BAY

N

Stanley

East Brigade: (Wallis)
2 coys Middlesex, Royal
Rifles of Canada,
Hong Kong

0   3 miles
0 1   3   5 km

Japanese lines of advance ....

Positions of most of each brigade, 25 Dec 1941 —————

When the battalion entrained, the men were disturbed to find that they were heading not for Halifax and duty in the war zone, but for Vancouver. This implied garrison duty in India, and more of the boredom they had already endured.

Waiting for the Canadians were two ships. The *Awatea* was a five-year-old liner from New Zealand with space for 540 passengers, commissioned by the British government. Her escort was an armed merchant cruiser, the *Prince Robert*. With an embarkation strength of 98 officers and 1,877 men – the Grenadiers and Rifles, a detachment of Royal Canadian Signal Corps, auxiliaries, and nurses Kay Christie of Toronto and May Water of Winnipeg – accommodation was cruelly cramped. All but 109 officers and men who went on the *Prince Robert* had to cram into the *Awatea*. The food was also deplorable, and everyone complained.

John Stroud recalled Brigadier Lawson's speech to the men after they had left Hawaii, informing them that their destination was Hong Kong. A groan greeted this news, but Lawson, who had been there before, assured them they would enjoy the place. While still aboard the *Awatea*, Stroud, who was in "B" Company, met a sergeant who persuaded him to transfer to the more prestigious Headquarters Company. (There were five companies in the Royal Rifles – "A," "B," "C," "D," and Headquarters.) Later, John found that he had been "up for sergeant" of "B" Company, although he was content to remain a private.

The ships reached Hong Kong on 16 November and disembarkation was completed on the 17th. Still en route were 212 vehicles for the Canadians – trucks, bren-gun carriers, and motorcycles. These were to be carried on the freighter *Don José* via Manila. With the arrival of the Grenadiers and Rifles, Gen. Maltby had more than 10,000 men in his garrison. He divided his force into Mainland and Island Brigades.

To lead the first, Maltby chose Brig. Cedric Wallis, a former commander of the 5/7 Rajputs who had lost an eye in World War I (and who thought the Hong Kong garrison needed fewer cocktail parties and more hard training). In his brigade were the Punjabis, Rajputs, the Royal Scots (depleted by malaria), and some Canadian signallers. Maltby put Brig. John Lawson in charge of the Island Brigade, and placed the two Canadian battalions and the Middlesex Regiment under him. The Middlesex men were all machine gunners, essential for manning the pillboxes along the coast and in the mountain passes, while both the Canadian battalions had machine gun companies.

Maltby did not attempt to hold all the New Territories; a fortified line, with redoubts and pillboxes, extended from Gin Drinker's Bay, northwest of Kowloon, to Port Shelter Bay on the east. The stronghold was the Shing Mun Redoubt, on higher ground overlooking the western end of the line. If the Japanese attack should come from occupied China, and the Gin Drinker's Line could not hold, Maltby planned to withdraw Wallis's Brigade to Hong Kong Island. One company of Punjabis was stationed close to the border with China, to destroy bridges and roads if necessary.

Naval and air support were laughable. In Victoria harbour lay the old destroyer *Thracian*, four gunboats, and eight motor-torpedo-boats (MTBs). At Kai Tak airstrip, east of Kowloon, were five obsolete craft – three Vildebeestes and two Walrus amphibians.

The two Canadian battalions went into barracks in Kowloon for training. British officers discounted rumours that the Japanese were massing along the Chinese border, but Lawson took them seriously. John Stroud remembered that the Indian troops impressed the Canadians, but they thought the British were soft from easy living. Relations between the British and Canadians were hardly cordial. Canadian rates of pay were higher, and rickshaw runners and friendly women ignored their erstwhile clients for the bigger tips the new arrivals offered. Inevitably, clashes followed.

Against the Hong Kong defenders the Japanese commander-in-chief, Lieut.-Gen. Taikaishi Sakai, committed Maj.-Gen. Tadayoshi Sano's 38th Division of nine large battalions in three regiments – Col. Doi's 228th, Col. Tanaka's 229th, and Col. Shoji's 230th. Seventy aircraft would support this

20,000-strong ground force.

On 8 December (the 7th beyond the international dateline in North America) the Japanese released their juggernaut, bombing the Americans at Pearl Harbor and Hawaii, the British in Malaya and Hong Kong, and later invading the American Philippines and the Dutch East Indies. Their motive was to carve out an empire rich in oil, rubber, and other resources that their rugged islands lacked.

The bombs that fell on Hong Kong on the 8th struck the Kai Tak airstrip and destroyed all five airplanes on the ground. They bombed the barracks at Sham Shui Po, but all the troops but two had already left for their stations. By 9 December, the vanguard of the three Japanese regiments had begun to move into the New Territories. The Punjabis blew up a bridge over the Sham Chun River that linked occupied China with the New Territories, and joined their regiment at the Gin Drinker's Line.

The Punjabis and one company of the Rajputs held the centre of this line; the other Rajputs were on the east, while the Royal Scots manned the west and the Shing Mun Redoubt. The 3rd battalion of Doi's 228th Regiment reached the redoubt in the afternoon, well ahead of its supporting artillery, which had been delayed by the Punjabi demolitions. More Japanese surged through the darkness that night, scattering the defenders in confusion. At daybreak on the 10th, Doi controlled the Redoubt. Wallis ordered a withdrawal to Golden Hill to avoid being cut off from the Rajputs and Punjabis, and Maltby sent him a company of the Winnipeg Grenadiers to reinforce the Royal Scots.

On the 11th, the Japanese took Golden Hill, and could now close the road that supplied the east part of the Gin Drinker's Line. At noon, Maltby ordered Wallis to begin evacuating his Brigade to Hong Kong Island. The Royal Scots and the company of Winnipeg Grenadiers descended into Kowloon, and the Rajputs and Punjabis made their way south to Devil's Peak, on a promontory overlooking the Island. While the Japanese bombed the power station, oil tanks, and the Kowloon dockyard, the two Canadian battalions left their barracks and moved to the island to take up positions Brigadier Lawson had assigned them. To John Stroud's dismay – he had been promised a motorcycle – the Canadians' vehicles had not arrived. (They never left Manila; the Americans used them in their unsuccessful defence of the Philippines.)

By the 12th, the Royal Scots and their Grenadier supporters had crossed to the Island on ferries. The Indian battalions had a harder time. From strong positions at Ma Lau Tong, the Rajputs fought a rear guard that repulsed the Japanese, with help from artillery firing from the Island. During the night of the 12th, the rest of the Punjabis crossed, and at first light on the 13th the *Thracian* and four MTBs rescued the Rajputs, who had to abandon their equipment. After all had gone, Wallis departed at 8:30 a.m.

At 9:00, a launch with a delegation and a white flag arrived at Victoria to demand surrender. Gov. Sir Mark Young frostily refused. A steep row of hills crosses the centre of Hong Kong Island, and a road leads from the north past Mount Nicholson, through the Wong Nei Chong Gap to Repulse Bay in the south. An enemy holding the Wong Nei Chong Gap could cut the island in two. Maltby was not certain whether the Japanese would land at Victoria, cross from Devil's Peak by the Lei U Mun Channel, or both. He divided his force into East and West Brigades.

In the East Brigade, under Brigadier Wallis, Maltby placed the Rajputs to the northeast and the Royal Rifles to the southeast, where the latter could move to the beaches if part of the Japanese force arrived by sea. Wallis set up headquarters in the Tai Tam Gap, between the two battalions. In the West Brigade, commanded by Brigadier Lawson, were the Royal Scots, Punjabis, and Winnipeg Grenadiers. Maltby assigned some Hong Kong Volunteers to each Brigade. Most of the Middlesex gunners took up positions at headquarters, in the Wong Nei Chong Gap, where Lawson was in command. (Maltby's whereabouts were not always clear; he may have stayed mainly in Victoria, in order to be in touch with the governor.)

The bombing continued. A Japanese reconnaissance party tried to cross the Lei U Mun Channel on the night of the 15th, but only a handful got ashore. On the 17th, Young again refused to surrender. The invasion of the Island began on the 18th, with a punishing air raid on Victoria, followed by heavy shelling. The enemy gathered at Devil's Peak and Kowloon for the assault that began at night. Maj.-Gen. Sano sent two battalions from each of the three regiments forward, leaving three battalions as a reserve.

Tanaka's 229th struck over the Leu U Mun Channel for Shau Ki Wan. Doi's 228th went towards Braemar Point, while Shoji's 230th went farthest west to North Point with orders to occupy the Wong Nei Chong Gap. The night was very dark; rain and smoke from burning oil tanks at Victoria obscured visibility. Taken by surprise, the garrison was not aware of what was happening until the Japanese were on the Island in strength. Tanaka's men overran an anti-aircraft battery manned by Hong Kong Volunteers, and slew the defenders in cold blood. More atrocities occurred at a medical post at Shau Ki Wan. At a battery at Pak Sha Wan, the Rajputs held out until noon of the 19th.

Most gallant were Hong Kong Volunteers fifty-five years of age and older, who held out at the North Point Power Station after they had been cut off. Two Middlesex platoons tried to relieve them but met with an ambush. At 4:00 p.m., out of ammunition, the Volunteers surrendered. While some of the enemy attacked shore defences, others pushed inland towards the Wong Nei Chong Gap.

At 2:00 a.m. on the 20th, Lawson sent detachments of the Winnipeg Grenadiers to take up high positions on Jardine's Lookout and Mount Butler,

National Archives of Canada, PA-11481 I, photo by Jack Hawkes

Canadian and British prisoners-of-war in Hong Kong awaiting liberation by men from HMCS *Prince Robert,* 30 August 1945.

northeast of the Gap. By 7:00, Col. Shoji's column was thrusting between the Gap and Mount Nicholson to the west of it. Lawson called on the Royal Scots, then to the northwest, to support Headquarters, but the Japanese ambushed them. By 10:00, the enemy had overrun the West Brigade's Headquarters. Lawson and his staff officers were gunned down as they ran for cover, and both Lawson and Col. Pat Hennessey were killed. Col. Shoji ordered full military honours at Lawson's burial and later a monument in memory of his valour.

The Royal Rifles of Wallis's East Brigade were faring badly. At 10:00, they tried to counterattack the Japanese on Sai Wan Hill, but were pushed back. A disappointed Wallis later claimed that the Rifles were "incapable of a real fight." He withdrew to high ground near Stanley village to regroup his force, a strategic error, for the Japanese were able to take control of the east half of the Island and the main reservoirs, leaving only those near Aberdeen to supply the entire Island. East Brigade lost most of its artillery, and in later attacks would lack covering fire.

After dark, Tanaka's regiment occupied Voilet Hill and cut the road that led from the Gap to Repulse Bay. The Winnipeg Grenadiers on Jardine's Lookout and Mount Butler were isolated. They held out on Mount Butler until 4:00 p.m., when they had no more ammunition. Here, Company Sgt.-Maj. John Osborn's courage merited a posthumous Victoria Cross. After lobbing back live grenades, he noticed one, too far gone to be tossed out, and he threw himself on it, protecting others and sacrificing his own life. The

loaned by John R. Stroud

Sai Wan Military Cemetery

Grenadiers at Wong Nei Chong Gap still held out.

At dawn on the 20th, six MTBs tried to block enemy reinforcements from landing, but two were sunk. The dead Lawson's West Brigade now came under the command of Col. H.B. Rose of the Hong Kong Volunteer Defence Corps. The Middlesex Regiment was doing battle in the north, the Royal Scots in the centre, and the main body of the Winnipeg Grenadiers in the south. The Punjabis were in reserve. A mixed force held Bennet's Hill, near Aberdeen. All were exhausted. That evening, Doi took Mount Nicholson, and Tanaka reached the south coast and took Shouson Hill.

Wallis's East Brigade, now cut off from the West Brigade, occupied a line across the peninsula north of Stanley, except for "A" Company, Royal Rifles, who had been dispatched with 200 civilians to the Repulse Bay Hotel to reinforce Middlesex troops and Volunteers. All day they had been resisting a thrust by Kanaka's men.

On the 21st, every counterattack failed, and the Brigades could not reunite. On the night of 22 December, the defenders evacuated the Repulse Bay Hotel, without atrocities. The Japanese were impressed by their courage. On the 23rd the Winnipeg Grenadiers still held out at Wong Nei Chong Gap, having no way to escape. At 7:30 that morning Shoji's 230th made a last assault. With all ammunition expended, and only a dozen free of wounds, the Grenadiers surrendered, and were well treated, although Shoji had lost 800 in the Gap and at Jardine's Lookout. By that time Doi had taken Mount Cameron, at the centre of the West Brigade's defences.

Under extreme pressure, Wallis ordered his East Brigade to withdraw well into Stanley peninsula. By the 24th, all nine Japanese battalions were on the Island. At 9:00 a.m. on Christmas Day, two civilians, captured at the Repulse Bay Hotel, arrived at Maltby's headquarters to ask for a three-hour truce, enough time to arrange a surrender. Maltby agreed to the truce, but not to surrender. At noon, the Japanese resumed their march towards Victoria. At 3:15 p.m., Maltby told Young that further resistance would be in vain. The defenders raised their white flags at 3:40.

On Stanley Peninsula, the Japanese went on a rampage so violent that what credit their fighting prowess had won quickly evaporated. They bayonetted wounded soldiers, raped women, and made conditions for the helpless prisoners a horrific nightmare. In the fighting, the British Commonwealth lost 2,133 killed and 1,300 wounded who, with the rest of the garrison, had to endure four years of harsh captivity. Japanese casualties in taking Hong Kong were about 3,000. Canada's losses were 23 officers and 267 other ranks killed, and 28 officers and 465 other ranks wounded. Worse was still to come, however.

At first, the prisoners of war stayed in camps in Hong Kong, and were forced to rebuild the Kai Tak airstrip. Some 129 died, among them Lieut.-Col. Sutcliffe of the Winnipeg Grenadiers, of beriberi and anemia in April. Early in 1943, Nurses Kay Christie and May Water, and a few men too seriously ill to be of any use, were repatriated. That year, one officer and 1,183 prisoners of other ranks were sent to Japan as slave labourers, chiefly in the mines. One hundred and thirty-five died from the cruel treatment. More than 550 of the 1,975 who left Vancouver in October 1941 never came home, and the health of many who did was forever impaired. The bodies of those who died in Hong Kong rest in the Sai Wan Bay War Cemetery on the Island; those who died in Japan lie in the British Commonwealth War Cemetery at Hodogaya, near Yokohama.

In 1942, the Canadian government came under fire for having sent the battalions. After much needling by George Drew, Leader of the Ontario Opposition, the federal government set up a Royal Commission, chaired by Sir Lyman Duff. To the surprise of few, it found evidence of mismanagement only over the dispatch of the vehicles. Hong Kong hardened the opposition to the King government's attempt to introduce conscription. Quebec, in particular, used the evidence of the waste of the two battalions as grounds for preventing the government from repeating such a blunder.

In 1992, a report Major-General Maltby had written fifty years before was unsealed. Maltby had accused the Canadians of cowardice. When news media contacted Hong Kong veterans they issued a scornful rebuttal, confirmed by Frank Abbott, historian at the Ryerson Polytechnical Institute. In a letter to the *Globe and Mail,* Abbott quoted Japanese sources that contradicted Maltby, and recalled in what high esteem Colonel Shoji of the Japanese 230th Regiment had held Canadian Brig.-Gen. John K. Lawson.

When the Hong Kong veterans came home in 1945, they found that they were entitled to exactly the same compensation as any other veterans – the severity of their treatment, longer time in captivity, and recurring ill health counted for nothing. As the clamour grew to compensate Japanese Canadians interned during the war, George Hees and Otto Jelinek, as ministers of veterans' affairs, both assured the veterans that the internees would not receive a penny; however, the Mulroney government yielded to pressure and paid the civilians. Such largesse has yet to be extended to soldiers who had four years torn from their lives through ill-judged decision by military brass and politicians.

Chronology of Important Dates in the Military History of Canada

875-1,000
Beginning of European interest in North America.

1004
Norse founded a camp at l'Anse aux Meadows, Newfoundland, and abandoned it two years later.

1390
Formation of the Iroquois Confederacy by Dekanawidah and his assistant Adodaroh (Hiawatha) uniting the Mohawks, Oneidas, Onondagas, Cayugas and Senecas into the Five Nations. (In 1722 the Tuscaroras joined, making the Six Nations.)

ca. 1420
Basque Whalers from France and Spain began to hunt in the Labrador Sea.

1481
British ''Merchants of Bristowe'' may have landed in Newfoundland, but they kept their activities secret to avoid competition from the French, Spanish and Portugese on the Grand Banks.

1494
Treaty of Tordesillas gave the Americas to Spain, who was too busy in the Caribbean and South America to notice the British and French in Newfoundland waters.

1504
St. John's Nfld. was established.

1506
A Norman fishing village was established on the east side of the Avalon Peninsula, Nfld.

1534
Jacques Cartier planted a cross on the Gaspé Peninsula, on the first of three voyages of exploration he made for France.

1576
26 August. British explorer Martin Frobisher claimed the land around Frobisher Bay for Britain.

1587
The Marquis de la Roche-Mesgoues was appointed the first Viceroy of New France by Henry IV of France.

1583
5 August. Humphrey Gilbert claimed Newfoundland for Elizabeth I of England.

1605
Founding of Port Royal (Nova Scotia) by Pierre du Gua, Sieur de Monts, and Samuel de Champlain, first capital of Acadia.

1608
Founding of Quebec by merchants led by Champlain.

1609
30 July. Champlain and his men defeated an Iroquois war party near Ticonderoga, Lake Champlain

1610
14-19 June. Champlain and his Huron and Algonquin allies defeated the Iroquois near the mouth of the Richelieu River.

1610-1611
Henry Hudson in his ship *Discovery* wintered in James Bay. Champlain sent Etienne Brulé to winter among the Hurons.

1612
Peter Easton used Harbour Grace, Nfld. as a base for his ten-vessel pirate fleet that plundered thirty English ships in St. John's harbour and raided French and Portugese ships at Ferryland.

1613
July. Port Royal was attacked, sacked and burnt by Capt. Samuel Argall, on orders from Sir Thomas Dale, Governor of Virginia, the first British expedition against Acadia.

Beverwyck (Albany, N.Y.) was founded as a trading post by the Dutch.

Récollet Father Joseph Le Caron reached Huronia (and returned to Quebec in 1616). 3 August. Champlain arrived in Huronia. 1 September-23 December. Champlain joined the Hurons for an expedition against the Iroquois. On 10 October. the Onondagas ambushed them, Champlain was wounded, and the French and Hurons retired to Huronia.

1616
17 June. William Vaughan founded a Welsh

colony at Trepassey Bay, Nfld.

1620

Late July Champlain began construction of Fort St. Louis on Cape Diamond, the first fort on the cliff at Quebec.

1621

The Iroquois began getting firearms from the Dutch.

10 September. James I granted land from Cape Gaspé to the St. Croix River to the Scotsman, William Alexander, despite French claims.

1622

July. The first Scots colonists reached Nova Scotia.

1624

Three Récollets founded a mission in Huronia (which was taken over by the Jesuits in 1626).

Temporary peace reigned between the French, Hurons and Algonquins and the Iroquois.

1625

19 June. First Jesuits reached Quebec.

1626

July. Jesuit Father Jean de Brébeuf founded a mission in Huronia (on the site of Penatanguishene).

1627

Britain and France were at war.

1629

19 July. Quebec was captured by Capt. David Kirke. Champlain and all the missionaries were sent to France.

1632

29 March. Quebec and Port Royal were restored to France by the Treaty of St.-Germain-en-Laye.

1633

22 May. Champlain and four Jesuit priests reached Quebec. The missionaries returned to Huronia in 1634.

1639

Jesuit Father Jérôme Lalemant founded Ste.-Marie-Among-the-Hurons (near Midland, Ont.).

1641

The Iroquois formally declared war on the French.

1642

August. The French built Fort Richelieu as protection for Montreal.

1642-1649 Destruction of Huronia

2 August. Jesuits Isaac Joques and René Goupil, en route to Quebec, were captured by Iroquois near Trois Rivières. Goupil was killed, the first Jesuit Martyr, and Joques escaped.

1644

30 March. Settlers were defeated by a large band of Iroquois intent on attacking Montreal.

1645

April. Attack on Fort Ste. Marie, stronghold of Acadian Charles de la Tour by his Acadian rival, Menou d'Aulnay. On the 13th, the 45 defenders surrendered, and most were hanged.

14 July. A peace was arranged between the Iroquois and French.

1646

September-October. Fathers Isaac Joques and lay brother Jean de La Lande were killed while on a peace mission to the Mohawks.

1648

Summer. Iroquois broke the peace by attacking the Jesuit missions of St. Joseph II and St. Michel in Huronia. Father Antoine Daniel was killed.

1649

16 March. A force of 1,000 Iroquois attacked St. Ignace and St. Louis missions. Fathers Jean de Brébeuf and Gabriel Lalemant were tortured to death.

14 June. The Jesuits abandoned Ste.-Marie among-the Hurons and moved to Christian Island to found Ste.-Marie II.

1650

Spring. Father Paul Ragueneau evacuated Ste.-Marie-II and returned to Quebec.

1653

Iroquois made a general peace with the French.

1654

3 July. Major Robert Sedgewick, commander on the New England coast, left Boston and attacked Acadia in reprisal for French attacks on British vessels. He captured Fort Ste. Marie, Port Royal and Fort Penobscot.

1655

3 November. By the Treaty of Westminster, Acadia was restored to France.

1660

May. Battle of the Long Sault of the Ottawa River (near the site of Hawkesbury). It was fought between 16 French and 44 Indian allies and some 800 Iroquois. All the French died.

1660

The French founded Plaisance, at Placentia Bay, Nfld.

1665

30 June. Alexandre de Tracy arrived in Quebec with 100 officers and 1,000 men of the Carnignan-Salières Regiment. The soldiers built a chain of forts along the Richelieu River.

1666

9 January-17 March. Sieur de Courcelle, Governor of New France, attacked the Mohawks. Of 500 French, 60 died of hunger and exposure.

14 September-5 November. Courcelle led a second expedition, of 1,500 men against the Mohawks. He burned many villages and claimed the land for Louis XIV of France.

1669

Voyage of the Nonsuch to Hudson Bay. Médard Chouard des Groseilliers established Charles Fort and returned to England with a cargo of furs.

1670

2 May. Charles II granted a charter to his cousin Prince Rupert and his associates as the ''Governor and Company of Adventurers Trading into Hudson's Bay''. Radisson and Groseilliers sailed with the first governor of the Hudson's Bay Company, Charles Bayly.

1671

2 June. Governor de Courcelle left Montreal and met with Iroquois leaders on Lake Ontario, who agreed to make peace.

1673

13 June. Robert Cavelier de La Salle began building Fort Frontenac (on the site of Kingston, Ont.).

17 July. The Dutch attacked Ferryland, Nfld.

August. The Dutch retook New York (New Amsterdam) from the British.

1674

9 February. By the Treaty of Westminster the Dutch restored New York (New Netherlands) colony to Britain.

10 August. Dutch Privateer Jurriaen Aernoutsz, unaware of the peace treaty, captured Penagouet, in Acadia, and took the governor, Jacques de Chambly, prisoner. After plundering French posts along the Bay of Fundy and capturing Jemseg (Saint John), Aernoutsz took his booty to Boston and claimed Acadia for Holland.

1675

The Iroquois attacked tribes friendly to the French.

1682

La Salle reached the Gulf of Mexico in April.

The French, including Radisson and Groseilliers, who had left the Hudson's Bay Company, built a fur post on the Hayes River close to Hudson Bay, captured York Fort on the Nelson River, and set up the *Compagnie du Nord*, to compete with the Hudson's Bay Company.

April. The Iroquois attacked tribes friendly to the French.

1684

York Fort was returned to the Hudson's Bay Company.

5 September. The Governor of New France, Joseph Le Febre de la Barre, with 700 French and 400 Indians, met the Iroquois

French and 400 Indians, met the Iroquois on Lake Ontario, who signed a treaty to keep the peace with the Miamis.

1686

20 March-June. Expedition under Pierre de Troyes and Pierre le Moyne d'Iberville, of 100 men, marched overland to Hudson Bay and seized the Hudson's Bay Company's three forts.

19 November. Britain and France signed the Neutrality Pact to settle the dispute over Hudson Bay. A commission would decide on the boundary between New France and Rupert's Land.

1687

17 June. Governor Jacques Denonville and De Troyes left Montreal with an expedition against the Senecas. Denonville left De Troyes and a garrison to build Fort Niagara on Seneca land.

1688

15 September. Because of Iroquois demands, Denonville ordered Fort Niagara demolished and abandoned.

1689

28 January. A French force left Trois Rivières to attack New England settlements.

1689-1697 King William's War

17 May. War was declared between Britain and France.

5 August. 1,500 Iroquois attacked Lachine, the worst disaster in the history of New France; 24 were killed, and 42 of 90 who were captured were never seen again.

October. Fort Frontenac was abandoned. Iberville surrendered Fort New Severn, on Hudson Bay, and he defended Fort Albany successfully.

13 November. La Chènage (near Montreal) was attacked by Iroquois and some settlers were massacred.

1690

22 January. At Onondaga, the Iroquois agreed to a peace treaty between England and the tribes of the Great Lakes.

8 February. Governor Frontenac organized war parties to attack British frontier settlements.

18 February. French and Indians led by Jacques Le Moyne and Nicolas D'Ailleboust de Manthet raided Schenectady, N.Y., massacred 60 inhabitants, and returned to Montreal with 50 horses laden with plunder.

18 March. The French, led by François Hertel de Rouville, attacked Salmon Falls, on the New Hampshire frontier, killed 34 and took 54 prisoner, burned buildings and slaughtered livestock.

19 May. William Phips, Provost-Marshal of New England, took a naval force to Port Royal, which surrendered on the 21st.

July. Iberville entered Hudson Bay with three small ships, raided Fort New Severn, and with booty returned to Quebec in October. 1691.

16 October. Phips was off Quebec with 37 ships and 2,200 men. Frontenac, who had 3,000 troops, refused to surrender, and Phips sailed away after some skirmishes.

1692

A British attack on Placentia was repulsed.

Governor Joseph de Villebon built Fort St. Joseph farther up the Saint John River (N.B.).

The Hudson's Bay Company rebuilt Fort Nelson and recaptured Fort Albany.

5 February. Abenakis massacred some British at York, Me.

22 October. Fourteen-year-old Madeleine de Verchères led a successful defence of the family fort against attacking Iroquois.

Autumn. Iberville, preying upon New England shipping, planned to plunder settlements, but found them too well guarded. He led two frigates and captured three prize ships before sailing for France in November.

1693

28 January. A force of Caughnawagas led by Nicolas d'Ailleboust de Manthet

attacked the Mohawk villages and captured 300 before a relief force under Peter Schuyler forced the French to withdraw.

The British retook Albany Fort and drove the French from Hudson Bay.

1694

16 January. French missionaries Louis-Pierre Thury and Sébastien de Billie led 230 Indians in an attack on Oyster Bay, Me., killing 100 settlers.

31 August. Seven French vessels were defeated by the English ships *William* and *Mary* off Ferryland, Nfld.

15 October. Iberville captured York Fort and renamed it Fort Bourbon. A new fur post was opened by the French at Michilimackinac by Antoine de Lamothe Cadillac.

1695

July. Frontenac sent Thomas Crisafy and 700 men to restore Fort Frontenac.

Autumn. Iberville sailed for France, where he received orders to attack British settlements on the Atlantic coast.

1696

A French campaign against Britain's coastal colonies began.

4 July. Frontenac left Montreal with 2,150 men to punish the Iroquois for attacks on French settlements.

14 July. Iberville and Simon de Bonaventure, a naval officer, captured the British ship *Newport* near St. John's.

August. Iberville reached the mouth of the Saint John River, lifted a British blockade that entrapped Governor Joseph de Villebon of Acadia, and captured a British frigate.

15 August. Iberville captured Fort William Henry, Me. from Capt. Pascoe Chubb, 25 Acadia-based British regulars and 240 Abenakis. Iberville sent 90 prisoners to Boston and sailed for Placentia 28 August. Capt. William Allen captured York Fort from the French.

Autumn. The French Governor of Placentia, Jacques de Brouillon, with Iberville, set out to expel the British from Newfoundland.

November. Iberville marched across the Avalon Peninsula, destroyed Ferryland, and captured St. John's on the 30th. Looting and burning continued until only Carbonear and Bonavista remained in British hands, when Iberville was ordered to Hudson Bay. Thirty-six settlements had been wrecked, 200 people killed.

1697

Spring. A British squadron and 200 soldiers under Sir John Gibson arrived at St. John's to serve as a garrison.

5-13 September. In Hudson Bay, Iberville with 5 ships defeated 3 British ships and captured York Fort.

20 September. The Treaty of Ryswick ended King William's War.

Newfoundland and Hudson Bay were ceded to Britain, and Acadia to France.

1700

8 September. Iroquois, Abenakis and Ottawas agreed to peace terms with the governor of New France, Louis de Callières.

1701

July. Detroit was founded by Cadillac and his lieutenant, Alphonse Tonty.

1702

1702-1713 Queen Anne's War (part of the War of the Spanish Succession).

15 May. England declared war on France.

1704

28 February. The French and Indians raided Deerfield, Mass., the worst of several led by Jean-Baptiste Hertel de Rouville; 54 settlers were killed and 120 taken prisoner.

20 June. Benjamin Church captured Les Mines (Grand Pré), Pipigiguit, Cobequid (Truro, N.S.) and Beaubassin at the head of Chignecto Bay, in retaliation for the Deerfield raid.

18 August. French and Indians destroyed the English settlement at Bonavista, Nfld.

the English settlement at Bonavista, Nfld.

1705

8 January. Daniel de Subercase, Governor of Placentia, Nfld., with 450 French troops, captured Bay Bulls, Petty Harbour, and the settlements at Conception and Trinity Bays, except for Carbonear.

1707

6 June. A British attack on Port Royal was repelled by Subercase, recently appointed Governor of Acadia.

20 August. A second British attack on Port Royal by John March leading Massachusetts militia was also repelled by Subercase.

1708

Militia at St. John's formed the Royal Newfoundland Regiment.

26 July. Hertel de Rouville and Jean-Baptiste Deschaillons left Montreal to attack Haverhill, Mass. They killed 15 British settlers, and lost 10 killed and 19 wounded.

14 December. Philippe de Costebelle, Governor of Placentia, and Joseph de Brouillon left Placentia to attack St. John's, which surrendered on 1 January 1709.

1709

July-November. A naval force from Boston under Samuel Vetch and a land force led by Francis Nicholson, prepared to attack Quebec. In October Britain cancelled the naval orders and Vetch did not sail. Nicholson withdrew after skirmishing with the French near Lake Champlain.

1710

29 September. Conquest of Acadia began. An expedition led by Francis Nicholson, a colonial naval force under Samuel Vetch, and a British squadron under Capt. George Martin, sailed from Boston against Port Royal. The French commander, Subercase, surrendered on 1 October. Port Royal became Annapolis Royal.

Simultaneously, a British fleet under Sir Hovenden Walker failed to capture the French settlement at Placentia Bay.

Winter. 80 British soldiers foraging outside Port Royal were massacred by Indians loyal to the French.

1711

July-September. An expedition under Sir Hovenden Walker failed to reach Quebec. In fog, his 9 vessels grounded on shoals in the Gulf of St. Lawrence, with the loss of 8 ships and 900 men, an episode called the "magnificent fiasco".

1713

11 April. The Treaty of Utrecht was signed. Acadia, Newfoundland and the shores of Hudson Bay, were ceded to Britain. France retained New France (Quebec), Ile St. Jean (P.E.I.), and Ile Royal (Cape Breton Island), and the right to fish and use parts of the Newfoundland shore.

August. The French planned a great new fortress at Havre à l'Anglois (Louisbourg).

1714

1 June. Governor Philippe de Costebelle surrendered Placentia to a British force under Capt. John Moody and moved to Ile Royale.

5 September. James Knight, Governor of Hudson Bay lands, and Henry Kelsey, arrived at York Fort to accept the surrender of all the Hudson Bay territories held by the French.

1715

27 June. William Stuart set out from York Fort to bring peace between the Crees and the Chipewyans. He achieved a truce by promising to build a fur fort at the mouth of the Churchill River.

1716

Louis de Louvigny with 400 Indians and 400 *coureurs de bois* defeated the Foxe Indians at Green Bay (Wisc.).

1719

7 March. The contract to build Louisbourg "the Gibralter of Canada" was awarded to Michel Isabeau. Director of fortifications was Jean de Verville, who recommended the site in 1716.

the site in 1716.

1720

British and Dutch traders opened a post a Oswego to deflect furs from the French posts.

1722

July. The French gave ammunition and aid to the Abenakis, who attacked the British settlement of Merrymeeting Bay, Mass. in retaliation for a British attack on the Abenaki village of Norridgewock.

September. 400 Noridgewocks, Hurons of Lorette and Abenakis destroyed British settlements along the lower Kennebec and Connecticut Valleys.

1726

The French established a permanent garrison at Niagara to check British and Dutch competition from Oswego.

1731

1731-1743 Pierre de La Vérendrye and his three sons built a chain of fur posts and explored as far west as the Red River.

1731

The French built Fort St. Frederic at Crown Point, Lake Champlain.

1736

8 June. Jean-Baptiste de La Vérendrye and 20 others were massacred on an island in Lake-of-the Woods by Sioux warriors.

1744

1744-1748 King George's War (War of the Austrian Succession)

15 March. France declared war on Britain.

3 May. Jean Duqesnel, commandant of Cape Breton, sent an expedition under Joseph Du Pont Duvivier against the British fishing station at Canso, which surrendered 24 May.

29 July. The French besieged Annapolis Royal, and withdrew on 2 October.

1745

24 March-17 June. Capture of Louisbourg. New Englanders under Gen. William Pepperrell sailed from Boston, and were joined by Admiral Peter Warren, Royal Navy, with sailors, at Canso. Louisbourg

surrendered on 17 June.

20 June. The French settlement at Three Rivers, P.E.I. was destroyed by New Englanders who had come to Louisbourg.

Note: The preceding dates for 1745 are according to the Julian Calendar. England did not adopt the Gregorian Calendar of 1582 until 1752. This has led to confusion between English and Continental dates. French sources date the siege of Louisbourg from 6 April to 30 June, with the attack on Prince Edward Island as 3 July. The latter dates were used in the chapter on Louisbourg.

1746

22 June-30 September. The Duc d'Anville left La Rochelle, France, with 54 ships to retake Louisbourg. After severe storms, the fleet sheltered in Chebucto Bay (Halifax) on 10 September. D'Anville died on the 27th and the fleet sailed for France on the 30th.

10 July. Capt. Jean de Ramezay reached Baie Verte, (N.B.) from Quebec with 700 Canadians and Indians, expecting to meet d'Anville.

1747

11 January. Capt. Nicolas de Villiers, Ramezay's 2nd-in-command, with 240 Canadians and 60 Indians, ambushed 500 British under Governor Arthur Noble at Minas (Grand Pré) on 31 January.

1748

18 October. The Treaty of Aix-la-Chapelle ended King George's War. Louisbourg, Prince Edward Island and Cape Breton Island were returned to France. Britain kept Acadia.

1749

The French started an agricultural settlement at Detroit.

9 July. Col. Edward Cornwallis arrived at Chebucto to found Halifax.

1 June. Abbé François Piquet opened a mission at La Présentation (Ogdensburg N.Y.). The French started a shipyard at Pointe au Baril (Maitland, Ont.).

October. Louis La Corne began fortifications at Beauséjour, on the Isthmus of Chignecto, to limit British settlement to peninsular Nova Scotia.

1750

16 April. Cornwalls sent Col. Charles Lawrence with 400 men to Chignecto to establish British authority. They confronted La Corne on the Missaguash River. La Corne burned the village of Beaubassen to prevent the British taking it.

September. Lawrence returned to Chignecto with a strong force, routed Abbé Le Loutre and his Indians and started work on Fort Lawrence. The French began work on Forts Beauséjour and Gaspareau.

1753

The French opened Fort St. Louis near the forks of the Saskatchewan River, completing a chain of posts controlling the headwaters of rivers flowing into Hudson Bay, to intercept furs en route to the Hudson's Bay Company forts.

The Governor of New France, the Marquis Duquesne, sent a military expedition to build a chain of forts from Lake Erie towards the Ohio Valley.

3 September. The Senecas demanded the removal of the French forts from the Ohio country.

11 December. Virginians under Maj. George Washington arrived in the Ohio country to counter the French occupation.

1754

28 May. Washington and the Seneca, Tanaghrisson, fought the Battle of Jumonville against the French led by Joseph de Jumonville. Washington retreated to Great Meadows and built Fort Necessity.

4 July. Battle of Great Meadows. This started the French and Indian War.

1755

2 June. With 2,000 British troops, Col. Robert Monckton landed at the Missaguash River and began besieging Fort Beauséjour. The French commander,

Louis Du Pont Duchambon de Vergor, surrendered on the 4th.

17 June. Fort Gaspereau, at Baie Verte, surrendered to Monckton's force. That day the French abandoned Fort Jemseg (Saint John N.B.), the last French fort in Acadia.

9 July. Battle of the Monongahela. The French under Daniel de Beaujeu, commander at Fort Duquesne, routed a British-American force under Gen. Edward Braddock near Fort Duquesne. Both Beaujeu and Braddock were killed.

28 July. Lieut. Gov. Charles Lawrence received approval of the Nova Scotia Council to deport Acadians who refused to take the oath of allegiance. (Thousands were expelled in September.)

1 September. French troops under the commander-in-chief, Baron Dieskau, operated against British troops under Col. William Johnson, who had attacked Fort St. Frédéric at Crown Point. Johnson also built a fort at the head of Lake George.

8 September. Battle of Lake George. Dieskau and France's Indian allies defeated 1,000 British and colonial troops under William Johnson. Afterwards the French began building Fort Carillon at Ticonderoga.

1756

1756-1763 The Seven Years' War (French and Indian War)

17 May. Britain declared war on France.

5 August. Oswego. The Marquis de Montcalm, commander of French troops, left Fort Frontenac with 3,000 men to attack the British forts at Oswego. The British garrison, under Col. James Mercer, who was killed, surrendered on 14 August. Britain lost control of Lake Ontario.

1757

21 January. The "Battle on Snowshoes". The French defeated Maj. Robert Rogers and his rangers near Ticonderoga.

26 July. Montcalm and the Chevalier de Lévis defeated a British force under

Col. Parker at Sabbath Day Point, Lake George.

3 August. With 6,200 French and Canadians and 1,800 Indians, Montcalm besieged Fort William Henry, defended by Col. George Munro. The fort surrendered on 9 August.

1758

May-July. Siege of Louisbourg. The British expedition left Halifax, the land force under Gen. Jeffrey Amherst, the naval force led by Admiral Edward Boscawen. The 157 ships carrying 27,000 men lay off Louisbourg on 2 June. The French commander, Augustin de Drucour, with 3,500 regulars, 4,000 sailors and militia, surrendered on 26 July.

8 July. Fort Carillon (Ticonderoga). Montcalm with 3,600 men defeated the British under Gen. James Abercromby with 6,000 regulars and 9,000 provincials, at Fort Carillon.

8 August. From Louisbourg, Capt. Andrew Rollo took a force to Ile St. Jean (P.E.I.) built Fort Amherst at Port-la-Joli (Charlottetown) and deported 3,500 Acadians to France.

27 August. With 3,000 men, Col. John Bradstreet took Fort Frontenac.

29 August. Wolfe left Louisbourg to destroy settlements around the Gaspé and at Miramichi.

14 September. Maj. James Grant and 800 British were defeated at Grant's Hill by French from Fort Duquesne.

25 November. Brigadier John Forbes took Fort Duquesne and renamed it Fort Pitt (Pittsburgh, Pa.).

1759

12 January. Wolfe was appointed commander-in-chief of the land force for the expedition against Quebec.

25 June. Gen. Wolfe arrived off Quebec with 8,500 men; the naval force of 168 ships was commanded by Admiral Charles Saunders.

24 July. A French force under François de Lignery, marching to relieve Fort Niagara, was ambushed and defeated by provincials, regulars and Indians under Sir William Johnson. The fort surrendered on the 25th.

26 July. The British occupied Fort Carillon, and on the 31st Fort St. Frédéric, both abandoned by the French.

31 July. Battle of Montmorency. Wolfe's men were repulsed when they landed on the Beauport shore east of Quebec.

7 September. Part of the British fleet moved above Quebec to Cap Rouge.

9 September. Wolfe spotted a landing site at l'Anse au Foulon.

13 September. Battle of the Plains of Abraham. About 4,000 British regulars under Wolfe defeated a like number of French — regulars, militia and Indians.

— Wolfe was killed and Montcalm died of wounds.

17 September. Chevalier de Lévis took command of the French army at Pointe aux Trembles and retreated to Montreal. The British army under Brigadier George Townsend entered Quebec on the 19th.

1760

9 February. On orders from Prime Minister William Pitt, Capt. John Byron began destroying the Louisbourg fortifications.

28 April. Battle of Ste. Foy. Lévis and 5,000 French defeated Brigadier James Murray and 3,900 British. Murray withdrew inside Quebec's walls.

16 May. Lévis abandoned the siege of Quebec when the British fleet arrived with reinforcements.

8 July. Battle of the Ristigouche. British ships under Capt. John Byron defeated a French relief force under François d'Angeac — the last naval engagement fought for New France.

16-25 August. Battle of the Thousand Islands. Amherst's army of 10,000 men arrived at Pointe au Baril, close to Fort Lévis, on an island in the St. Lawrence. The 400 French defenders surrendered on

25 August.
Three armies were converging on Montreal
— Amherst's that had assembled at
Oswego, Haviland's from Lake Champlain,
and Murray's from Quebec.
8 September. Vauderuil surrendered
Montreal to Amherst.
29 November. The French at Detroit
surrendered to Maj. Robert Rogers.
1761
14 February. The British occupied
Michilimackinac.
1762
27 June. French troops under Charles
d'Arsac de Ternay captured Fort William,
at St. John's Nfld.
7 September. Col. William Amherst left
Louisbourg with 1,500 troops to retake St.
John's. They landed at Torbay on the 13th
and drove the French back into Fort
William on the 15th. The French
commander, Joseph d'Haussonville,
surrendered on the 18th. This was the last
encounter between Britain and France in
North America.
1763
10 February The Treaty of Paris ended the
Seven Years' War. France ceded all her
North American possessions to Britain,
except St. Pierre and Miquelon, and part of
Louisiana, retaining fishing rights on the
Grand Banks.
May-June. Pontiac's uprising. The Ottawa
chief's warriors captured all the posts west
of Niagara except Detroit.
1764
12 August. Col. John Bradstreet led a force
against the Delaware and Shawnee
Indians. He avoided a fight, and conducted
peace talks at Presqu'lle (Erie Pa.).
1765-1774 The British Parliament passed
a series of "Intolerable Acts" that put the
American colonists in a rebellious frame of
mind.
1774
5 September. The 1st Continental Congress
met in Philadelphia to air grievances over

Britain's Intolerable Acts.
1775
May. Capture of Fort Ticonderoga by
American rebels led by Ethan Allen and
Benedict Arnold; capture of Crown Point
by Seth Warner.
9 June. The Governor of Canada, Guy
Carleton, declared martial law and called
for volunteers to augment his force of 800
British regulars.
Summer. The first American Loyalists
came into Quebec Province. Some served
as volunteers under Carleton.
September. The American rebels began a
two-pronged invasion of Canada, one,
under Brigadier Richard Montgomery,
along the Richelieu River, the other, by
Col. Benedict Arnold, down the Chaudière
River directly towards Quebec.
18 October. Montgomery captured Fort
Chambly.
3 November. St. Jean surrendered to
Montgomery after a long siege.
11 November. Carleton evacuated
Montreal, and Montgomery occupied it on
the 12th.
13 November. Arnold reached the Plains of
Abraham and retreated to Pointe aux
Trembles to await the arrival of
Montgomery.
17 November. Charlottetown (P.E.I.) was
captured by American privateers.
5 December. Arnold and Montgomery
began their siege of Quebec.
31 December. The rebel assault on Quebec
was repulsed by Carleton and Col. Allan
Maclean. Montgomery was killed. The
siege continued until the Spring.
1776
26 January. Eustache de Lotbinière, a
Canadian priest, was appointed chaplain
to serve Canadians who joined the
American rebel army.
1 April. 1,124 American Loyalists arrived
in Halifax from Boston. Many had taken
refuge there, and when the British army
left Boston they had to leave, too.

6 May. Arrival of the British fleet to lift the siege of Quebec.

20 May. Battle of the Cedars. A force of 40 regulars under Capt. George Forster, and 200 Indians, defeated 400 American rebels at their outpost to the west of Montreal.

8 June. American rebels were defeated at Trois Rivières by Brigadier Simon Fraser and the 24th Regiment.

18 June. Sir John Johnson reached Montreal with 200 followers from the Mohawk Valley. On the 19th, at Fort Chambly, Carleton gave him a warrant to raise the King's Royal Regiment of New York.

28 June. Battle of Valcour Island. While pursuing the rebels up Lake Champlain, Carleton's fleet defeated ships commanded by Benedict Arnold.

13 October. Carleton defeated an American rebel fleet at Crown Point.

6 November. Americans from Machias, Me. attacked Fort Cumberland, N.S. and were repulsed.

1777
June-October. Gen. John Burgoyne led an army of 9,000 men south from St. Jean along Lake Champlain to reach Albany. Col. Barry St. Leger led a smaller force from Oswego through the Mohawk Valley to meet Burgoyne at Albany. Neither got there.

5 July. Burgoyne captured Fort Ticonderoga.

6 August. Battle of Oriskany. Sir John Johnson, John Butler and Joseph Brant led a force of Loyalists and Indians and ambushed reinforcements under Gen. Nicolas Herkimer.

15 September. John Butler received a warrant to raise a regiment of rangers.

17 October. Burgoyne surrendered at Saratoga N.Y. to rebel Gen. Horatio Gates.

1778
February. France signed an alliance with the American rebels and promised military aid.

27 June. Gen. Frederick Haldimand arrived as governor-in-chief of Canada (Quebec).

3 July. John Butler raided Wyoming, Pa.

11 November. John Butler's son Walter led rangers and Indians in an attack on Cherry Valley N.Y.

1779
Impressment into the Royal Navy was made legal in Canadian ports.

17 June. Brigadier Francis McLean founded a fort at Castine, Me. as an outpost for Halifax.

25 July. Francis McLean beat off an American rebel attack.

1781
28 August. Annapolis Royal was raided by American privateers.

18 October A British army under Lord Charles Cornwallis surrendered at Yorktown, Va., after which Britain began negotiating for an end to the war, even though she had won military control of the northern colonies.

1782
1 July. American privateers attacked Lunenburg, N.S.

9-24 August. On Hudson Bay, Fort Prince of Wales and York Fort surrendered to a French force under Jean-François de Galaup Comte de Laperouse.

30 November. Britain and the United States agreed on preliminary peace terms.

1783
18 May. 7,000 American Loyalists arrived at Parrtown (at the mouth of the Saint John River) as settlers.

3 September. The Treaty of Paris between Britain and the United States ended the American Revolution.

13 December. 30,000 Loyalists had reached Nova Scotia and New Brunswick.

1784
May-October. About 9,000 Loyalists settled in Ontario. They were allowed to go because the Iroquois wanted them settled nearby as a safeguard against American encroachment.

25 October. Governor Haldimand granted a tract of land along the Bay of Quinte and another on the Grand River to the Iroquois.

1788

John Meares arrived with two trading ships in Friendly Cove, Nootka Sound, and opened a trading post.

1789

5 May. Start of the Nootka Incident. The Spanish warship *Princesa* commanded by Estaban Martinez, arrived at Nootka to enforce Spain's claim to the west coast.

4 July. At Nootka, Martinez seized the British ship *Argonaut*

14 July. Martinez seized the British ship *Princess Royal*.

1790

10 April. Spain began erecting forts at Nootka.

24 July. Spain agreed to offer reparations to Britain for the seized ships.

28 October. The Nootka Convention was signed in Madrid. Spain agreed to give up claim to exclusive ownership of the west coast.

1792

Late September. Francisco de la Bodega y Quadra evacuated the Spanish base at Nootka Sound, although sovereignty had not been resolved.

1794

19 November. Jay's Treaty was signed. Britain agreed to evacuate the forts that were on United States territory in 1796.

1795

28 March. The Spanish evacuated their base at Friendly Cove, Nootka Sound.

1803

22 March. Massacre by Muquinna's Nootkas of 25 crew of the U.S. ship *Boston*, a trading vessel, in the Sound of Nootka. (Two survivors were rescued from the Indians in 1805.)

1807

22 December. United States passed the Embargo Act to stop all trade with foreign ports, in retaliation for Britain's Orders-in-Council and Napoleon's Decrees that interfered with American maritime rights.

1809

22 December. United States passed the Non-Intercourse Act which reopened trade to all nations except Britain and France.

1811

3 May. The Hudson's Bay Company agreed to sell Lord Selkirk 300,000 square kilometres (116,000 sq. mi.) for a colony at Red River.

1812

19 June. United States declared war on Britain.

A few days after the U.S. schooner *Julia* fought a naval engagement off Brockville with the British brig *Earl of Moira* and schooner *Duke of Gloucester. The Julia* took shelter in Ogdensburg harbour, and the other two retired to Kingston for repairs.

3 July. Capt. Frederic Rolette captured American Gen. William Hull's schooner *Cayahoga* and found Hull's battle plan.

12 July. Hull and 2,500 American troops occupied Sandwich.

17 July. A British party led by Capt. Charles Roberts captured Michilimackinac.

5 August. Indians led by Tecumseh cut Hull's supply line to Detroit.

8 August. Hull withdrew to Detroit.

13 August. Gen. Isaac Brock reached Amherstburg with 300 reinforcements from Toronto and Niagara.

14 August. Tecumseh and 600 Indians joined Brock to besiege Detroit.

15 August. The American garrison at Fort Dearborn (Chicago) was massacred by Indians.

16 August. Hull surrendered Detroit to Brock.

19-20 August. The U.S.S. *Constitution* defeated the British ship *Guerriere* off Nova Scotia.

1 September. Commodore Isaac Chauncey was appointed commander of American naval forces on the Great Lakes.

21 September. American riflemen led by Capt. Benjamin Forsyth raided Gananoque.

9 October. British ships *Detroit* and *Caledonia* were captured on Lake Erie by Capt. Jesse Elliot.

13 October. Battle of Queenston Heights. American troops under Gen. Stephen Van Rensselaer were defeated by a combined force of British, Canadians and Indians. Brock was killed in action, and Gen. Roger Sheaffe assumed command.

9-10 November. Gen. Henry Dearborn and 2,000 Americans attacked Odelltown (Que.), and were driven back to Lake Champlain by Col. Charles de Salaberry and his Canadian Voltigeurs.

22 January. Gen. Henry Proctor and 500 troops and 800 Indians under Tecumseh defeated the Americans at Frenchtown (Ohio).

7 February. Capt. Benjamin Forsyth and 200 riflemen raided Brockville and carried off 52 men.

22 February. A force led by Col. ''Red George'' Macdonell, captured the fort at Ogdensburg N.Y.

March. The 104th Regiment marched through the snow from Fredericton N.B. to Quebec City and lost only one man.

27 April. York, the capital of Upper Canada, was attacked by an American force under Gen. Zebulon Pike.

8 May. The Americans left York after burning the government buildings.

15 May. Capt. Sir James Yeo, R.N., took command of the Provincial Marine at Kingston.

27 May. Capture of Fort George, at Niagara, by Chauncey and Dearborn. The defenders, led by Gen. John Vincent, withdrew to Burlington Heights.

29 May. Yeo and Sheaffe attacked Sackets Harbor. The Americans, under Brigadier Jacob Brown, forced the British to withdraw.

1 June. H.M.S. *Shannon* captured the U.S.S. *Chesapeake* off Nova Scotia.

5-6 June. Battle of Stoney Creek. Gen. Vincent and Col. John Harvey defeated an American force under Brigadiers William Winder and John Chandler. The Americans withdrew to Forty Mile Creek.

8 June. Yeo's ships arrived at Forty Mile Creek and the Americans withdrew all the way to Fort George.

21-24 June. Battle of Beaver Dam. 570 Americans under Col. Charles Boerstler were ambushed by Lieut. James FitzGibbon with 50 regulars, and 400 Indians. 462 Americans were captured.

5-30 July. The British raided Fort Scholsser, Black Rock, and Plattsburgh N.Y.

10 September. Americans under Commodore Oliver Perry defeated a British naval force under Commodore Robert Barclay at Put-in Bay, Lake Erie.

18 September. American Gen. William H. Harrison forced Gen. Proctor to evacuate Detroit. Proctor moved up the Thames Valley accompanied by Tecumseh and his warriors.

6 October. Battle of Moraviantown. Harrison defeated Proctor, and Tecumseh was killed.

16 October. Sale of Fort Astoria (at the mouth of the Columbia River) by the Pacific Fur Company partners to partners of the North West Company. The fort was proclaimed British territory.

26 October. Battle of Chateauguay. Americans under Gen. Wade Hampton were defeated by Canadians under Col. Charles de Salaberry.

November. An American force of 8,000 men under Gen. James Wilkinson left Sackets Harbor expecting to link up with Gen. Hampton for a joint attack on Montreal.

11 November. Battle of Crysler's Farm. Wilkinson's subordiantes Brigadiers Boyd and Brown, were defeated in a rearguard action by Col. Joseph Morrison's regulars and Canadians.

30 November. Capt. William Black, R.N.,

arrived off the mouth of Columbia River in the armed sloop *Racoon*. On the 13 December. Black named Fort Astoria Fort George.

10 December. The American garrison evacuated Fort George (Niagara) and moved to Fort Niagara, N.Y. On the 11th they burned Newark (Niagara-on-the-Lake).

18 December. Col. John Murray and 500 British and Canadian troops captured Fort Niagara, N.Y.

18-30 December. Gen. Phineas Riall, with a party of Indians, burned Lewiston, Manchester, Fort Schlosser, Black Rock and Buffalo, N.Y.

1814

16-24 January. British troops raided Madrid, Salmon River, Malone and Four Corners, N.Y.

February. Americans raided Port Talbot (Ont).

30 March. Gen. James Wilkinson and 4,000 American troops, occupied Odelltown, Que., and were defeated by the British at Lacolle before they retreated to Plattsburgh.

6 May. Yeo captured Oswego and appropriated supplies.

15 May. 500 Americans raided, looted and burned Port Dover and Long Point, Lake Erie.

18 May. British reinforcements led by Col. Robert McDouall reached Michilmackinac to prevent the Americans from seizing it. In reserve were the Michigan Fencibles, commanded by William McKay, raised among Canadians living close to Lake Michigan.

20 May-6 June. The British blockaded Sackets Harbor.

30 May. Bateaux carrying British seamen went up Sandy Creek, off Lake Ontario near Sackets Harbor, to elude pursuing ships. The bateaux were ambushed by the Americans.

3 July. Brigadier Jacob Brown led American troops across the Niagara River to capture Fort Erie.

5 July. Battle of Chippawa. Brown's troops defeated Gen. Riall's 1,800-man force.

11 July. A British force from Halifax under Gen. Sir John Sherbrooke captured Eastport, Me., attacked Castine on 31 August. and Machias on 10 September. Eastern Maine was then in British hands.

18 July. 150 Michigan Fencibles under William McKay, and Indians from Green Bay, marched for the Mississippi. At Prairie-du-Chien (Iowa) they forced the U.S. gunboat *Governor Clark* to withdraw, and the garrison surrendered.

25 July. Battle of Lundy's Lane. Americans under Gen. Jacob Brown faced British and Canadians under Gen. Gordon Drummond. After heavy losses on both sides, the Americans withdrew, and the British claimed a victory.

4 August. At Michilimackinac a garrison of 200 under Col. Robert McDouall held off an attack by 750 Americans under Col. George Croghan.

14 August. The American ships *Niagara*, *Tigress* and *Scorpion* attacked the H.M.S. *Nancy* near Washaga Beach. Her commander, Lieut. Miller Worsley, burned her to prevent capture.

15 August. The British under Drummond began a siege of Fort Erie. Drummond was repulsed.

3 September. Lieut. Miller Worsley and 77 men in canoes captured the *Tigress*, at anchor northeast of Michilimackinac.

5 September. Using the *Tigress* and her American colours, Worsley captured the *Scorpion*.

10 September. The *St. Lawrence*, the largest wooden ship ever built on fresh water, was launched at Kingston.

11 September. Gen. Sir George Prevost was defeated on Lake Champlain by American Capt. Thomas Macdonough, and a British land force was repulsed from Plattsburgh.

October. The Americans lifted the blockade

of Kingston when the *St. Lawrence* was ready to sail.

5 November. The Americans destroyed Fort Erie and retired across the Niagara River.

24 December. The war ended with the signing of the Treaty of Ghent.

1815

15 June. Many of Selkirk's settlers left Red River out of fear of the fur traders.

25 June. Métis Cuthbert Grant attacked the fort at Red River, and the rest of the settlers left.

September. Colin Robertson and the Governor of the Hudson's Bay Company territories, George Semple, arrived at Red River to restore the settlement.

1816

19 June. Massacre of Seven Oaks. Cuthbert Grant's mounted column was escorting Red River carts full of pemmican when Governor Semple and 25 men went to intercept him. In the skirmish Semple and 19 of his men were killed.

13 August. Lord Selkirk led a private army of discharged veterans and captured Fort William, the headquarters of the North West Company. He arrested some of the partners and sent them to Montreal for trial for the massacre at Seven Oaks. Selkirk sent Miles Macdonell and 140 men to recapture Fort Douglas (headquarters of the Red River settlement) and Fort Daer (Pembina N.D.).

1817

28-29 April. The Rush-Bagot Agreement, limiting armaments on the Great Lakes, was signed in Washington D.C.

1818

20 October. Fort Astoria was restored to the Americans.

1819

22 February. By the Treaty of Florida Blanca, Spain gave up her claim to the Pacific coast north of the 42nd parallel.

1823

Work began on new fortifications for Quebec City (which were completed in 1832).

1824

18 May. William Lyon Mackenzie, the future rebel leader, published the first issue of his *Colonial Advocate*.

30 November. Construction began on the Welland Canal.

1826

8 June. Mackenzie's printing press at York was wrecked by Tory youths.

21 September. Work began on the Rideau Canal.

1827

6 August. In London, representatives of Britain and the United States agreed to continue co-dominion of the Pacific Northwest, with either country free to end the arrangement on 12 months notice.

24 September. The Talkotin and Chilkotin tribes on the upper Fraser River were at war. Hudson's Bay Company men gave the weaker Talkotins arms, and the Chilkotins withdrew.

1828

1 July. Alexander McLeod, chief trader of Fort Vancouver, led an attack on the lodge of the Challum Indians because they had murdered a Hudson's Bay Company clerk and his escort the previous January.

1829

27 November. The Welland Canal was completed to Port Robinson (and to Port Colborne in 1833).

1832

29 May. The steamer *Pumper* made the first trip through the Rideau Canal. (The Grenville and Carillon Canals, on the Ottawa River were completed in 1833, connecting Kingston with Montreal by an inland route safer than the St. Lawrence.)

Summer. Work began on the present Fort Henry at Kingston.

1834

17 February. The Lower Canada Assembly adopted the ''Ninety-Two Resolutions''.

27 March. Mackenzie became mayor of the

newly chartered City of Toronto.
18-29
June. Confrontation on the Stikene River between the Russians and Peter Skene Ogden on the Hudson's Bay Company ship *Dryad*. The Russians refused to let Ogden proceed upstream, and the *Dryad* withdrew.

1836
26 January. Sir John Colborne was appointed commander of forces in both the Canadas.
Late December. William Slacum, aboard the U.S. brig *Loriot* was spying in the Pacific Northwest. Afterwards the American settlers along the Columbia River opposed Hudson's Bay Company rule. Slacum sought to discredit Britain, and the United States determined to gain sovereignty over the west coast as far north as the 49th parallel.

1837
7 May. By the Declaration of St. Ours, Louis Joseph Papineau was chosen leader of the Lower Canadian *Patriotes*.
30 June. Mackenzie founded a Committee of Vigilance for Upper Canada.
October The 24th Regiment left Toronto, Kingston and Penetanguishene for Lower Canada at the request of Sir John Colborne.
6 November. *Patriote* Thomas Brown led the *Fils de la Liberté* in a street fight in Montreal against members of the Doric Club.
23 November. Battle of St. Denis. 2,000 British troops under Col. Charles Gore were defeated by *Patriotes* led by Wolfred Nelson.
25 November. Battle of St. Charles. Col. George Wetherall defeated the *Patriotes* after marching from Fort Chambly.
5 December. Mackenzie led 800 rebels down Yonge Street towards Toronto. His vanguard under Samuel Lount was dispersed by a picket posted at the edge of the city.
7 December. Volunteers under Col. James

FitzGibbon defeated Mackenzie's rebels near Montgomery's Tavern. Mackenzie fled to the United States.
13 December. Colborne defeated the *Patriotes* at St. Eustache.
15 December. *Patriotes* at St. Benôit surrendered to Colborne.
29 December. The American steamer *Caroline* was burnt in the Niagara River by Canadians under Capt. Andrew Drew.

1838
5 January. U.S. President Van Buren issued a Neutrality Proclamation forbidding U.S. citizens taking sides in the Canadian revolt.
26 February-3 March. Americans occupied Pelee Island, and were routed by British and Canadian troops led by Col. John Maitland.
28 February. A raid from Vermont into Lower Canada, led by Robert Nelson and Cyrille-Hector-Octave Coté, was dispersed by the milita.
30 March. Lord Durham was appointed governor general to investigate unrest in the Canadas.
29-30 May. Burning of the *Sir Robert Peel*. A gang led by Bill Johnston destroyed the steamer off Wellesley Island in the upper St. Lawrence River.
11-22 June. The Short Hills Raid. In Pelham Township, Niagara area, Americans and exiled Canadians were dispersed by the milita.
9 November. *Patriotes* who crossed from Vermont, led by Robert Nelson and Cyrille Coté, were dispersed at Lacolle and Odelltown.
11-16 November. Battle of the Windmill near Prescott (Ont.). 200 Americans and Canadian exiles occupied the windmill. After they surrendered, eleven were hanged at Kingston.
3 December. Battle of Windsor. American raiders were dispersed by militia and regulars.
10 December. The defeat of the *Patriotes*

who occupied the village of Beauharnois ended the second Lower Canadian Rebellion.

1839

4 February. Lord Durham submitted his report recommending the union of the Canadas.

All year. Indians of Bute Inlet, on the B.C. coast, were exterminated by the Yuculta Indians who lived along Johnstone Strait.

8 February. The "Aroostook War". Lumbermen of Maine and New Brunswick clashed because the border was not defined.

1840

23 July. The Act of Union of Upper and Lower Canada received Royal assent, to take effect 10 February 1841.

1842

American settlers on the Columbia River were calling for a U.S. boundary at 54 degrees, 40 minutes "or fight".

9 August. The Webster-Ashburton Treaty settled the boundary between Maine and New Brunswick.

1843

March. Fort Victoria, on Vancouver Island, was opened as the headquarters of the Hudson's Bay Company in the area.

1844

The Democratic candidate in the U.S. federal election, James Polk, campaigned on the slogan "Reoccupation of Oregon, Re-Annexation of Texas", although the U.S. had never owned either territory.

July. Cowichan Indians attacked Fort Victoria. Chief Trader Roderick Finlayson fired grape shot that shattered the Indians' nearby lodge, and a cannon ball that pierced a canoe in the harbour.

1846

15 June. The Oregon Boundary Treaty was signed. The boundary lay along the 49th parallel and the Strait of Juan de Fuca.

1856

29 January. The Victoria Cross was awarded to Alexander Dunn for gallantry at the Charge of the Light Brigade, the first Canadian to receive it.

1857

22 June. The Canadian Rifle Regiment was sent to Red River to counter American influence.

1861

8 November. The *Trent* Affair. U.S.S. *San Jacinto* stopped the British steamer *Trent* and seized two Confederate agents en route to Europe, which brought Britain and the United States to the brink of war.

30 December. The 62nd Regiment was sent to New Brunswick, the first of four regiments dispatched to Canada because of the *Trent* crisis.

1864

19 October. Confederate soldiers who had infiltrated Montreal raided St. Albans, Vt. and robbed banks of $90,000.

20 October. The Canadian militia was called out because of rumours of Fenian attacks.

1865

23 March. The British parliament voted £50,000 for Canadian defence after the Union ship *Kearsarge* sank the British-built Confederate ship *Alabama*.

1866

7 March. 10,000 Canadian militia were called out because of anticipated attacks by Fenians.

10 April. An attempt by Fenians to land on Campobello Island failed.

31 May.-2 June. Battle of Ridgeway. After crossing the Niagara River, Fenians led by John O'Neill defeated the Canadian militia at Ridgeway and withdrew to Fort Erie.

3 June. A relief force of British regulars and Canadian militia entered Fort Erie, but the Fenians had withdrawn towards the American side.

7 June. 1,000 Fenians crossed from Vermont into southern Quebec and plundered around Pigeon Hill, but retreated when the Canadian militia approached.

19 June. On a train filled with passengers and troops, Timothy O'Hea put out a fire before it could ignite gunpowder aboard. O'Hea was awarded the Victoria Cross, the only time it was given for valour within Canada.

1867

6 November. The new Parliament of Canada adopted a resolution for the entry of Rupert's Land and the Northwest Territory into Canada. (The Act for entry passed on 31 July 1868.)

1868

22 May. The first Dominion Militia Act was passed, but active units were not formed for three years.

1869

August. A government survey crew under John S. Dennis alarmed the Métis at Red River, who feared they would not be allowed to keep their lands.

11 October. A survey party at St. Vital, Man., was stopped by Louis Riel and 20 other Métis.

19 October. The Métis formed a National Committee at St. Norbert, Man., with Riel as secretary and John Bruce as president.

30 October. Métis refused to let William McDougall, the new Lieutenant Governor of Rupert's Land, enter the Red River colony.

2 November. Riel's Métis stormed Fort Garry (the site of Winnipeg), occupied it, formed a provisional government and proclaimed Riel its president.

26 November. Canada refused to take over Rupert's Land on 1 December as agreed because of Métis opposition. Prime Minister John A. Macdonald would not pay the Hudson's Bay Company for the land until McDougall could guarantee peaceful possession.

6 December. Governor General Lord Lisgar proclaimed a pardon if the Métis dispersed peacefully.

7 December. The Métis foiled an attempt by English-speaking Canadians to sieze Fort Garry. Among them was Thomas Scott, an Oangeman from Ontario.

1870

January. Riel summoned a convention which agreed to form a provisional government to negotiate terms of entry into Confederation.

9 February. The Métis convention elected Riel president of Red River.

4 March. Thomas Scott was executed by firing squad, Riel's most serious blunder. Ontario viewed it as murder.

5 March. Britain and Canada agreed to a military expedition to Red River, and selected Col. Garnet Wolseley, the Deputy Quartermaster-General in Canada, to lead it.

May. The expedition, of the 60th Rifles and Ontario and Quebec militia units, prepared to move on Red River by way of Lake-of-the-Woods.

15 May. The Act establishing Manitoba as a province came into effect. 1,400,000 square miles (566,000 ha.) were set aside for the Métis.

25 May. Fenians under John O'Neill went to Eccles Hill, in southern Quebec, and were dispersed by the militia under Col. Osborn Smith.

15 July. The Hudson's Bay Company lands were annexed to Canada as the Northwest Territories.

24 August. Wolseley's expedition moved on Fort Garry. The Métis leaders fled and Riel reached the United States.

17 September. Riel made a secret visit to St. Norbert, Man. to persuade the Metis not to support Fenian invaders.

1871

5 October. Fenians under William B. O'Donoghue crossed the border into Manitoba and seized the Hudson's Bay Company post at Pembina. They were followed by American troops and arrested. Riel again returned in secret to assist the government.

11 November. The last British troops left

Quebec City, except for a small garrison that remained at Halifax.

1872

The Dominion Lands Act granted free homesteads to settlers in Manitoba. The influx of people dismayed the Métis, and many left to form new settlements on the Saskatchewan River.

January. The Ontario Legislature offered a reward of $5,000 for the capture of Louis Riel.

1873

Late May. The Cypress Hills Massacre. Ten American wolf hunters accused the Assiniboine Indians of stealing horses. In the fighting one wolfer and 36 Indians were killed.

23 May. An Act of Parliament set up the North West Mounted Police to keep peace between traders and Indians.

1876

1 June. Royal Military College opened in Kingston, to train officers for a Canadian regular army and the militia.

1884

5 June. Métis led by Gabriel Dumont visited Riel in Montana and he agreed to go to Saskatchewan and help them protect their rights from encroaching settlers.

8 July. Riel arrived at Duck Lake, on the North Saskatchewan River.

15 September. A force of 386 *voyageurs* under Col. Frederick Denison set sail for Egypt to assist in the rescue of Gen. Charles Gordon, then besieged at Khartoum, Sudan. Gen. Garnet Wolseley, who had commanded the expedition to Red River, asked for the *voyageurs* to help ascend the Nile. The expedition reached Khartoum on 28 January. 1885, but the city had fallen and Gordon was dead. This was Canada's first overseas military undertaking.

16 December. Riel's petition on Métis grievances was sent to Ottawa.

1885

January. The Canadian government agreed to form a commission to investigate Métis grievances.

11 March. From Fort Carlton, 32 km. from Batoche, N.W.M.P. Superintendent Leif Crozier warned Ottawa that rebellion was about to erupt in the Northwest.

18-19 May. At his headquarters at Batoche, Riel siezed hostages and proclaimed a Métis provisional government with himself as president, and Gabriel Dumont as adjutant-general.

21 March. Riel demanded the surrender of the N.W.M.P. detachment at Fort Carlton.

26 March. At Duck Lake the Métis defeated a detachment of N.W.M.P. led by Sup't Crozier.

30 March. Chief Poundmaker and 200 Crees attacked Battleford and the white settlers sought shelter at the N.W.M.P. barracks.

1 April. At Frog Lake, 9 whites and mixed bloods were murdered by Crees led by Wandering Spirit.

2 April. A three pronged expedition form the railway line was set in motion, under the overall command of Gen. Frederick Middleton, commander of the Canadian militia. Gen. Thomas Strange would go to Calgary and march for Edmonton; Col. William Otter would move north from Swift Current and relieve Battleford; Middleton would move north from Qu'Appelle towards Batoche.

15 April. N.W.M.P. Inspector Francis Dickens abandoned Fort Pitt after white civilians under his protection decided to surrender to Big Bear.

24 April. Middleton's force was badly mauled at Fish Creek. On the same day, Otter relieved Battleford.

2-3 May. At Cut Knife Hill, Otter's force withdrew after meeting stiff resistance from Poundmaker's Crees.

9-12 May. Battle of Batoche. The government forces broke Métis resistance decisively. Riel surrendered on 15 May. Dumont escaped and reached the United States.

25 May. Poundmaker surrendered to Middleton near Battleford.

27–28 May. At Frenchman's Butte, Alta., Big Bear retreated from Strange's force.

3 June. Steele Narrows – the last battle on Canadian soil. A detachment of N.W.M.P. under Samuael Steele fought with Crees under Big Bear, but the Cree chief escaped.l

2 July. Big Bear surrendered at Fort Carleton.

16 November. Riel was hanged at the N.W.M.P. barracks in Regina.

27 November. Wnadering Spirit and 7 other Indians were hanged for the nurders committed at Frog Lake in April.

1889

19 February. Canadian government pardoned Gabriel Dumont for his part in the Northwest Rebellion.

1890

12 May. Gen. Frederick Middleton convicted of looting furs during the Northwest Rebellion; he resigned 24 June.

1899

11 October. Britain declared war on Boers of South Africa.

30 October. 1st Canadian Contingent sailed from Quebec for South Africa, arrived Cape Town 29 November.

1900

21 and 27 January, 21 February. 2nd Canadian Contingent left Halifax for South Africa in stages.

18–27 February. 1st Canadian Contingent fought in Battle of Paardeberg.

16 March. Strathcona's Horse sailed for South Africa, arrived 10 April.

25 April. Canadians fought at Israel's Poort, South Africa.

23 December. 1st Canadian Contingent arrived in Halifax.

1901

8 March. Strathcona's Horse arrived in Halifax from South Africa.

1902

14 January. Canadian Mounted Rifles sailed from Halifax for South Africa.

31 May. Treaty of Vereening ended the South African (2nd Boer) War.

1904

24 June. North West Mounted Police designated "Royal."

1906

The last British soldiers left Canada, replaced at Halifax by a garrison under the Canadian government.

1907

28 November. The 10th Parliament authorized a National Battlefields Commission.

1914

1 August. The Duke of Connaught, the Governor General, offered Canadian troops to Britain (Britain accepted 6 August).

4 August. Britain declared war on Germany and Austria-Hungary; Canada was automatically at war.

18 August. The Canadian Parliament passed the War Measures Act.

29 August. Princess Patricia's Canadian Light Infantry sailed for England.

3 October. 1st Canadian Contingent, 33,000 strong, sailed for England.

1915

6 January. The "Princess Pats" went into action in France.

14 January. The 1st Canadian Division arrived in France from England.

10 March. Canadians fought at the Battle of Neuve Chapelle.

16 March. 2nd Canadian Division began arriving in England.

3 May. At Ypres Dr. John McCrae wrote "In Flanders Fields."

15 June. Canadians saw action at Givenchy, France.

30 November. To date, Canadian casualties were 539 officers, 13,017 other ranks killed.

1916

3–20 April. 2nd Canadian Division fought at St. Elio, Belgium.

2–13 June. Canadians saw action at Mount Sorell.

1 July. Newfoundland troops captured

Beaumont-Hamel; it was the beginning of Battle of the Somme.

4 September. Canadians reinforced part of the Somme Line, near Courcelette.

15 September. Canadians captured Courcelette.

8 October. James Richardson received the Victoria Cross at the Somme.

25 October. 4th Canadian Division attacked on the Somme.

11 November. Sam Hughes resigned as Minister of Militia and Defence.

1917

9 April. Easter Monday. Four Canadian divisions and one British brigade captured Vimy Ridge. It was first time that all four divisions attacked together.

2 June. William "Billy" Bishop received the Victoria Cross for his role in the air war.

15 August. Canadian success at Hill 70, near Lens, France.

1 September. By this date, 33,587 Canadians had been sent to the Canadian Expeditionary Force.

26 October–30 November. Canadians fought at Passchendaele, Belgium.

6 December. Disastrous explosion in Halifax Harbour claimed 1,800 lives, injured 4,000 others, and left 6,000 homeless.

1918

28 March. Anti-conscription riots in Quebec City. 4 civilians were shot by soldiers.

21 April. Canadian pilot Roy A. Brown received credit for downing Manfred von Richthofen (the Red Baron).

8 August. Canadians attacked Amiens, France. It was the start of "Canada's Hundred Days" that ended on 11 November.

26 August–2 September. Canadians cut through Hindenburg Line.

27–30 September. Canadians attacked remaining part of Hindenburg Line at Canal du Nord.

9 October. Canadians captured Cambrai, France.

21 October. Canadian mission for Siberia appointed, to be based at Vladivostock.

11 November. Armistice ended World War I: 628,462 Canadians served, 424,589 of them overseas. 60,661 were killed.

1920

1 February. Royal North West Mounted Police became Royal Canadian Mounted Police (and absorbed the former Dominion Police).

15 November–18 December. 1st meeting of League of Nations in Geneva; Canada was a founding member.

1936

26 July. King Edward VIII dedicated Vimy Memorial in France.

1937

1,250 Canadians joined Mackenzie-Papineau Battalion to fight against Franco's Spanish Nationalists.

1939

3 September. Britain declared war on Germany.

10 September. Canada, now empowered to make the decision, declared war.

16 September. Canada pledged one division to be sent to Britain.

13 November. Maj.-Gen. Henry D.G. Crerar set up Canadian Military Headquarters in London, England.

17 December. British Commonwealth Air Training Plan signed in Ottawa.

1940

Canada began massive construction of naval vessels on coasts and Great Lakes.

13–14 June. 1st Canadian Infantry Brigade landed in France, withdrew with loss of six men after fall of France.

14 July. Canadian Lieut.-Gen. Andrew G.L. McNaughton received command of the British 7th Armoured Corps, consisting of Canadian, British, and New Zealand troops.

1941

Women's divisions of the Canadian Army and Royal Canadian Air Force were formed.

14 August. Atlantic Charter signed by

Churchill and Roosevelt at Placentia
Bay, Newfoundland, to protect ships
from German submarines.
27 October. Two Canadian infantry battalions, 1,975 men, sailed from
Vancouver to reinforce the Hong Kong
garrison.
7 December. Canada joined Britain and
the United States in declaring war on
Japan.
8 December. (7 December, North
American time) Japanese moved into
Kowloon, Hong Kong mainland.
18 December. Japanese began landing
on Hong Kong Island.
25 December. Garrison at Hong Kong
surrendered. 290 Canadians had been
killed, 264 more died later in prison
camps.
1942
Ten new squadrons were added to
Canadian Bomber Group.
Montrealer George "Buzz" Beurling,
serving with R.A.F., was credited with
the downing of 15 enemy aircraft.
May. Battle of St. Lawrence. Submarine
U-553 torpedoed British steamer Nicoya
and Dutch vessel Leto.
19 August. Dieppe Raid by 5,000 men
of seven regiments of 2nd Canadian
Division, 1,000 British, American, and
Free French; 907 Canadians killed, 946
taken prisoners.
1943
1 January. An R.C.A.F. bomber group
began operating from British bases.
10 July. 1st Canadian Infantry Division
and 1st Canadian Tank Brigade took
part in invasion of Sicily, which fell on
16 August.
15 August. Canadian and American
troops occupied Kiska Island in the
Aleutians, abandoned by the Japanese
before they landed.
3 September. 1st and 2nd Canadian
Brigades and tanks were in the force
invading the Italian mainland.
21 December. 1st Canadian Division
began fighting the Battle of Ortona,
and entered the town on the 28th.

1944
20 March. Lieut.-Gen. H.D.G. Crerar
took command of 1st Canadian Army,
which was in England, taking part in D-
Day landings.
23–31 May. 1st Canadian Corps, in Italy,
broke through German line across Liri
Valley, close to Monte Cassino.
6 June. 3rd Canadian Division, 2nd and
3rd Armoured Brigades, landed on
beaches at Courselles, St. Aubin, and
Bernières, Normandy, between British
and Americans. Caen fell 9 July.
17 August. 1st Canadian Army took
Falaise and with allied forces encircled
the Germans, ending campaign in
Normandy; 5,000 Canadians died.
40 August–3 September. 1st Canadian
Corps, in Italy, cut the German line on
Foglia River, and penetrated Po Valley.
1 September. 1st Canadian Army liberated Dieppe.
1 October. 2nd Canadian Division
crossed Antwerp Canal; port was
opened for allied ships 28 November.
1 October–8 November. British and
Canadians drove Germans from
Beveland and Walchern.
1945
8 February. 1st Canadian Army attacked
Germans in Reichswald on offensive
into Germany, helped cut Siegfried
Line on 10 March.
25 April–26 June. Canadian representatives attended United Nations
Conference in San Francisco that
approved U.N. Charter.
28 April. Canadians and Germans in
Holland agreed to a truce.
4 May. Fighting ended in Canadian sec-
tor near Wilhelmshaven, Aurich and
Elmden. Germans surrendered on 5th.
7 May. Germany surrendered to western
allies, and to Soviets on 8th.
4 July. Canadians entered Berlin as part
of British garrison.
6 August. V.J. Day. 80,000 Canadians
who had volunteered to serve in the
Pacific were now not needed.
2 September. Official surrender of

Japan.

In World War II, 1,086,771 Canadians (including 49,252 women) served in the armed forces; 41,992 died.

1949

31 March. Newfoundland confederated as Canada's 10th province.

4 April. Canada joined North Atlantic Treaty Organization (N.A.T.O.).

1950

26 June. House of Commons informed that North Korean troops were pouring into South Korea.

30 June. Three Canadian destroyers ordered to join U.N. forces in Korea.

1951

22 January. Fourth destroyer authorized for Korea.

23 February. Canadian troops fought Chinese invaders in Kapyong Valley.

1 May. Government resolved to form 25th Canadian Infantry Brigade for Korea.

4 May. 27th Infantry Brigade formed for N.A.T.O. duty in Europe.

2–25 November. Offensives against Canadians by Chinese troops.

15 November. Part of 27th Brigade arrived in Hanover, West Germany.

1953

27 July. Armistice ended Korean War. Of 21,940 Canadians who served, 314 were killed, 1,211 were wounded, and 33 were captured; 7,000 stayed on garrison duty until November 1954.

Since the Korean War, apart from support duties during Operation Desert Storm, Canadian troops have worked mainly as peacekeepers in many countries.

Recommended Reading

Chapter 1: Acadian Civil War
Macdonald, M.A. *Fortune and La Tour: The Civil War in Acadia.*
    Toronto, 1983.
Dictionary of Canadian Biography. Vol. 1. Biographies of Charles de
    Saint-Etienne de La Tour and Charles de Menou d'Aulnay.

Chapter 2: Quebec, 1629
Trudel, Marcel. *The Beginnings of New France.* Translated by
    Patricia Claxton. Toronto, 1973.
Dictionary of Canadian Biography. Vol. 1. Biographies of the Kirkes.

Chapter 3: Iberville, Hudson Bay, and Newfoundland
Laut, Agnes C. *The Adventurers of England on Hudson Bay.*
    Chronicles of Canada Series, Toronto, 1914.
Newman, Peter C. *The Company of Adventurers.* Markham, Ontario, 1985.
Dictionary of Canadian Biography. Vol. 2. Biography of Pierre Le Moyne
    d'Iberville, of his father Charles, and some of his brothers.

Chapter 4: Louisbourg, 1758
Downey, Fairfax. *Louisbourg: Key to a Continent.* Englewood, New York,
    1965.
Grinnel-Milne, Duncan. *Mad Is he? The Character and Achievements of
    James Wolfe.* London, 1963.
McLennan, J.S. *Louisbourg: From Its Foundation to Its Fall.* Sydney,
    Nova Scotia, 1961; 1918.

Chapter 5: Fort Frontenac 1758
Fryer, Mary Beacock, and Adrian G. Ten Cate. *Pictorial History of the
    Thousand Islands.* Brockville, Ontario, 2d ed., 1982.
Snider, C.H.J. *Tarry Breeks and Velvet Garters.* Toronto, 1958.
Dictionary of Canadian Biography. Vol. 4. Biography of John Bradstreet.

Chapter 6: Sainte-Foy, 1760
Stacey, C.P. *Quebec 1759: The Siege and the Battle.* Toronto, 1959.
Dictionary of Canadian Biography. Vol. 4. Biography of James Murray.

Chapter 7: Quebec 1775–1776
Fryer, Mary Beacock. *Allan Maclean: Jacobite General.* Toronto: Dundurn Press, 1987.

———. *King's Men: The Soldier Founders of Ontario.* Toronto: Dundurn Press, 1980.

Chapter 8: Little York, 1813
Benn, Carl. *Historic Fort York, 1793–1993.* Toronto, 1993.

Stacey, C.P. *The Battle of Little York.* Toronto: Toronto Historical Board, 1971.

Chapter 9: Fort Astoria, 1813
Stanley, G.F.G. *The War of 1812: Land Operations.* National Museum of Man, 1973.

Chapter 10: Crysler's Farm, 1813
Berton, Pierre. *The Invasion of Canada 1812–1813.* Toronto, 1980.

———. *Flames across the Border 1813–1814.* Toronto, 1981.

Chapter 11: Battle of the Thames, 1813
Richardson, John. *War of 1812.* Edited by Alexander Casselman. First published 1842. Reprint. Toronto: Coles, 1974.

Chapter 12: Lundy's Lane, 1814
Hitsman, J. Mackay. *The Incredible War of 1812.* Toronto, 1965.

Chapter 13: Windsor, 1838
Fryer, Mary Beacock. *Volunteers and Redcoats, Rebels and Raiders.* Toronto: Dundurn Press, 1987.

Chapter 14: Red River, 1870
Senior, Hereward. *The Last Invasion of Canada: The Fenian Raids 1866–1870.* Toronto, 1991.

Stanley, G.F.G. *Toil and Trouble: Military Expedition to Red River.* Toronto: Dundurn Press, 1989.

Chapter 15: Fort Whoop-Up, 1874
Hannon, Leslie. *Forts of Canada: An Illustrated History.* Toronto, 1969.

Chapter 16: Cut Knife Creek and Hill, 1885
Beal, Bob and Rod MacLeod. *Prairie Fire: The 1885 North-West Rebellion.* Edmonton, Alberta, 1984.

Steele, Col. S.B. *Forty Years in Canada: Reminiscences of the Great North-West.* Toronto, 1915.

Chapter 17: Paardeberg, 1900

Haycock, Ronald J. *Sam Hughes: The Public Career of a Controversial Canadian.* Waterloo, Ontario, 1986.

Marquis, B.A., T.G. *Canada's Sons on Kopje and Veldt.* Toronto, 1900.

Morton, Desmond. *The Canadian General: Sir William Otter.* Toronto, 1974.

Miller, Carman. *Painting the Map Red: Canada and the South African War, 1899–1902.* Montreal and Kingston, 1993.

Smith-Dorrien, Sir Horace Lockwood. *Memories of Forty-Eight Years' Service.* London, 1925.

Chapter 18: Hong Kong, 1941

Ferguson, Ted. *Desperate Siege: The Battle of Hong Kong.* Toronto, 1980.

Government of Canada, Department of Veterans Affairs. *Commemoration: Canadians in Hong Kong 1990.*

Stewart, Adrian. *The Underrated Enemy: Britain's War with Japan December 1941–May 1942.* London, 1987.

Vincent, Carl. *No Reason Why: The Canadian Hong Kong Tragedy, an Examination.* Stittsville, Ontario, 1981.

Index

Illustrations are in bold type.
Ships' names are in italics.
Regiments are listed together under Military Units.